NORTHWOOD
CARNIVAL GLASS
1908 – 1925
Identification & Value Guide

Carl O. Burns

COLLECTOR BOOKS
A Division of Schroeder Publishing Co., Inc.

The current values in this book should be used only as a guide. They are not intended to set prices, which vary from one section of the country to another. Auction prices as well as dealer prices vary greatly and are affected by condition and demand. Neither the author nor the publisher assumes responsibility for any losses which might be incurred as a result of consulting this guide.

Searching For A Publisher?

We are always looking for people knowledgeable within their fields. If you feel that there is a real need for a book on your collectible subject and have a large comprehensive collection, contact Collector Books.

On The Cover

Marigold Tornado vase
Ice blue Peacock at the Fountain water pitcher
Amethyst Good Luck bowl

Cover design: Beth Summers
Book design: Holly C. Long

Collector Books
P.O. Box 3009
Paducah, KY 42002-3009
www.collectorbooks.com

CONTENTS

DEDICATION

This book is dedicated to two of the "pioneer" carnival glass collectors, Eleanor Hart and John Stewart. Both became active in carnival glass in the 1960s and did a great deal to promote the hobby at a time when there were no more than a few hundred collectors, worldwide. Eleanor and John were the first two people I met within the carnival glass world, and I was fortunate to have both of them living near me at the time. They became my "mentors" in my early days of carnival collecting in the late 1960s and early 1970s, offering me encouragement and sharing their knowledge. John Stewart passed away in the mid 1980s, and there is hardly a day when I do not think of him. Eleanor Hart passed away in the summer of 2000, after a lengthy illness. We shared many wonderful times together. Both are so sadly missed, but lovingly remembered.

ABOUT THE AUTHOR

Carl Owen Burns has spent nearly 33 years buying, selling, collecting, and researching carnival glass. He is also a full-time antique dealer, as were his parents before him. Of Scottish and Irish ancestry, with a touch of Native American Abnaki blood thrown in for good measure, he has traced his family's roots in North America back to the French and Indian Wars of the 1750s. His great-great-great-great uncle was the Scottish poet, Robert Burns. He is an active member of several national and international carnival glass societies and has lectured about the glass around the country.

Nearly equal to his passion for old carnival glass is his interest in Imperial slag glass, produced from 1959 through the 1970s, and his love of rock & roll, blues, and folk music is evident in his collection of well over 1,000 LPs. An avid outdoorsman, trout fishing, canoeing, and photographing wildlife take up a good part of his spare time. He lives with his wife, Marsha, in the mountains of western Maine.

This is his fourth book on carnival glass. Two of his prior works, *Imperial Carnival Glass 1909 – 1931* and *Dugan/Diamond Carnival Glass 1909 – 1931* are available from Collector Books. An earlier work, *Collector's Guide to Northwood's Carnival Glass,* now out of print, has become a collector's item in itself.

ACKNOWLEDGMENTS

Without the encouragement, support, and participation of a great many wonderful people, this book would not be a reality today. All of the people listed here participated in this project in many ways. Some provided invaluable information about and photographs of many extreme rarities that would otherwise not have appeared in this book. Others graciously opened up their homes to me and allowed me to photograph glass from their collections. They all deserve far more praise and recognition for their efforts than space will allow here. They are all devoted to the promotion of the carnival glass collecting hobby and will forever have my sincerest appreciation for all they have done.

First, a very special note of thanks goes to two of the finest people in the carnival hobby, Diane and Dean Fry, for coming to my rescue at "the eleventh hour" with nearly 50 photographs of some of the most beautiful carnival shown in this book.

Secondly an equal appreciation goes to Maurice "Moe" Myers & Pam MacDonald, Robert & Darlene Hurst, and Eleanor C. Hart for allowing me to photograph glass from their collections. And to my loving partner in life, Marsha Burns, who also provided glass but more importantly, put up with me during all the trials and tribulations that occurred during the preparation of this book.

And to all of the following people, who participated in countless ways, goes my heartfelt thanks. Some contributed solely to this book and others were major contributors to my previous book on Northwood Carnival. Some are sadly no longer with us and are dearly missed and fondly remembered. We are all indeed members of a great fraternity.

Harry Atwater
Rich Brazel
John & Lucile Britt
Mike Carwile
Richard Cinclair
Kevin & April Clark
Richard Conley
Dave Doty
Richard Fenton
Adam Fikso
Michel Filion

Rick & Debbie Graham
Don & Becky Hamlet
Steve Jennings
Donald E. Kime
Roland Kuhn
Yolanda & Jim Lewis
Michel Marbach
Lee Markley
Rick McDaniel
Sam McGill
Tom & Sharon Mordini

Neil Panciera
Carry L. Parsons
Orval Plotts
Randy & Jackie Poucher
John D. Resnick
Travis & Jennifer Reyan
Casy Rich
Marnen & Betty Robertson
Mary Rockwell
Dennis Sutton
Greg Warhol

INTRODUCTION

Just think of the name "Northwood" and visions of Peacocks, Acorn Burrs, Grape & Cable, Hearts & Flowers, Rose Show, and a veritable myriad of dazzling colors, in masterpieces of the mould-makers art, spring instantly to mind. Regardless of the fact that it was only one among many types of glass produced by the legendary Harry Northwood, no other name has become more synonymous with the beautiful iridescent glass that we have come to call "carnival." There is a mystique about the name. It is spoken in tones of near reverence. Heads turn and faces light up at the mere mention of it. It is something sacred. It is something to be eagerly sought and highly treasured when found. It is the standard by which all other carnival glass seems to be judged. It is Northwood!

Harry Northwood was not the first to produce this beautiful glass. Nor was his production longevity of it equal to that of his major competitors. Imperial, Fenton, and Dugan/Diamond certainly manufactured it for a much longer time span. Fenton made a far more diverse variety of color variations. Dugan/Diamond and Fenton both made a greater variety of patterns and Imperial's penchant for diversity of functional shapes is almost endless. So, what is it about Northwood? Why does the "aura" of perfection surround the name? Why do we tend to place Harry's glass so high on the pedestal of desirability? Is it because so much of his glass is signed? No, I think not. Is it because we feel his product was of a superior quality?

No, as far as brilliance and clarity, other glasshouses, like Millersburg, equaled or surpassed the glass quality produced by Northwood. Is it because of the high monetary value that many of Northwood's pieces have attained? Perhaps, for some, but not for the true lovers of his glass. It is something much more than all of these things. It is something not seen, touched or even experienced by the physical senses: something felt; something recognized and acknowledged, yet never clearly defined by our minds. To hold a piece of Northwood carnival in your hands is not a physical act. It is an experience anchored deep within us. A chord is struck. There is a poetry here. Not of the spoken word, but of the entire essence of the piece. The mind seems to transcend the physical presence of the glass and begins to wander through a delightful garden of beautifully balanced color, shape, and design. We like it there and want to stay. We want to experience this place again and again. We must have this. It is Northwood!

I cannot further define this "Northwood mystique," I will not attempt to do so. And, I hope no one else ever does. Something about the beautiful glass produced by Harry Northwood would be lost if this were done: something far greater than any monetary value. Something that is a part of us would be gone: that wonderful spark inside of us that says, "It is Northwood!"

WHAT IS CARNIVAL GLASS?

Contrary to what is often portrayed on television and in films, the average households of the late Victorian era were, in reality, rather drab and colorless places. The average wage earner of that period often worked for $10.00 – $12.00 a week, if that. Elaborate and colorful household trimmings were simply beyond the financial reach of most people. Only the wealthy could afford the colorful, more elaborate clothing, decorative items, and other possessions that often defined their financial stature to others.

By the end of the Victorian era, at the onset of what is now called the Edwardian period, this began to change. The benefits of the Industrial Revolution gradually became more and more available to the average wage earner. Tired of the strict lifestyle constraints imposed by the Victorian philosophy, the average citizen began to demand, and get, a better deal. The rapid growth of industry, combined with an ever expanding and improving transportation network resulted in a greater availability of more varied goods, at a lower cost. Still, one of the most appealing art forms of the day, the handmade, expensive, iridescent art glass, much of which was imported from Europe, remained out of the reach of most consumers. Costing from $10.00 to as much as $20.00, a week's wages or more for most, these items were simply not affordable by the masses.

During the winter of 1907 – 1908 when the Fenton Art Glass Company introduced to the trade their new, inexpensive, colorful iridescent wares, the glass we have come to call "carnival" took the market by storm. Priced at from five to 25 cents per piece, average homemakers of the period at last had the opportunity to add some color and charm to their daily lives and add it they certainly did! It became the most popular form of decorative glassware in American history. Within a few months, glasshouses such as Northwood, Imperial, Millersburg, Westmoreland, Dugan, and the U.S. Glass Company introduced their own inexpensive, pressed iridescent lines, which would dominate the glass market for the next 20 years.

The process by which it was made is a relatively simple one. Molten glass, in any number of colors, was pressed in a mould in the conventional manner. It was removed from the mould, shaped by hand and quickly sprayed, while still hot, with an iridizing solution composed of various metal salts. The effect of this on the hot glass resulted in the beautiful, multicolor iridescent blend. One of the most frequently used sprays was a ferric chloride solution, which resulted in an orange or "marigold" iridescent color. Other formulas using such elements as tin chloride and chloride of antimony produced different iridescent effects and colors. The temperature at which the hot glass was sprayed could also be altered to produce different effects. The hotter the glass when sprayed, the more satiny the iridescence. Brilliant, more transparent, and shiny effects could be produced by spraying at a slightly cooler temperature.

Over the course of its 20-plus years of production, the glass was marketed by the manufacturers, wholesalers, and retailers under many different trade names. It was not originally called carnival glass nor was it made exclusively for the purposes of premium or give-away. It was sold through numerous retail outlets around the country and abroad, just like any other manner of goods. Each manufacturer had their own names for the glass. Northwood often marketed his as "Golden Iris," early Fenton iridescent lines were often called "Iridyl," and Millersburg often advertised their lines as "Radium." Wholesalers and retailers used a variety of colorful names to promote the glass, such as "Mexican Aurora," "Pompeian," "Venetian Iridescent," and a whole host of others.

It was not until the 1930s, long after major production of the glass had ceased, that the term "carnival glass" came into use. In fact, the earliest reference to this term that I have been able to find is from a "Purasnow" brand flour promotion from about 1937 – 1938. During this period, remaining stocks of the glass were often sold off, at pennies on the dollar, to carnivals, circuses, sideshows, and even movie theatres, to be given away as prizes, premiums, and enticements. Thus, the name carnival glass came to be, and that is the term we use for it today.

HARRY NORTHWOOD

It is not my intent or purpose in this book to fully document in detail the life and career of Harry Northwood. That has already been done by others. Our focus here is to document the variety, values, and availability of his pressed, patterned, iridescent glass made between 1908 and 1925 and to provide a general guide for collectors. Still, a better sense of perspective regarding this can be gained with a basic outline of the man himself and the artistry he created.

Born on June 30, 1860, at Wordsley, Kingswinford, in the Stourbridge district of England, Harry Northwood had glassmaking in his blood from the moment he took his first breath. He was the son of John Northwood, already a prominent figure in the glass industry and famed for his glass carvings that we know today as "cameo glass." At just 14 years of age, Harry Northwood served his first apprenticeship in the trade at the famed Stevens & Williams works. His father had been schooled in the classical tradition and had a penchant for visiting museums, often with sketchbook in hand. It is likely that young Harry often accompanied his father and the seeds of the artistic skills that were to blossom years later and a continent away were no doubt planted on these outings.

Harry Northwood, his mind likely aglow with eagerness, anticipation, and the excitement common to all young men as they journey into the adventure of adulthood, arrived in America on November 1, 1881. It did not take him long to secure employment as a glass etcher at the Hobbs Brockunier Glassworks in Wheeling, West Virginia, ironically the very factory that would one day bear his name and from which his most famous creations would come. Within a year, he was joined by his young cousin Thomas Dugan, also destined for fame in the American glass industry.

Harry did not stay long at Hobbs Brockunier. After his marriage to Clara Elizabeth Beaumont in 1882, he moved around quite a bit, as young men are apt to do. He was employed for a time by La Belle Glassworks of Bridgeport, Ohio, but soon moved on to the Phoenix Glass Company of Phillipsburg, Pennsylvania. Eventually, he ended up back at La Belle where he quickly worked his way up to plant manager. However, the La Belle plant was destroyed by fire in September of 1887. At the ripe old age of 27, Harry found himself unemployed and with a family to support. He decided that the time had come to place his destiny in his own hands.

Just two months later, Harry Northwood, in company with several other investors, purchased the vacant Union Flint Glass Factory in Martins Ferry, Ohio, and the first glasshouse to bear his name was born. Production commenced in January of 1888, and his artistic genius became rapidly apparent. Mould-blown Opalescent, Rubina, and Cased Glass lines were among his early creations at Martins Ferry. Many designs such as Leaf Mold, Leaf Umbrella, Royal Oak, and Royal Ivy, all eagerly sought by collectors today, originated there. The success he enjoyed over the next four years at Martins Ferry enabled Harry to begin planning a more ambitious venture.

A decision to relocate was made in 1892. Northwood's financial success at Martins Ferry had enabled the construction of a brand new facility. By October of that year the Northwood Glass Company of Ellwood City, Pennsylvania, was up and running. However, the firm's initial success was short-lived. Perhaps he had moved too fast, expanded too quickly, and overextended himself financially. Within three short years, lawsuits from creditors resulted in serious financial problems for the firm. By February of 1896, production had ceased, and Harry Northwood once again sought greener pastures elsewhere. It would not take him long to find them.

Just two months later, the Northwood Glass Company of Indiana, Pennsylvania began operations in the factory that had once housed the Indiana Glass Company. Here, Harry Northwood produced his first "Ivory Glass," what we call custard glass today. Pressed Opalescent Glass lines, like Alaska and Klondike (Fluted Scrolls), also originated here. For the first time in his career, Northwood adopted a trademark, the word "Northwood" written out in script, and many examples of his wares produced at Indiana bear this mark. Northwood's young cousin Thomas Dugan was the plant manager, and his growing artistic influence can be clearly seen in several of Northwood's lines that were produced there. In fact, Thomas Dugan was very soon destined to make his own name well known to the trade.

By 1899, competition from the newly formed U.S. Glass Company had increased alarmingly. U.S. Glass was a combine of 19 different glasshouses, all of whom employed non-union labor. In an effort to counter this competition, Northwood joined a similar co-operative in 1899, the National Glass Company. The factory would now operate as the Northwood Works of the National Glass Company, but Harry Northwood accepted a position as National's London representative. Actual ownership of the Indiana factory was transferred to Thomas Dugan and he in turn, in September of 1899, deeded it over to National. Harry Northwood returned to England to assume his duties there, but it was destined to be a short trip indeed. Within just two years, National was in serious financial trouble and had to reorganize. Part of that reorganization included the sale of the Indiana plant back into the hands of Thomas Dugan, perhaps to help finance the building of National's new plant in Cambridge, Ohio. Harry Northwood severed his ties with National. He returned to the United States and wasted little time in making his presence felt.

I guess one could say that at this point Harry Northwood returned "home" to where his career in America had its roots. In 1902 he purchased the empty factory in Wheeling, West Virginia, that had once housed his first employer, Hobbs Brockunier. By the fall of that year, H. Northwood & Co. was in operation. During the next six years a dazzling variety of glass emerged from the Northwood plant at Wheeling. Tableware, novelties, lamps, crystal, colored, slag, and opalescent lines all proved enormously successful. It was here, in 1905, that Northwood adopted his now famous "underlined N in a circle" trademark. The financial woes and problems of earlier years must now have seemed a distant memory to Harry. The future seemed bright indeed, and his most famous creations lay just over the horizon.

When the Fenton Art Glass Company developed an inexpensive iridizing process and introduced their new, pressed, iridescent glass lines in the winter of 1907 – 1908, they took the glass market by storm. These lines were an overnight success with the buying public. Other glasshouses scrambled to develop their own iridescent lines and gain a quick share of the new market. The era of the glass we call "carnival" had begun, and Harry Northwood was quick to realize its potential. By mid-spring of 1908, his own iridescent line which he called "Golden Iris" (marigold) was ready for market. Iridized lines in amethyst, green, and cobalt blue base colors soon followed. In January of 1910, Northwood introduced a new pattern line, designed specifically for iridescent production, that would soon become one of the largest, most popular, and widely recognized pattern glass lines in American glass-making history: Grape & Cable. The astounding financial success of this line enabled further expansion of Northwood's iridescent output and the years of 1911 – 1912 saw the emergence of the greatest variety of iridescent patterns and colors in the firm's history. January of 1912 saw the introduction of new pastel iridescent colors, what we today call white, ice blue, and ice green. Northwood's famous aqua opalescent color followed close on their heels.

The years 1914 – 1915 saw a successful, albeit short, revival of Northwood's custard glass production, followed in 1916 by the simpler, artistic iridescent shapes we now call stretch glass. Harry Northwood was indeed at

the zenith of his career, but we can only guess what future artistic innovations in glass-making he may have already envisioned. In the summer of 1918, Harry Northwood fell seriously ill, retiring to his home on Front Street in Wheeling. News reports of the time describe his illness simply as "liver problems." Quite suddenly, on February 4, 1919, the creative genius of Harry Northwood ended at the age of 58.

The factory that bore his name continued operation for six more years, but without the innovative genius of its creator, the firm seemed to lack direction. There was some brief success with a few lines that were produced between 1920 and 1925, but nothing compared to the earlier "glory" years under the leadership of the master. Gradually, mention of the firm's wares faded from the trade journals. On December 12, 1925, production ceased forever at H. Northwood & Co. of Wheeling, West Virginia.

NORTHWOOD IRIDESCENT GLASS PRODUCTION

Most of the soon-to-be major producers of the glass we now call carnival reacted quickly to the introduction of the this new ware by the Fenton Art Glass Company. Fenton had first displayed the glass to the trade during the winter of 1907 – 1908. Within a few months, most of Fenton's competitors were ready to introduce their own iridescent lines, and Harry Northwood was no exception. By the spring of 1908 his new iridescent line which he called "Golden Iris" was ready for the market. The name Golden Iris refers to what we now call marigold. This was not only the first iridescent color produced by Northwood, but also by most of the firms that were to quickly jump on the iridescent glass bandwagon.

No doubt Harry Northwood was quick to realize the potential to be found in this new iridescent glass. It was certainly made to order for showing off elaborate designs and pattern detail. But, mould making and the creating of patterns in which to best express this new art form took time and money. So, many existing moulds already in use for other types of glass were rushed into iridescent production. These were, in effect, temporary measures, used until new designs more appropriate for this new ware could be created, and most of these patterns saw relatively short iridescent production runs. This accounts for why some Northwood Carnival items are found primarily in marigold and are in very short supply today. Patterns such as Cherry & Cable, Northwood's Nearcut, Valentine, the Intaglio Lines (Cherry, Strawberry, and Peach & Pear) and Northwood's version of Waterlily & Cattails are all good examples of this. All of these patterns were in non-iridescent production just prior to 1908. As new, more appropriate designs were created within the following months, these older patterns were all dropped from iridescent production.

By January of 1909, Northwood added two more iridescent colors to his line. We know them as amethyst and green. A wider variety of patterns also began to appear; some like Beaded Cable, Daisy & Plume, Star of David and Wild Rose were still being culled from pre-iridescent production lines. Others, like Finecut & Roses and Vintage Grape, had been purchased from the Jefferson Glass Company. Northwood often marketed his new amethyst color as "Wine Ruby." His first green iridescent line, introduced that year, was called "Alaskan Iridescent." He had discovered that a most unusual color effect could be achieved by spraying the marigold iridizing solution (ferric chloride) over a green base glass. This resulted in a bronze-like or often copper-like iridescent effect. A fairly extensive variety of bowls, compotes, bonbons, vases, and other novelty shapes can be found with this treatment. In 1909 Northwood also produced his first cobalt blue carnival, but for some as yet unknown reason, the color was not produced in quantity until about two years later.

The year 1910 would prove to be a banner one indeed for Harry Northwood and for iridescent glass production in general as well. In January of that year at the Pittsburgh Glass Exhibition, he unveiled his newest pattern creation, designed specifically for iridescent production. While it was sold and advertised under many different trade names, we have come to know it as Grape & Cable or Northwood's Grape. To say that this new pattern was successful would be a considerable understatement. It took the market by storm! A good example of its popularity is to be found in the fall 1910 Butler Brothers wholesale catalog. There are many assortments of Northwood carnival in that catalog. All but two of them are comprised solely of Grape & Cable items! Other well-known Northwood Carnival patterns also made their debut that year. Three Fruits, Northwood Strawberry, Grape Leaves, and Rosette, to name just a few, all made their first appearances in iridescent form in 1910. By now the majority of the activity at the Northwood plant was involved with the production of iridescent wares. Due in large part to the success of the Grape & Cable line, 1910 ended as one of the firm's most profitable years. And Harry Northwood would soon use these profits to greatly expand his iridescent production even further.

The period from 1911 through 1912 saw this rapid expansion take place. In many ways they were the "boom" years of iridescent glass production at Wheeling. An astounding variety of new iridescent colors and newly created patterns emerged from the Northwood plant, more than in any other time frame in the entire era of Northwood's carnival production. Patterns such as Hearts & Flowers, Embroidered Mums, Nippon, Acorn Burrs, Corn Vase, Bushel Basket, Daisy & Drape, virtually all of Northwood's famous "Peacock" designs, and far too many more to list all date from this period. The largest production runs of cobalt blue carnival, not only for Northwood but for his competitors too, began in earnest at this time, as evidenced by that color's proliferation in the wholesale catalogs. Northwood also introduced three new carnival colors to the trade in January of 1912. He called them "pearl, azure, and emerald," but we have come to know them as white, ice blue, and ice green. The era of the pastels had begun. Almost simultaneously with the introduction of the pastel colors came another, totally new iridescent effect: aqua opalescent carnival. Current evidence suggests that Harry Northwood began production of this color early in 1912 to fill a contract for the Mortimer Glass Company. He would shortly thereafter be marketing the color on his own as well. (See the section on Northwood's aqua opalescent carnival for more detailed information about this.) But, there was a downside to all this rapid expansion. The cost of creating and marketing so many new patterns and colors, combined with an expansion of the work force necessary to meet the demand, took its toll. The year 1912 surprisingly ended with the firm operating in the red!

The next three years were somewhat more conservative ones for the Northwood firm, as far as iridescent production was concerned. While many existing patterns and colors continued to be very successful sellers, comparatively few new ones were created, nothing close to the "boom" years of 1911 – 1912. There were however some noteworthy events relating to iridescent production. In February of 1914, Harry Northwood filed for a patent on his Peacock at the Fountain pattern. It was granted five months later. Northwood had been producing the design since 1912, so this may have been done at this time in an attempt to halt one of his major competitors from copying the pattern. The Diamond Glass Company of Indiana, Pa. (formerly the Dugan Glass Co.) had been doing exactly that! The second event took place from 1914 – 1915. For the second time in his career, Harry Northwood turned to the production of custard glass. Many of his most popular iridescent patterns, like Peacock & Urn, Grape & Cable, Three Fruits, Grape Arbor, Grape & Gothic Arches, and many others all underwent custard glass production at this time. Some of these pieces were iridized in two different effects. Some were given a delicate, transparent, pastel iridescent treatment that allowed the ivory color of the custard glass to show through. These examples are called "pearlized custard" by collectors today. The other iridescent treatment used was that of a heavy, marigold color iridescent overlay, known today simply as marigold on custard. Examples of both of these iridized custard treatments are rarely found today. Production of them was obviously quite limited, as was this entire custard glass "revival" attempt by Harry Northwood. It lasted for only two years. One new carnival pattern line that we can tentatively date to this time period is that of Northwood's rare Diamond Point Handled Basket. A November 1915 trade journal reports about a new Northwood line of pressed crystal novelties in a raised "diamond and ribbon" effect, designated as Northwood's #42 line. This sounds like a pretty fair description of the Diamond Points Basket, which is primarily found in non-iridized crystal. However, examples in marigold, amethyst, and cobalt blue carnival are also known. If this #42 line was indeed Northwood's Diamond Point Basket, any iridescent production of it would have to have occurred after November of 1915.

By 1916 production of the glass we have come to call carnival was no longer the mainstay of Northwood's production. Some have speculated that Northwood's production of it ended altogether by that year. Granted, almost no glass that can be categorized as true Northwood carnival appears in any of the general wholesale catalogs after 1917. Then again, there is surprisingly little Northwood glass of any kind in the wholesale catalogs after 1917! Yet the firm remained in business until 1925. How do we account for this? While we do not know for sure, I have a theory I will share with you. From about 1917 onwards, Northwood seems to have abandoned many of his old wholesale marketing techniques. By that time, America was becoming more deeply involved in the war in Europe. Manufacturing costs were rising as more and more materials and resources were being used in preparation for war. Manpower was being lost to military service. A marked increase in the wholesale prices of the glassware assortments in the wholesale catalogs during the 1915 – 1918 period reflects a growing inflation. In order to survive under these conditions, a smart businessman like Harry Northwood must surely find ways to either cut his costs or raise his profit margin. In effect, I think he simply "cut out" the middleman. I think he began to turn away from selling his glass to general wholesalers like Butler Brothers and Charles Broadway Rouss. By marketing his glass direct from the factory to retailers he could likely increase his profit levels by from 25 to 50 percent. This is only theory mind you, but it would certainly explain the lack of Northwood glass, including carnival, in the general wholesale catalogs from 1917 onward. So, did the production of Northwood carnival cease altogether around 1916 – 1917? I think not, and there is a fair amount of evidence to suggest that it continued, albeit on a very limited basis, right up until the plant ceased operations in 1925. This evidence can be found by examining some of the other wares and colors developed by the Northwood firm from 1916 onwards.

In 1916, Northwood introduced his first iridescent lines of the type we call stretch glass today. These lines were primarily produced in several newly developed colors. One of these is called topaz, a brilliant, pastel canary yellow color. It will fluoresce under ultraviolet light, and collectors today often refer to it as vaseline. Some patterned Northwood carnival items like the Hearts & Flowers plate, Bushel Basket, Thin Rib vase, and Four Pillars vase are found in this color, sometimes with a marigold iridescent overlay, but more often with a pastel iridescence and even a stretch effect to the iridescence. Celeste blue was another of the new colors developed for stretch glass, and several patterned Northwood carnival items are known in this color, complete with stretch effect iridescence. The color called "russet," Northwood's version of olive green, was also developed primarily for stretch glass, and it was not introduced until 1920. Yet, patterned carnival pieces both with stretch iridescence and with the more normal, carnival, multicolor iridescence are known in this color. One of the last colors developed by the Northwood firm was called "rosita amber." It is a dark, almost "root beer" color that bears a striking similarity to the carnival color we call "horehound." Yet, this color was not introduced until 1925, just a few months before the plant closed. I think I have made my point here. These colors developed for stretch glass, yet all known in "classic" carnival forms,

present strong evidence for at least some continued production of carnival glass by Northwood after 1917.

If you require further evidence for Northwood carnival production after 1917, then look no further than plain old common sense. Northwood's major, surviving competitors in the production of iridescent glass were Fenton, Diamond, and Imperial. All three of those firms continued to produce carnival glass through the late 1920s. Both Diamond and Imperial produced right up into 1931. So there was still a market for it after 1917, and Harry Northwood was certainly no fool. Nor was the management of the Northwood firm after Harry's death in 1919. Why would they simply abandon to their competitors the production and marketing of the most successful type of glassware the Northwood firm had ever produced? The answer, to my way of thinking, is simple. No way! During the lean years of World War I (and the even leaner ones that followed), maintaining at least some share of the carnival glass market would surely be a major priority. Granted, it may have been on a far more limited basis than in past years, but I'm convinced that at least some of the beautiful glass we call carnival continued to be made at H. Northwood & Co., of Wheeling, West Virginia, right up until the end, in December of 1925.

THE NORTHWOOD TRADEMARK

During the 1800s few American glasshouses trademarked their wares. It was not considered necessary, as there were comparatively few of them in existence to begin with from the period between 1840 through the 1870s. This began to change in the 1880s as the glass industry in America rapidly expanded during the boom years of the Industrial Revolution. By the turn of the century and through the early years of the twentieth century, more and more glasshouses began to adopt trademarks, so that the buying public could distinguish their wares from those of their competitors.

Harry Northwood was one of the first to establish this practice in 1898, at his factory in Indiana, Pennsylvania. He adopted a trademark consisting of the name Northwood, written out in script. This mark can be found on many of his custard glass and opalescent glass lines produced at that location. After moving to Wheeling, West Virginia, in 1901, he adopted a new trademark, the now well-known underlined, capital letter "N" enclosed within a circle. He registered this trademark in 1905. Only glass made at his Wheeling,

West Virginia, plant bears this trademark, and it is the one most commonly found on his iridescent wares. Not all pieces of Northwood Carnival bear this mark however. There are numerous examples of his carnival that are unsigned, and there are several reasons for this. There are some pieces that either due to shape or pattern design will simply not accommodate a trademark. Northwood is also known to have produced iridescent wares for independent jobbers, like the Mortimer Glass Company, and on contracted special orders for other customers. These items would therefore, naturally, not be trademarked. Also, use of this trademark seems to have diminished from about 1916 – 1917 onward. Few examples of his lines from that period bear it. In fact, after Harry Northwood's death in 1919, trademarked wares from the Northwood firm's final six years of production are almost non-existent.

The only other Northwood trademark found on any of his iridescent lines is that of the word "Northwood," spelled out in block style letters. It is found only occasionally on the fitting collar of some of his iridescent gas and electric light shades. Some Northwood items, primarily those that are deep in shape, like Grape & Gothic Arches water pitchers, tumblers. berry bowls, and table set pieces, have a distinct circle without the "N" on the interior center of the base.

This is not a trademark of any kind. It is merely a circular mark made by the "plunger" used in the moulding process.

Today, the copyright to the Northwood trademark is owned by the American Carnival Glass Association. This prevents any American-based firm from copying it. The A.C.G.A. has thus rendered a service of incalculable value to all collectors of Northwood Glass.

NORTHWOOD PASTEL CARNIVAL GLASS

What is pastel carnival glass? It is simply glass of a much lighter, pastel shade of color than that which is found on the more vivid shades like marigold, green, amethyst or cobalt blue. It has a frosty, translucent texture with a delicate, multicolor iridescence. You do not need to hold the piece to light to determine its base glass color, as it is quite obvious from first glance. We call these colors white, ice blue, and ice green today.

For many years it was assumed that production of these pastel colors dated very late in the carnival era and that these colors were created to boost waning interest in iridescent glass. Nothing could be further from the truth! In fact, Northwood introduced these three new colors in January of 1912, at the very height of the iridescent glass production boom. His original names for them were pearl (white), azure (ice blue), and emerald (ice green). Reports in trade journals of the period described them as "being of a much lighter and more delicate tone than anything heretofore offered to the trade." There is no doubt that Northwood was the first to offer these new colors. Other

carnival producers, like Fenton and Dugan, soon offered their own versions of these colors, but their production of them would never come close to matching Northwood's. Harry Northwood was without question the "king" of pastel carnival glass.

Variations on these colors were soon added to the line as well. Potash was added to the molten glass batches to give an opalized effect to the edge. Thus, colors we know today as ice green opalescent and ice blue opalescent were created. Other slight color tone variations were soon created and thus we have pastel colors like sapphire blue.

Northwood's white, ice blue, and ice green carnival colors are in very high demand today, and few items made in them are all that easily found. Many are extremely rare. The rarity of one pastel color over another varies greatly from pattern to pattern and shape to shape. Generally, white is the most available followed by ice blue and ice green, in that order. But I repeat, this is a *very* general ranking, and there are numerous exceptions to this which you will find noted in the pattern texts of this book.

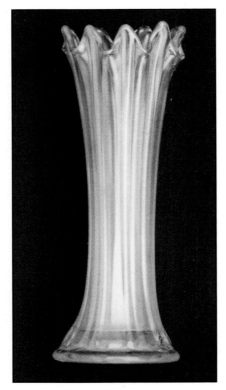

White

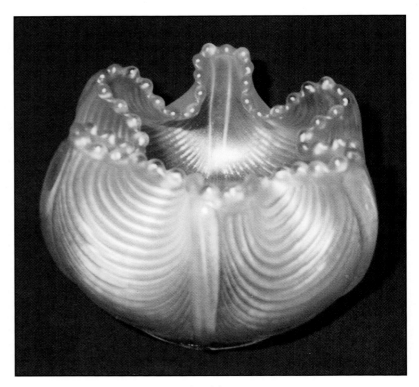

Ice blue

Ice green

NORTHWOOD PEACH OPALESCENT CARNIVAL GLASS

Considered by many to be one of the most beautiful carnival glass colors, peach opalescent is essentially marigold carnival with pearl-white, opalized edges and/or undersurfaces. Potash was added to the hot, crystal glass resulting in the opalized effect. Then it was sprayed with ferric chloride iridizing spray to produce the marigold iridescent coloring.

The Dugan Glass Co. of Indiana, Pennsylvania, was the largest producer of this iridescent/opalescent color combination. In fact, Thomas Dugan was the first to produce it and was likely the originator of the color. Northwood also made some peach opalescent, but it is so rare that it can only be considered experimental on his part. Currently, less than a dozen examples of true Northwood peach opalescent carnival are known to exist. These include a Grape & Cable 2-handled bonbon, two known Beaded Cable rosebowls, a Ruffles & Rings footed bowl, and a handful of Northwood Strawberry plates. And herein lies one of the major mysteries surrounding Northwood's iridescent production. A tantalizingly vague reference to what sounds like a description of the color is found in a January 1909 trade journal, reporting on Northwood's display at the Pittsburgh Glass Exhibition. It describes Northwood's new iridescent line "on which the applied color is subsequently accentuated by a coating of dead white for a second background." It certainly sounds like a reporter's description of peach opalescent, and the 1909 time frame of this quote coincides precisely with Dugan's earliest production of the color. It would indeed seem the logical time for Northwood to introduce his version of the color as well, in order to capture a share of the market. But there are problems here. Two of the four known patterns in Northwood's peach opalescent (Grape & Cable and Northwood's Strawberry) did not yet exist in 1909; they were first marketed in 1910. The other two did exist (Beaded Cable and Ruffles & Rings), but two lonely pieces would certainly not make much of a display. Certainly not enough to warrant a reporter writing about them in a trade journal. Also, if Northwood had committed himself to the production of this color, enough so as to make a display of it at the exhibition and presumably take orders for it, then...where is all of it? If so, surely more than just 10 or 12 pieces of it would have survived the years and be known today.

It has been suggested that this trade journal quote may instead be in reference to Northwood's marigold on custard glass. This can be discounted for two reasons. First, Northwood did indeed make custard glass with a marigold iridescent overlay. But this occurred during 1914 – 1915, when Northwood attempted a brief revival of custard or "ivory" glass, as it was called then. He is not known to have produced any custard glass at his Wheeling plant prior to 1914. Secondly, virtually all of the patterns known in marigold on custard did not exist in 1909. They are all patterns that were created during the 1910 – 1914 period, with most of them dating 1912 – 1914.

So, just exactly what this quote refers to and why Northwood apparently chose to produce so little peach opalescent, a very popular seller with his major competitor Thomas Dugan, remains shrouded by the mists of time. We may never know the answer. Regardless, the rarity of Northwood's peach opalescent is something every collector should bear in mind. Keep your eyes peeled. Who knows? You may just be lucky enough to find a piece. There must surely be undiscovered examples out there somewhere.

Northwood Aqua Opalescent Carnival Glass

Considered by many to be the ultimate expression of iridescent color artistry, the production of Northwood's aqua opalescent carnival glass, like his peach opalescent carnival, is shrouded in mystery. No assortments of the color have ever surfaced in any existing wholesale catalogs, so it was obviously not intended to be marketed to the general retail trade in the usual manner. In fact, no mention of the color, nor any advertising for it, has ever surfaced in any existing Northwood advertising or literature. Yet, there is virtually no doubt that Northwood made it, and in fact, was the largest producer of the color. So, when was it made? And, for whom was it made? While we don't have all the answers as yet, a few pieces of the puzzle are slowly starting to fall into place.

A 1912 trade journal report contains two tidbits of information that have been key factors in opening the door to the mystery surrounding Northwood's production of aqua opalescent carnival. Both refer to a man named George Mortimer and the success of the Mortimer Glass Company's "new iridescent lines," including "a number of specialties" that he carried. George Mortimer? The Mortimer Glass Company?

George Mortimer was actually a well-known figure in the glass industry in the early 1900s. Prior to the iridescent glass production era, he had worked at several prominent glasshouses, including Fenton and Northwood. In 1908, he went on his own and founded the Mortimer Glass Company. Mortimer was an independent "jobber," that is, he did not actually manufacture glass himself. He contracted with various factories to produce glass for him, which he then marketed as his own product. This was not an uncommon practice then and is still not uncommon today. (A good present day example is the L. G. Wright Glass Company, which closed just over two years ago.) Could aqua opalescent carnival glass have been made by Northwood for George Mortimer? This may well be the case. Let's look at the evidence.

1. The date of these quotes, 1912, coincides precisely with the time that virtually all the patterns Northwood is known to have produced in aqua opalescent were in production.

2. Bearing in mind that the quotes are referring to "new iridescent lines," the quote of "a number of specialties" implies something unique, out of the ordinary, different from other iridized wares.

3. Any glass made by Northwood for an independent jobber such as Mortimer, who was going to market the glass as his own product, would certainly not be signed with the Northwood trademark. An unusually large percentage of Northwood aqua opalescent pieces are not trademarked. (This could also account for the fact that many other unusual colors of Northwood carnival are not trademarked as well. It's possible some of these other colors may also have been made for Mortimer or other independent jobbers.)

4. Mortimer had been previously employed by both Northwood and Fenton, so he had obvious ties to both of them. Is it therefore merely coincidence that Northwood and Fenton were the two primary producers of aqua opalescent carnival? I think not.

As is the case with most detective work, answers to questions usually lead to more questions, and this case is no exception. If aqua opalescent was a color uniquely made by Northwood for George Mortimer, then what about all the signed examples that exist? What about Fenton's aqua opalescent carnival pieces? What about the two known pieces of Millersburg's aqua opalescent carnival? All very valid questions, and there are answers. We must first answer the mystery of the two Millersburg aqua opalescent Ohio Star vases, the only Millersburg pieces known in that color. The time frame is the key here. Consider the following scenario. It was 1912. George Mortimer had an idea for a completely new iridescent color effect. He needed someone to produce it for him. He first went to Millersburg with his idea, and they made a couple of sample or "test" pieces for his approval. He may well have been very pleased with them, as they are beautiful.

However, by early in 1912 Millersburg was in serious financial difficulty and had already been forced to reorganize as the Radium Glassware Company. They would, in fact, cease operations altogether by June of that year. George Mortimer, hesitant to enter into a production contract under those circumstances, likely saw the handwriting on the wall and decided to take his business elsewhere.

So, to whom did George Mortimer go to with his idea: Northwood or Fenton? My bet is on Harry Northwood. Mortimer goes to Northwood with his idea. Test pieces are run. He is pleased with the results, and a contract with Northwood to produce the glass is secured. The glass is made, George Mortimer markets it, and it is hugely successful. When the contract has been fulfilled, Mortimer tries for a second contract with Northwood to produce more glass.

But Harry Northwood is a shrewd business man. He is no doubt envious of the success Mortimer has enjoyed marketing this unique iridescent color and realizes he has a real winner. Rather than enter into a second contract with Mortimer, he decides to produce and market the glass himself. Very few glass makers of the era ever filed for exclusive patents on their wares. If Mortimer had no patent on the color, then anyone was free to produce it.

And that is exactly what Harry Northwood did. The color line was expanded to include many more shapes and patterns, thus easily explaining the existence of all the signed Northwood aqua opalescent items. They were made and marketed by Northwood after his contract with Mortimer had expired.

George Mortimer may have then gone to Fenton or perhaps not. Fenton did make the color, but apparently in relatively few shapes and patterns. It is far more rare than Northwood's. Perhaps Mortimer did contract with Fenton to produce some of the color. It is also possible that he did not and Fenton merely produced some of it on their own to compete with Northwood. We may never know the answers to this part of the mystery, but one thing is certain: Northwood, by this time, had no doubt captured the lion's share of the market on this beautiful color. Perhaps Fenton tried it, but could not gain a profitable enough share of the market to warrant larger production of the color. Perhaps they made it for Mortimer in small quantities, but by then Northwood had cornered the market on the color, so Mortimer just gave up. All these questions remain unanswered, for now. But the scenario I have presented here is based upon the few tiny bits of the puzzle that are known to us at present. And they do seem to fit. Perhaps one day more definitive information on the production circumstances surrounding this beautiful and immensely popular Northwood carnival color will come to light.

Aqua opalescent

THE NORTHWOOD-JEFFERSON MOULDS

Not all of the patterns that Northwood used for his iridescent creations originated at the Northwood factory. Some are now known to have been purchased from other glasshouses. The Jefferson Glass Co. was located in Follansbee, West Virginia. They were a major producer of decorative glass during the late 1800s and very early 1900s, one of the largest producers of non-iridized opalescent pattern glass. Their designs such as Tokyo and Swag with Brackets are well known to collectors of opalescent glass. But by 1907, Jefferson had decided to relocate and shift their production away from the decorative glassware market. They became a major producer of functional, practical glass items, specifically for the architectural and newly blossoming automotive trades.

In 1908, Harry Northwood purchased several of their moulds. Two facts have confirmed this. First, several patterns known to have been produced in iridescent form by Harry Northwood after 1908 appear in non-iridized forms in pre-1907 Jefferson factory catalogs. Secondly, a surviving memo written by Harry Northwood specifically refers to iridescent production problems with "a mould purchased from Jefferson."

We can now confirm that Northwood purchased at least four pattern moulds from Jefferson, all of which quickly found their way into iridescent production: Finecut & Roses, Meander, Ruffles & Rings, and Vintage Grape. All of these patterns appear in pre-1907 Jefferson catalogs. They also appear among Jefferson opalescent glass assortments in the Butler Brothers wholesale catalogs right up into mid 1908. Then, they suddenly vanished from the Jefferson assortments late in 1908, only to magically reappear in Northwood iridescent assortments a few months later. This leaves little doubt as to where Northwood obtained the patterns.

Meander, Ruffles & Rings, and Vintage Grape all found their niche in iridescent form as secondary exterior designs, combined with a variety of other Northwood primary, interior patterns. Finecut & Roses became one of the most popular Northwood carnival patterns, made in rosebowls and footed candy dishes, in an extensive array of iridescent colors.

When found unsigned and in non-iridized opalescent colors, pieces in these patterns are all pre-1907 Jefferson products. It is possible that Northwood may have purchased other moulds from Jefferson, or even other glasshouses, but for now, these are the only ones we know of for certain.

NORTHWOOD CARNIVAL GLASS COLORS

A wide variety of iridescent colors emerged from the Northwood factory between 1908 and 1925. Many were regular production colors, some saw very limited production, likely made only for specific customers, and some are merely slight variations of standard production colors. In some cases it is doubtful that some of these slight variations were even intended as separate color entities, but merely the result of a poorly mixed batch of some other color. Quality control as we know it today did not exist then. There were no machines or computers to regulate constant temperature or precise chemical mix when a batch of glass was made. It was all done by eye and hand, so variations in color tone and density are quite common. Still, carnival collectors today qualify many colors as separate entities, so as they say, "When in Rome...."

The names of the Northwood carnival colors presented here are the ones that are used and accepted by most collectors today. In many cases they are not the original names used by the manufacturer, but have come to be the names most widely used today.

MARIGOLD: An orange iridescent effect usually applied to a clear base glass. Ferric chloride spray was used to achieve this. It may range from a light, pastel tone to a dark, rich, "pumpkin" effect. It was the first iridescent color used by Northwood, starting in 1908.

CLAMBROTH: Some collectors refer to this as "champagne" or "ginger ale," very descriptive terms. The iridescent effect is that of a very light, ginger ale-colored tone over a clear base glass. It is rarely found on Northwood pieces, but some examples do exist.

PEACH OPALESCENT: Marigold with a white opalized edge and/or undersurface. The opalizing was achieved by adding potash to the hot glass. Dugan was the major producer of this color. Northwood apparently only experimented with the color. Fewer than a dozen pieces of true Northwood Peach opalescent are known to exist.

AMETHYST/PURPLE: There are two color tones involved here, but it is doubtful that they were originally intended as such. Purple is just that: a deep purple color. Amethyst tends to have a more reddish or even rust-colored tone, but both were really intended as the same color. They are merely the results of variations in the chemical mix or temperature when a batch of glass was made. Northwood often advertised this color as "wine ruby." For reasons of convenience, we shall use the general name "amethyst" when referring to these colors in this book.

BLACK AMETHYST: Virtually opaque unless held directly to a very strong light source. It will show a strong, dense red or exceptionally deep purple tone when held to such light. It is actually an iridized version of Northwood's opaque "ebony" color.

LAVENDER: A delicate pastel shade of purple with pastel iridescence. Think of a very light purple of the same pastel tones as ice blue or ice green.

VIOLET: Often called "wisteria," this is a very light shade of lavender, only with a distinct blue tint to it. It is literally the color of a violet, with a soft, pastel iridescence, and violet is the term most accepted by collectors. This is an extremely rare color for Northwood and known only on a few pieces.

GREEN: May range from a medium to a very dark, rich, emerald tone. Northwood produced large quantities of it between 1909 and 1912; less from 1912 onwards.

ICE GREEN: A very light, translucent shade of green with a delicate, frosty iridescence. The color was introduced in January of 1912.

LIME GREEN: Very similar to ice green, but just slightly darker and "sharper" in tone. Some pieces have an extremely faint tinge of yellow in them. It is doubtful (in my opinion) that this was ever intended as a separate color, but more likely the result of a slightly "off-color" batch of ice green.

ICE GREEN OPALESCENT: Ice green with an opalized edge and/or undersurface, a very rare Northwood color.

LIME GREEN OPALESCENT: Lime green with an opalized edge and/or undersurface, also very rarely seen.

RUSSET: Northwood's version of olive green, this color was introduced late in Northwood's iridescent production, circa 1919.

WHITE: A delicate, translucent white with a frosty, pastel iridescence. Northwood introduced this color in January of 1912, calling it "pearl iridescent."

COBALT BLUE: A dark blue color, often marketed as "royal blue."

ICE BLUE: A translucent pastel blue with a delicate, frosty iridescence. Introduced in January of 1912 and called azure by Northwood.

ICE BLUE OPALESCENT: Ice blue with opalized edges and/or undersurfaces, a very rare Northwood color.

POWDER BLUE OPALESCENT: Just slightly darker and denser in color tone than ice blue opalescent. Probably nothing more than the result of a slight chemical or temperature variation during the manufacturing process.

CELESTE BLUE: A shade darker and richer in tone than ice blue, this color was primarily used for production of what is called stretch glass today. On occasion a patterned carnival glass piece surfaces in this color, usually with the "onionskin" stretch effect to the iridescence. This color was marketed by Northwood in 1916.

SAPPHIRE BLUE: The color of sapphire or "sky blue," this color is very similar in tone to celeste blue, but examples do not have the stretch effect to the iridescence. Rarely found.

RENNINGER BLUE: This color was so named because the first known examples of it turned up at the famous Renninger's Antique Market in Pennsylvania, and continued to be found in that area for some time. It is a very difficult color to describe, lighter than cobalt blue, but much darker than ice blue or sapphire. It is somewhat like a pastel shade of teal, but with a strong blue tone. (See Northwood's Peacocks elsewhere in this book for a good example of the color.)

TEAL: A dark to medium color with strong blended blue/green tones.

AQUA: Turquoise, a pastel blue/green blend.

AQUA OPALESCENT: Aqua with opalized edges and/or undersurfaces. In production during the 1912 – 1914 time frame and a very popular color with collectors today.

HOREHOUND: Northwood's unusual version of amber, it is so named because of its resemblance in color to old-fashioned horehound candy. It is not unlike a root beer color and is often found with a slight lavender tint in the glass. (See Bushel Basket for an example of this color.)

HONEY AMBER: A light pastel version of amber, with a definite "honey" tone. Rarely seen.

NORTHWOOD CARNIVAL GLASS COLORS

SMOKE: A translucent, smoky gray color, sometimes with a very light lavender tint to it. A rare color for Northwood.

VASELINE: Actually a brilliant canary yellow base glass. Sometimes found with a marigold iridescent overlay, but most Northwood examples are all-over yellow with a rich, pastel iridescence. Some examples have stretch effect iridescence. Most will glow under blacklight. This color dates from the 1916 period.

MARIGOLD ON CUSTARD: Opaque custard glass with a marigold iridescent overlay. Dates circa 1914 – 1915.

PEARLIZED CUSTARD: Custard glass with a very delicate, pastel "rainbow" iridescence. No marigold coloring to this. Dates circa 1914 – 1915.

BLUE SLAG: An opaque blue glass with a swirled, "marbleized" effect with a dark, heavy iridescent overlay. Extremely rare. Only a handful of pieces known.

IRIDESCENT EFFECTS

Not only did Northwood produce an extensive variety of iridescent base glass colors, but also a variety of different iridescent effects and treatments. These are effects that have nothing to do with the base glass colors. They were achieved by alterations in procedure, temperature, and the iridizing solution applied to the hot glass.

SATIN IRIDESCENCE: This is the effect most often found on Northwood carnival. It is a rich, multicolor iridescence with a soft satiny patina, often with considerable gold tones in the iridescence. It was achieved by spraying the iridizing solution onto very hot glass. The hotter the glass, the more satiny the effect.

RADIUM IRIDESCENCE: This term is most often used with reference to Millersburg carnival glass, as they were the primary producers of this effect. It has a brilliant, transparent, almost "mirror-like" multicolor iridescence that allows the base glass color to show through without holding the piece to light. Northwood seldom used it, but examples do surface on rare occasion. It was achieved by spraying the iridizing solution onto the glass at a cooler temperature than for the satin effect.

ALASKAN IRIDESCENCE: Northwood marketed this unusual effect in 1909, and Alaskan iridescence is his original name for it. It is green base glass with the marigold (ferric chloride) iridescent spray applied to it. The result is an unusual color combination of marigold over green, often with a soft, "bronze-like" or even "copper-like" color tone to the overall iridescent effect.

ELECTRIC IRIDESCENCE: This term probably causes more confusion than any other. Electric iridescence is a positively brilliant, stark, almost glowing effect, usually with a very heavy, almost neon blue tone as the predominate color in the iridescent effect. This effect was actually achieved by spraying the glass twice, with two different iridescent spray solutions. First, the glass was sprayed with the usual ferric chloride solution. Then a second spray of either chloride of antimony or tin chloride was quickly applied. The result was the brilliant electric blue iridescence so eagerly sought by today's collectors. In his personal notes, Harry Northwood mentioned this process, noting that it "gives blue colors and is rich." This electric blue iridescent effect is found not only on pieces of blue base glass, but on amethyst, green, and occasionally, marigold pieces. It can be found on virtually any vivid base glass color.

STRETCH IRIDESCENCE: This effect has a pronounced "onionskin" effect, or "stretch marks" to the iridescence effect. This is achieved by shaping the piece after the iridizing solution has been applied, whereas with the normal carnival iridizing process, the piece was shaped prior to the application of the iridizing spray. This can also be achieved by reheating the already iridized glass after it has cooled. A slight expansion of the cooled glass, when reheated, causes the stretch effect. This effect is most often associated with the plain, unpatterned wares known as stretch glass today, but on occasion, patterned examples, in several of Northwood carnival designs, were made with this effect. It is most often found on the more pastel colors, like lavender, celeste blue, and vaseline, but examples in amethyst, cobalt blue, green, and even marigold are also known with stretch effect to the iridescence.

THE WHOLESALE CATALOGS

Among the most valuable tools in researching glass are the wholesale merchandise catalogs. During the years between 1880 and 1940, the bulk of the general merchandise offered to the retailers in this country was sold through several large wholesale firms, like G. Sommers & Co., Charles Broadway Rouss, and the king of them all, Butler Brothers. This latter firm was by far the largest of these, with showrooms and warehouses in several large American cities. Their showroom in Chicago covered nearly five acres! Through their huge 300 – 450 page wholesale catalogs titled "Our Drummer," Butler Brothers offered every conceivable type of merchandise, from chewing gum to automobiles, to the nation's retailers. Clothing, furniture, tools, toys, jewelry, sporting goods, pottery, china, and of course, glassware were all offered to the trade.

The glassware was offered in assortments, all of which were packed at the factory of origin, and it is this feature that makes these catalogs such valuable research tools. For example, if a piece of carnival glass in a previously unknown pattern were to surface, these catalogs could help identify the item's maker. If it turned up in an assortment of glassware that con-tained patterns known to have been made by Northwood, then there is no question that your mystery piece also originated at the Northwood plant.

These catalogs, which were updated and revised several times a year, also offer interesting insight into the manner in which carnival glass was marketed, revealing original trade names used to market and promote the glass, the wholesale prices at which it was sold, and perhaps most importantly, a valuable time line for dating when certain patterns, shapes, and colors were produced. Throughout this book you will find selections relating to Northwood carnival glass taken from these catalogs. I hope they will add to your enjoyment and that you will find them an interesting perspective with regards to your carnival glass collecting.

You will also find several pages reprinted from the 1906 Northwood factory catalog. The only known Northwood catalog, it pre-dates carnival production by two years and offers many pattern lines carried over into iridescent production. Since these lines may relate directly to their later carnival versions, I have included them for your enjoyment.

REPRODUCTIONS & FAKES

It would be wonderful if I could say there were no reproductions or fakes with regards to Northwood's carnival glass, but sadly such is not the case. Sooner or later, virtually anything of value or desirable to the collector will be reproduced, and Northwood carnival glass is no exception. Some of these reproductions have been around for more than 25 years, and some have only recently appeared on the market. Worse still, over the last five years these reproductions and fakes have grown in number at an alarming rate. More and more new carnival pieces are coming out of Taiwan every day, and several American glasshouses now own moulds that originated at Northwood, Dugan, Imperial, and many others. We have actually reached a point in time where examples of new glass are outnumbering the old in shops, antique malls, and flea markets.

In many cases, newer carnival glass tends to have a more gaudy and garish tone to the iridescence. It is often very bright, shiny, has a somewhat "slippery" feel to it, and lacks the smooth, subtle blend of colors that is found on the old. But this is not a hard, fast rule. As time passes, many companies producing new carnival glass are getting the hang of it, and there are examples turning up that come closer and closer to the look of old carnival. One thing to look for is the weight and thickness of the glass. Most new glass is deliberately made thicker and heavier than the old. Glass is proportionately far more expensive to produce now than it was 75 – 100 years ago, and this is done as a cost-saving method to cut down on breakage and loss during production.

What follows is a listing of companies that have reproduced or are currently reproducing Northwood items in both iridescent and non-iridescent forms.

THE L.G. WRIGHT GLASS COMPANY

This firm was established back in the late 1930s. Wright actually produced no glassware themselves, but rather acted as a "jobber" firm. They owned the moulds, but would have other glasshouses make items for them and then market the finished products as their own wares. In the late 1930s, L.G. Wright travelled around buying up moulds. He went to Indiana, Pennsylvania, and purchased many carnival glass moulds that had been salvaged from the old Dugan/Diamond Glass Co., after fire had destroyed that plant in 1931. He also acquired some Northwood moulds around the same time. It is not currently known whether these were acquired by Diamond after Northwood closed in 1925, or whether Mr. Wright also travelled to Wheeling, West Virginia, and purchased them there. But he definitely did own and reproduce some Grape & Cable pieces, so he obviously obtained the moulds somewhere.

Starting around 1970, L.G. Wright began marketing new carnival glass items. Most were made in old Dugan/Diamond moulds and patterns, but for some inexplicable reason Wright chose to mark some of these items with a *very* misleading trademark, a slight variation on the old Northwood mark, that to this day fools a lot of people. A comparison of the original Northwood trademark and the L.G. Wright trademark used in the early 1970s is shown below.

Old Northwood trademark

L.G. Wright trademark

Wright used this trademark on carnival glass items, custard glass, and opalescent glass, so **beware of this mark.** It is *not* an old Northwood trademark, and this glass is still seen frequently on the market today. In the mid 1970s, L.G. Wright abandoned the use of this mark in favor of a less stylized "W" in a circle. The firm went out of business in 1999. Unfortunately, all of the moulds owned by Wright were sold at auction. Some have ended up in Taiwan, and others were purchased by many existing glasshouses, so future reproductions of Northwood and Dugan patterns are virtually assured!

THE MOSSER GLASS COMPANY

Mosser began making new carnival glass items in the 1970s and still does so today. They often leased moulds from L.G. Wright for their own use. They also now own some Northwood and Dugan moulds, some of which were purchased at the L.G. Wright mould auction in 1999. Around 1980, Mosser marketed several carnival glass items that contained a blatantly deceptive trademark. Many of these were in Northwood's Grape & Cable pattern. They included butter dishes and both large and small footed banana bowls, in the colors of ice blue, cobalt blue, ice green, and amber. The piece that seems to cause the most confusion is the Grape & Cable butter dish. The old Northwood one has fluted, sawtooth-like edge points on the base. The Mosser reproduction has a broadly scalloped base. A comparison of the old Northwood trademark with the mark used by Mosser is shown below.

Old Northwood trademark

Mosser reproduction

The American Carnival Glass Association owns the rights to the old Northwood trademark. This new mark used by Mosser was deemed too similar to that of the old Northwood mark to be considered anything other than deceptive. Legal action was taken on behalf of the A.C.G.A., and Mosser was forced to abandon use of this mark. Still, examples of these pieces turn up on today's market, so be advised. Many other new Mosser carnival items are either unmarked or bear a capital letter "M."

MADE IN TAIWAN

Reproductions from Taiwan of many carnival glass items began showing up on the American market in the early 1980s, and they are now proliferating at an alarming rate! New pieces of patterns originally made by Northwood, Dugan, Fenton, and even Millersburg, are flooding the market, in both iridized and non-iridized forms. Most are sold here through import houses like A.A. Importing Co. and Castle Imports, among others. They are marked only with foil labels reading "Made In Taiwan," which, of course, are easily removed. The problem is that because these items are manufactured outside the United States, there is little that can be done to stop them.

CURRENT KNOWN REPRODUCTIONS

Listed here are items that are currently known reproductions of Northwood patterns, in both iridized and non-iridized forms. These are the ones that I am aware of at present, and I have attempted to be as thorough as possible. However, new reproductions are appearing on the market so fast that it is virtually impossible to be 100 percent timely. There will no doubt be others by the time you read this book.

CHERRY & CABLE: Massively reproduced in a wide variety of colors and shapes. Some shapes were never originally made. Old pieces are documented *only* in marigold. New pieces include butter dish, creamer, spooner, covered sugar, celery vase, cracker jar, water pitcher, tumbler, stemmed goblet, and a full line of miniature children's toy pieces (never made originally) in carnival colors of purple and pastel green opalescent. Non-iridized pieces are being made in color stained crystal, custard glass, chocolate glass, ruby, cobalt blue, and pink. Most are made by Mosser.

DRAPERY ROSEBOWL: Made in aqua opalescent carnival by Fenton. The Fenton version rests on three scrolled feet, while the Northwood original is collar based. Trademarked with the Fenton logo, so should present no problems.

FRUITS & FLOWERS BONBON: Made in amethyst carnival by Fenton in the 1970s. Trademarked with the Fenton logo, so no problem here. A 14" chop plate and large ruffled bowl was also marketed in amethyst carnival by L.G. Wright in the 1970s. They are marked with the L.G. Wright mark shown previously.

GOOD LUCK: Bowls and 14" chop plates have been reproduced in marigold, amethyst, cobalt blue, and green. They are believed to be coming from Taiwan and are marked on the back with a grossly oversized "N" with no circle or underline. Iridescence on these is very gaudy and metallic looking.

GRAPE & CABLE: Unfortunately a lot of reproductions here and more surely on the way! Reproductions by Mosser include large and small footed banana bowls in ice blue and amber; butter dishes in ice blue, cobalt blue, ice green, and amber. Hatpin holders in purple, cobalt blue, green, ruby, and amberina are coming out of Taiwan. Water sets in amethyst carnival recently appeared on the market, maker currently uncertain. Non-iridized reproductions of the butter dish, creamer, spooner, water pitcher, tumbler, and hatpin holder exist in purple, cobalt blue, pink, green, ruby, amberina, custard glass, and chocolate glass, some from Taiwan, others by Mosser. Several other items including large ruffled bowls, humidors, and handled baskets were all made by Fenton in limited editions for various customers in a variety of iridized and non-iridized forms, but all clearly bear the Fenton Logo.

HEARTS & FLOWERS: The only item here is a large 11" dome-footed bowl, made in amberina and amethyst by Fenton in the 1970s. It is marked with the Fenton logo and is a size and shape never made by Northwood.

PEACOCKS (PEACOCKS ON THE FENCE): Bowls, believed to be from Taiwan, in marigold, cobalt blue, and green. The pattern goes nearly to the edge of the bowl, unlike on the old ones. Marked with the huge, oversized "N" on the base with no circle or underline. Very gaudy "mirror-like" iridescence.

SINGING BIRDS: Tumblers in cobalt blue, amethyst, and ice blue opalescent carnival. Possibly made by Summit Art Glass Co., but uncertain as of this writing.

NOTES ON COLLECTING

There is certainly enough variety within the field of Northwood's carnival glass to satisfy any collecting tastes. Whether your tastes run to bowls, plates, compotes, rosebowls, bonbons, water pitchers, tumblers, mugs, vases, table sets, or punch sets, there is something within the vast array of shapes made by Northwood to please everyone. Many collectors specialize within particular areas. Some concentrate on plates, some on bowls, some on pitchers and tumblers. That's entirely up to you. My own philosophy is one of variety. The seemingly endless possible combination of shapes and colors is really what carnival glass is all about. A varied collection is more interesting, presents a better representation of this diversity, and also broadens the education of the collector. It can pay off in other ways, too. A varied collection will attract the greatest possible interest on the part of prospective bidders when the time comes to sell. Collecting fads come and go. With these fads come fluctuations in prices paid by prospective bidders at a carnival glass auction. For example, if you have built an entire collection comprised of compotes and rosebowls and those two shapes are not especially in vogue when you are ready to sell, you will not realize the highest potential return on your investment. With a varied collection, there is something there for everyone, thus attracting a better bidding crowd.

Building a collection of Northwood carnival is most definitely a challenge today. Twenty-five or 30 years ago it was relatively easy. Examples of quality pieces were abundant at shops, shows, local auctions, and flea markets. You could pick and choose what you wanted to buy, confident in the knowledge that there would always be more "down the road." A collection of 100 – 300 pieces or so could be accumulated in a relatively short period of time. You would then cull the collection, keeping your best or favored pieces. The rest was sold, and the funds used to upgrade. This process was frequently repeated, resulting in an ever higher degree of quality to your collection. Little attention was paid to actual values of the pieces we bought, as prices were only a fraction of what they are today. We bought what we liked with little regard to investment return. This is how a collection was built.

Things have certainly changed! It would be virtually impossible to build a collection in this manner today. Not only have values reached levels not even dreamed of 20 or 30 years ago, but the glass is simply not available in any degree of abundance today. Quality pieces of carnival glass are few and far between in shops, local auctions, and flea markets. One can no longer be confident that there will always be more down the road. It takes time, patience, and money to build a quality collection today. Gone forever are the days when we could pick and choose, cull and upgrade at our leisure. Collections today, by necessity, are built slowly with careful consideration given to shape, color, iridescence, and price before a purchase is made. Better now to invest the hard-earned dollar in fewer pieces, but of higher quality, because the odds are you will *not* find another one down the road! My best advice is to buy what appeals to you, but buy the best possible quality of color, shape, and iridescence that your collecting budget will allow.

Peacocks ruffled bowl

Greek Key pie crust edge bowl

PATTERN: ACORN BURRS

One of the most eagerly sought and highly treasured of all Northwood carnival patterns, Acorn Burrs is truly a masterpiece of the mould maker's art. Many feel it is Harry Northwood's finest effort and rightfully so. Unusually high relief, fantastic pattern detail, and not so much as a centimeter of wasted space combine in breathtaking fashion, placing Acorn Burrs very high on the list of must-have patterns.

Originally advertised as Northwood's Chestnut line (which is what the design really depicts), Acorn Burrs was made in a full line of functional pieces that include berry set, table set, water set, and punch set. As can best be determined at this time, the berry set, table set, and water set seem to have entered production during the 1910 – 1911 period. All three of these sets are known only in marigold, amethyst, and green, which were Northwood's primary production colors during this time. The punch sets underwent a much more extensive production. They are known in marigold, amethyst, green, white, ice blue, ice green, and the ultra-rare aqua opalescent. This tends to confirm that the punch set was added to the line at a later date. Northwood did not introduce his pastel carnival colors until January of 1912, so production of the punch set had to have taken place after that date. The existence of the rare aqua opalescent examples reinforces this, as research has now revealed a 1912 – 1914 time frame for the production of this color. No examples of the berry set, table set or water set have ever surfaced in any of the pastel colors. Perhaps they were no longer in production during the 1912 – 1914 period. It is also possible that Harry Northwood simply chose not to make them in the pastel colors, for reasons that remain unknown.

One other fact about this design further tends to confirm the above mentioned production time frame. A handful of Acorn Burrs punch cups is known in cobalt blue. Research has now revealed that most of the major carnival producers did not begin full production of this color until the 1912 period. No cobalt blue carnival appears in any of the existing wholesale catalogs until that time. A cobalt blue Acorn Burrs punch base has also been reported, but I have been unable to confirm its existence. To the best of my knowledge, no cobalt blue Acorn Burrs punch bowl has ever been confirmed.

The only other item known in this design is a most unusual whimsey vase, which was swung from the tumbler mould. Only one example, in amethyst, has been reported. Mention should also be made of the souvenir or "etched" examples that are sometimes found. Punch cups and tumblers are known with an etched name and date on them, around the plain top band. Some bear the date 1912 while others have a 1914 date.

Value wise, Acorn Burrs always brings top dollar. The demand for this design far outweighs supply, so don't expect to find these pieces at bargain prices. The berry set, table set, water set, and punch set are found most often in marigold and amethyst. Green turns up far less often, especially in the water set and punch set. As to the punch set, the ice green examples seem to be the rarest of the three pastel colors. Of course, the magnificent aqua opalescent punch sets command the top billing. I personally know of only three complete sets, with a few punch cups scattered about in collections.

Shapes & Colors Known

Berry, table or water set:
    marigold, amethyst, green
Punch set: marigold, amethyst, green, white, ice blue, ice green, aqua opalescent (punch cups known in cobalt blue)
Whimsey vase: amethyst

Many collectors consider the Acorn Burrs punch set, shown here in amethyst, to be the most beautiful of any carnival punch set by any maker.

C1987, "Rustic" — 11 in deep bowl separate stand, full ht. 11 in., 12 handled cups, relief nut and leaf embossing, all over dk. metallic iridescent finish. 3 sets in bbl., 60 lbs.. Set, **$1.60**

This unique punch bowl base is an example of Northwood's iridescent Luna line which was introduced early in 1912. Luna, densely textured and almost opaque, was used exclusively for the production of electric light shades. If the matching bowl and cups should ever surface, this unique set would rank with the aqua opal Grape & Cable punch set and the Wisteria whimsey vase as the top three rarities in the entire field of carnival collecting.

For many years we had nothing more than an educated guess of a 1912 time frame for the production of the Acorn Burrs punch set. We were right on the money! This ad, from a newly discovered spring 1912 Butler Brothers catalog, offers the set with 12 cups, something we usually associate with the larger banquet size sets like the Grape & Cable banquet punch set.

Although it is called Acorn Burrs today, the exquisite detail of its original name, Chestnut, is clearly revealed on the water pitcher and creamer, both in amethyst.

PATTERN: BASKET OF ROSES

If you're really on your toes, you just might discover a real bargain here. Many people confuse this very scarce pattern with the more readily available Fenton design called Wreath of Roses. While the two patterns do have many similarities, there are enough major differences to easily distinguish between the two. Northwood's Basket of Roses is found only on a collar based, two-handled bonbon, while the Fenton Wreath of Roses is found on a stemmed, two-handled bonbon. The center portion is unpatterned, and the exterior carries the famous Northwood's Basketweave pattern. Fenton's Wreath of Roses has a rose in the center and a Wide Panel exterior pattern. Basket of Roses has fewer roses and rosebuds than on the Fenton look-alike, and most examples carry the Northwood N in a circle trademark. The background may be plain or stippled.

The other major difference is an important one, and it concerns rarity and value. While Fenton's Wreath of Roses bonbons are quite readily available in many carnival colors, this is certainly not the case for Northwood's Basket of Roses bonbons. They are quite rare in any color and always command much higher prices. Marigold, amethyst, and cobalt blue are the only colors reported to date. Most of the known cobalt blue examples have the stippled background. A green example would be a terrific find, but none has been confirmed to date. I've also been amazed that no white examples have turned up, as that color entered production right around the same time as did cobalt blue.

I would guess that there are likely fewer than 100 of these bonbons known, so keep your eyes peeled for this one. There are still probably some of them hiding out there somewhere.

Shapes & Colors Known

Bonbon: marigold, amethyst, cobalt blue

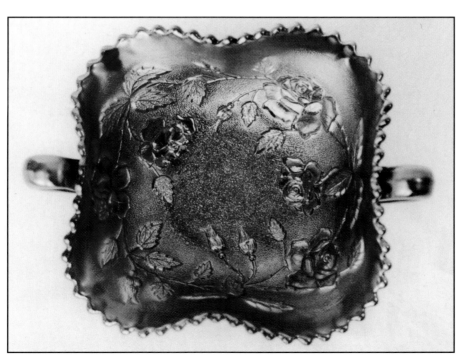

Northwood's Basket of Roses bonbon in amethyst. Note the stippled background on this example.

One of the most recognized of Northwood's carnival patterns, Basketweave was used primarily as an exterior design on bowls, plates, compotes, and bonbons, with a wide variety of interior designs. The pattern saw its greatest use during the 1908 – 1912 period. From 1912 onward, use of the design diminished in favor of a more simple ribbed exterior on most items.

The pattern also appears on the exterior surface of bowls, plates, and compotes that have a plain, unpatterned interior. Collectors refer to these plain items as "Northwood's Rainbow." These items are most often found in amethyst, but marigold and green examples exist as well.

Northwood's distinctive Basketweave pattern, most often used on the exterior surface of pieces like this very scarce white Fruits & Flowers bonbon.

Shapes & Colors Known

Bowl, 8" – 9": marigold, amethyst, green
Plate, 9": marigold, amethyst, green
Compote: marigold, amethyst, green
(Used primarily as an exterior pattern with a variety of interior designs.)

Harry Northwood certainly got his money's worth out of the mould for this very popular design. The pattern first appeared in 1903, as part of his Mosaic (purple slag) line, followed three years later by opalescent production. In 1909 the pattern began a lengthy carnival glass production run, becoming a staple of Northwood's iridescent production for nearly six years and was revived yet again for custard glass during the 1914 – 1916 period. So, it would seem that this design was every bit as popular with the buying public then as it is today.

While only two carnival shapes are known, it is the wide variety of colors available that makes this design a collector's favorite. The three-footed, crimped top rosebowl is the most popular of the two because it shows the pattern to best advantage. It is still reasonably available in marigold, amethyst, cobalt blue, and green, the latter of which is most often found with the Alaskan iridescent treatment. However, rich emerald green examples, with all-over brilliant, multicolor iridescence do exist, but these are seldom found and highly treasured. White and aqua opalescent are the next most available colors. They actually do turn up with fair regularity, but are quite popular with collectors and will always command a good price. The non-opalized aqua examples are much harder to find, as are the few known teal examples. Ice blue and ice green examples are quite scarce and always in high demand. Very rare ice blue opalescent and ice green opalescent examples are also known, and these are very close to the top of the rarity list for this design. Two known marigold on moonstone examples are known and have commanded big prices when they changed hands. But the top honors go to the two known peach opalescent examples, two of only a handful of true peach opalescent Northwood carnival pieces known. Mention should also be made of a single known example in Persian blue, a semi-opaque, translucent light blue shade with a marigold iridescent overlay. Were it not for the fact that this single known example has damage, it would surely rank in value with the peach opalescent.

The only other known shape is a flared, three-footed candy dish, fashioned from the same mould. It is found in a more limited range of colors, including marigold, amethyst, green, cobalt blue, white, ice blue, ice green, and aqua opalescent. Most are reasonably available, but the aqua opalescent examples are actually much harder to find than the rosebowl of the same color. Still, this is not as popular a shape as the rosebowl, as it does not show the pattern well, especially on the darker colors.

Both the rosebowl and candy dish may be found with either a plain or rayed interior, and the Northwood trademark is nearly always present on the interior surface.

Shapes & Colors Known

Rosebowl: marigold, amethyst, green, cobalt blue, white, ice blue, ice green, teal, aqua, aqua opalescent, ice blue opalescent, ice green opalescent, marigold on moonstone, persian blue, peach opalescent, horehound
Candy dish: marigold, amethyst, green, cobalt blue, white, ice blue, ice green, aqua opalescent

The Beaded Cable rosebowl in aqua opalescent, a highly popular color still readily available in this shape.

Two views of a Beaded Cable rosebowl. The first shows the brilliant iridescence and the second, held to daylight, reveals the unusual horehound base glass color, quite scarce in this pattern. Note the slight lavender tint in the base, typical of many of the examples found in horehound.

The arrival on the scene of what we now call carnival glass during the winter of 1907 – 1908 caught many of the soon-to-be major producers off guard. In an effort to gain a quick share of this new market, existing moulds for items already in non-iridized production were rushed to the forefront, until new, more appropriate designs could be created. Such is the case with Northwood's Beads. It is among Harry Northwood's earliest carnival efforts, dating circa 1908 – 1909. The design was already in production in non-iridized crystal and colored ware, in a full line that included berry set, table set, water set, and various sized bowls and plates. Pattern glass collectors know it as Pods & Posies.

The carnival version is confined to the exterior surface of 7" – 9" bowls, with a plain, unpatterned interior. The Northwood trademark is usually present, and the only colors reported to date are marigold, amethyst, and green. Most of the green examples, which seem to be the most frequently found, have the Alaskan iridescent treatment. The amethyst ones are actually rather scarce, but even they will usually not command a high price or a great deal of interest. The combination of pattern, shape, color, and iridescent quality are what carnival glass is all about. So, when you have only one shape, a limited color range (often with only average or below iridescent quality, as do many of these bowls) and the pattern confined to the exterior surface, the collector interest and demand just aren't there.

Shapes & Colors Known

Bowl, 7" – 9": marigold, amethyst, green

Northwood's Beads is found only on the exterior of 8" – 9" bowls, like this one in marigold.

In recent years some collectors have begun calling this pattern Northwood's Raspberry. Northwood did make a Raspberry pattern, but this design shows enough differences that I feel the traditional name, given to it by Marion Hartung, should be used.

The design is a simple yet effective one, found primarily on the interior of stemmed compotes. The exterior carries the Basketweave pattern, and most examples are signed with the Northwood trademark. Amethyst is probably the most often seen color, followed by marigold and green, in that order. Scarce white examples are also known, indicating that the design was still in production circa 1912, when Northwood introduced his pastel colors.

As a primary pattern, Blackberry is found only on the stemmed compote. However, it was also used as an interior design on some examples of the Daisy & Plume footed rosebowl and 7" – 9" bowls. In that form, the pattern is known in a wider variety of colors. For further information, see the text on Daisy & Plume, in this book.

Shapes & Colors Known

Compote: marigold, amethyst, green, white
* Also found as an interior design on some Daisy & Plume pieces.

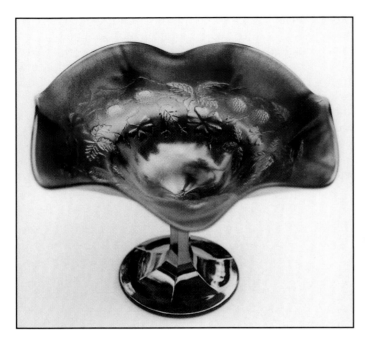

Northwood's Blackberry stemmed compote in amethyst.

Two distinctly different moulds were used to make the Blackberry compote. These are best illustrated by the exterior views shown here. Note that the green example on the left has a much thicker stem, which slopes more gradually into the bowl of the compote, and has a slightly larger diameter on the pedestal foot than its amethyst counterpart on the right.

PATTERN: Blackberry & Rays

One might tend to think this pattern is a simple combination of Northwood's Blackberry and Smooth Rays. One would more or less be correct in that assumption. One might therefore pass it up at a antique shop or show with nothing more than a casual glance. And one would come to regret that because one is not likely to see another example! Found only on the interior of stemmed compotes, Blackberry & Rays is really a very rarely found pattern. I'd be extremely surprised to learn of more than a dozen or two examples known! While examples may not set any price records, it is probably one of the most under-appreciated and under-valued items in Northwood carnival. Only three colors have been reported to date: marigold, amethyst, and green. Surprisingly, there seem to be far fewer marigold examples known than there are amethyst and green. The Northwood trademark is usually present. Blackberry & Rays has all the characteristics of the 1909 – 1910 production time frame.

One of the often overlooked Northwood carnival rarities: the Blackberry & Rays compote, shown here in green.

PATTERN: Blossoms & Palms

This early Northwood iridescent effort dates circa 1908 – 1910 and is one of the designs carried over from pre-carnival opalescent production. It is so strikingly similar to Northwood's Wild Rose that I strongly suspect it is merely a variation of it, or at the very least served as the inspiration for Wild Rose. It is found only on the exterior surface of 8" – 9" bowls, often with the Northwood's Grape Leaves interior pattern. It is also found with a plain interior, and the Northwood trademark is usually present. With a plain interior, only three colors have been documented to date: marigold, amethyst, and green, with marigold far and away the most commonly seen. The edge may be broadly ruffled or have the three in one style crimping.

"GOLD IRIDESCENT" SALAD DISH ASSORTMENT.

Will sell everywhere and even at "double profit" prices if you choose.

1C1832—Average diam. about 9 in., 3 fancy shapes, all footed, crimped edges, allover golden iridescent luster, radiant rainbow hues, decorations burnt in and will not wear off. 2 doz. each 3 styles. Total 6 doz. in bbl., 104 lbs. Per dozen, **87c**

In recent years a rumor started circulating that Northwood did not produce any carnival glass with the three in one style edge crimping. Hopefully this Northwood assortment of Blossoms & Palms bowls, from a 1909 Butler Brothers catalog, will lay that myth to rest. Two of the three bowls shown clearly have the three in one edge crimping.

The Blossoms & Palms pattern shows through quite nicely from the exterior surface of this rare ice blue Grape Leaves bowl.

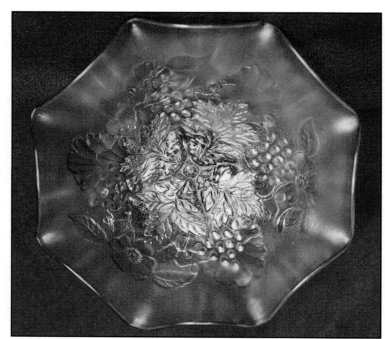

PATTERN: Blossomtime & Wildflower

This unusual compote with its rather unique stem is yet another example of an existing mould rushed into carnival production, circa 1909. The interior Blossomtime pattern was added to the Northwood's Wildflower compote, which had been in production in non-iridized form for several years.

The production history of this compote in iridized form is quite interesting albeit somewhat confusing. Based on current research, the following scenario seems most likely. The Northwood Wildflower compote with a plain interior had been made in non-iridized crystal, emerald green, and decorated emerald green since 1905. In 1909 this compote, with a plain interior, entered briefly into carnival production in marigold, amethyst, and green. Shortly thereafter, the Blossomtime interior design was created, using a new interior mould plate, and carnival production in the aforementioned colors continued. At some point thereafter, the Wildflower exterior design was abandoned in favor of a plain exterior, for reasons that remain unknown. Perhaps the Wildflower exterior mould plate was simply no longer useable.

So, there are three variants here: Blossomtime with the Wildflower exterior; Blossomtime with a plain exterior; and Northwood's Wildflower with a plain interior. All can be found in marigold, amethyst, and green. The iridescent quality on most examples is excellent, and the Northwood trademark is usually present. The Blossomtime version is particularly popular with collectors and always in demand. All three versions of this compote are rather difficult to find.

Shapes & Colors Known

Compote, all three versions: marigold, amethyst, green

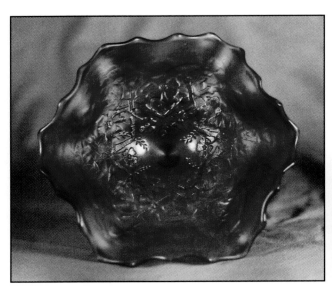

Two views of the Blossomtime compote in marigold. Note the unusual stem. When found with a plain interior, the compote is called Wildflower.

PATTERN: Bullseye & Leaves

One of Northwood's earliest iridescent offerings, carried over from pre-carnival opalescent production, Bullseye & Leaves dates circa 1908 – 1909 and is found only on the exterior surface of 7½" – 9" ruffled bowls. The interior is plain, and the Northwood trademark is usually present. The edge is usually broadly ruffled, but some examples with the three in one edge crimping are known. As is the case with most exterior only designs, there is not a whole lot of collector demand and interest here. Only two colors, marigold and green, have been reported to date. The green examples are often found with Northwood's Alaskan iridescent treatment.

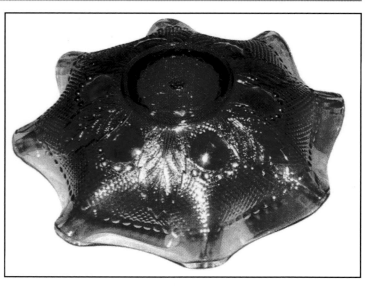

Bullseye & Leaves is one of Northwood's earliest iridescent offerings, dating circa 1908 – 1909.

Shapes & Colors Known

Bowl, 7½" – 9": marigold, green

PATTERN: Bushel Basket

With two shape variations known, in a seemingly endless variety of carnival colors, Northwood's Bushel Baskets are truly a collector's delight. They must have been extremely popular with the buying public at the time of their production as well, for despite nearly four decades of active collecting, many of the colors are still quite available. Harry Northwood certainly got a lot of mileage out of this mould. Production of the Bushel Basket spanned a good many years, from 1910 through the early 1920s, in a wide variety of iridized and non-iridized colors. We know this because some of the colors in which it is found, both iridized and non-iridized, were not introduced by Northwood until the late teens through early 1920s. There are a round version and an eight-sided version. The round version stands roughly 4¾" tall, while the eight-sided version may vary from 4" to 4¾", as the handles tend to be flared outward more than on the round basket.

In non-iridized form, the round Bushel Basket may be found in crystal with fired-on gold decoration, blue, vaseline, and flint (clear to white) opalescent, custard glass with nutmeg stain, and opaque black (ebony).

The carnival version entered production during the 1910 – 1911 period and was produced in an amazing variety of colors. Still reasonably available are examples in marigold, amethyst, cobalt blue, white, aqua opalescent, and ice green. Harder to find are the green, ice blue, horehound, lavender, and aqua baskets, but they do turn up from time to time. Smoke, teal, and lime green are all quite scarce. The rest of the colors all fall into the rare to extremely rare category. These include lime green opalescent, ice blue opalescent, sapphire blue, celeste blue, and vaseline. Only a relative handful of examples is known in these

Shapes & Colors Known

Round bushel basket: marigold, amethyst, green, cobalt blue, white, ice green, ice blue, aqua, aqua opalescent, horehound, lavender, smoke, teal, lime green, lime green opalescent, ice blue opalescent, sapphire blue, celeste blue, vaseline
Eight-sided bushel basket: marigold, amethyst, green, cobalt blue, lavender, white, ice blue, ice green, horehound, Renninger blue, aqua
Round bushel basket, plain handle: amethyst, green
Eight-sided bushel basket, plain handle: amethyst

five colors. Giving the top honors in rarity to any of these five colors is a very tough judgment call, but I'll go with a two-way tie between the sapphire blue and vaseline.

The variety of colors known in the eight-sided version is considerably more limited, but there's still a lot to hunt for. Marigold, amethyst, cobalt blue, lavender, and white are all still available, with the white examples the most commonly found. Green, horehound, ice green, ice blue, and Renninger blue are all much

scarcer. Non-opalized aqua examples top the rarity list.

Mention should also be made of a third variation that turns up on rare occasion. On this version, the portion of the handles that joins the body of the piece is plain, without the "twisted rope" effect. This version can be found in either the round or eight-sided variant. The round version is known in amethyst and green, while the eight-sided version has been reported only in amethyst, to date. Not all examples of the Bushel Basket are signed.

Shown here are two of the rarest colors for the round Bushel Basket: sapphire blue and vaseline. Rest assured that both of these have beautiful multi-color iridescence. The photos here have been back-lighted to show the true base glass colors. Fewer than a dozen of each of these are known.

The eight-sided Bushel Basket in green, a very scarce color for this version.

37

PATTERN: BUTTERFLY

Introduced in 1910, Northwood's Butterfly is a classic example of the effectiveness of simplicity. The single butterfly against the Stippled Rays background jumps out at you. The pattern is found only on the interior of collar based, two-handled bonbons in a limited range of colors. There are two versions: one with a plain exterior and one with an unusual "threaded" exterior.

The plain backed version is not terribly difficult to find in marigold or amethyst, but the green examples may take some patient searching. I know of two rare examples in smoke, an unusual color for Northwood. The threaded exterior examples are quite scarce to very rare in any color, but the amethyst ones do turn up on occasion. Cobalt blue and marigold are much harder to find. Both the green and ice blue are extremely rare with relatively few examples known. Be prepared to part with some serious cash for an example in either color!

The existence of the ice blue examples confirms that the design was still in production in 1912 when Northwood introduced his pastel colors, so it seems odd that no white or ice green examples have yet been reported. Something to bear in mind: There may well be one hiding out there someplace!

Shapes & Colors Known

Bonbon plain exterior: marigold, amethyst, green, smoke

Bonbon threaded exterior: marigold, amethyst, green, cobalt blue, ice blue

A very rare Northwood Butterfly bonbon in ice blue, with the threaded exterior.

The amethyst Butterfly bonbon with a plain exterior, on the left, is a real beauty and still not too difficult to find. The marigold example with the threaded exterior on the right is another story. These are very scarce.

38

Yet another design rushed into iridescent production, Cherry & Cable (sometimes called Northwood's Cherry) holds the distinction of being Harry Northwood's first "full line" pattern to undergo carnival production in 1908. The design was already a staple of the firm, having been in production in color stained crystal for several years. In that form, it was produced in a berry set, table set, water set, a massive banquet size punch set with unusual stemmed punch cups, a covered cracker jar, and a handled celery vase. Carnival shapes known are limited to the berry set, table set, and water set, and all have been reported only in marigold.

In iridescent form, the design's production seems to have been a relatively brief one, lasting only about two years. By the 1909 – 1910 period Northwood had expanded his iridescent lines to include colors of amethyst and green. No old Cherry & Cable items have surfaced in those two colors, so it would seem that iridescent production of this pattern had ended by that time. By then, new, more elaborate patterns were being created specifically for iridescent production.

All carnival items in this pattern are very difficult to find, and some are actually quite rare. Tumblers are probably the most available item, but they don't come cheap. They are a favorite with tumbler collectors and

always command respectable prices. The water pitchers are quite rare, with relatively few known. Often overlooked are the berry sets. While they may not command the popularity, attention, and prices of the water set and table sets, they are actually harder to find.

Nearly all examples carry the Northwood trademark. The marigold color and iridescence often shade to clear toward the base of many pieces, especially on the water pitchers and tumblers, but there are examples with solid, rich marigold color and iridescence, top to bottom.

Unfortunately this design has suffered from massive reproduction, in both iridized and non-iridized form, for many years. At some point after the demise of H. Northwood & Co. in 1925, Westmoreland acquired the moulds to Cherry & Cable. They reproduced the pattern in non-iridized crystal, color stained crystal, and milk glass. With the passing of Westmoreland in the mid-1980s, the moulds were acquired by the Mosser Glass Co., and herein lies the biggest problem for carnival collectors. Not only has Mosser reproduced this design in iridescent form, but they actually expanded it, creating moulds for shapes never originally produced by Northwood. These include stemmed goblets and a full line of miniature children's toy dishes, all items that Northwood never made.

This is a current listing of Cherry & Cable reproductions. Unfortunately, there will likely be others in the future.

Reproductions by Westmoreland
Crystal & color stained crystal: butter dish, creamer, spooner, covered sugar, celery vase, water pitcher, tumbler, covered cracker jar
Milk glass: butter dish, creamer, spooner, covered sugar, celery vase, water pitcher, tumbler, covered cracker jar

Reproductions by Mosser
Purple carnival glass: butter dish, creamer, spooner, covered sugar, celery vase, water pitcher, tumbler, covered cracker jar, stemmed goblet, miniature table set, water set, berry set
Ice green opalescent carnival glass: covered cracker jar, stemmed goblet, water pitcher, tumbler (many items in this color feature fired-on gold decoration on the cherries and the cable)

Mosser has also reproduced many Cherry & Cable items in the following: custard glass, chocolate glass, pink, cobalt blue, and crystal

If you are aware of these reproductions, the problems should be minimal. Just remember that, as far as carnival is concerned, the old pieces are known ONLY in marigold; all others are reproductions.

Shapes & Colors Known (old only)

Berry set, table set, water set: marigold

Northwood Cherry & Cable water pitcher and tumbler in marigold, the only iridescent color Northwood is known to have produced for this pattern.

PATTERN: CONCAVE DIAMONDS

It is not my intention in this book to delve into the world of what is commonly called stretch glass. That's a whole separate field in itself, and there are already excellent references on that subject. The Northwood Concave Diamonds pattern does indeed fall into that category, but in this case an exception is being made. Not only is this design eagerly sought by stretch glass collectors, carnival collectors have also embraced it, so it is included here as a "fringe" member of the carnival family. The pattern is actually part of a line Northwood introduced in 1917, called "satin sheen." It was made in a variety of shapes and colors, most of which are pastel shades, and includes some of the last iridescent colors developed by the Northwood firm.

The covered tankard water sets are among the most popular items in this line. They consist of a tall, roughly 11¾" covered tankard pitcher, matching tumblers, often with a widely flared edge, and coasters. The pitcher is mould-blown with a separately applied handle. While this set is very hard to find in any color, the most often seen is a shade of medium pastel blue that most collectors have assigned to the category called "celeste blue." In actuality, this color was called Venetian blue by Northwood. The pitcher, tumblers, and coasters are also known in topaz yellow, often referred to as vaseline by many collectors. The tumblers are also known in russet, Northwood's version of olive green, a color introduced around 1920. To the best of my knowledge, no matching water pitcher in the russet color has yet surfaced, but some must surely be out there.

Another very scarce and desirable item is the two-piece guest set, or tumble up, as it is sometimes called. Guest sets were common to the early 1900s. They were filled with water and placed in guests' bedrooms for their convenience. The set consists of a small, 6½" tall, bulbous pitcher, with a separately applied handle, and a 3½" tall tumbler. The tumbler has an oversized marie (collar base) which allows it to be inverted and placed over the neck of the pitcher, thus forming a cover. They are known in all the aforementioned colors, plus an iridized opaque blue color that Northwood called "jade blue." This set was Northwood's #559, and it is very scarce in any color.

Other known shapes include a 6⅛" tall bulbous, flared vase (Northwood's #618), a 6" crimped top vase (Northwood's #613), and a very rare pickle castor in a silver plated frame. The vases are known in Venetian blue, jade blue, and topaz yellow. The pickle castor, oddly enough, is known only in marigold.

Shapes & Colors Known

Covered tankard pitcher: Venetian blue, topaz yellow
Tumbler: Venetian blue, topaz yellow, russet
Guest set: Venetian blue, topaz yellow, russet, jade blue
Vase, either style Venetian blue, jade blue, topaz yellow
Pickle castor: marigold

The Concave Diamonds covered tankard. While collectors today refer to this color as celeste blue, Northwood originally called it Venetian blue.

40

One of the most popular Northwood carnival novelty items, the Corn vase made its debut during the 1911 – 1912 period and was one of the first items to be produced in Northwood's new pastel colors. They stand roughly 6½" tall and are usually signed with the Northwood trademark. The underside of the base may be plain or patterned with corn husks.

Color wise, there's a lot to collect here. White, ice green, and amethyst are by far the most available colors. Green will be much harder to find, and most of the others will present a real challenge. The marigold examples are surprisingly scarce. Other known colors include aqua, lime green, ice blue, teal, black amethyst, and an unusual color collectors call Coke bottle green. Remember the color of the old Coke bottles? Topping the rarity list is the ever popular aqua opalescent. Only a handful of examples is known in that color, and they will command very serious prices when offered for sale. Oddly, I know of no cobalt blue examples. This seems strange since 1912 was a major production year for that color, but none have surfaced to date.

Shapes & Colors Known

Plain vase: marigold, amethyst, white, green, ice green, lime green, aqua, Coke bottle green
Husk patterned base: marigold, amethyst, white, green, ice green, ice blue, lime green, black amethyst, aqua, teal, aqua opalescent

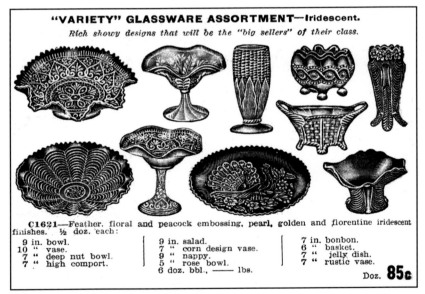

"VARIETY" GLASSWARE ASSORTMENT—Iridescent.
Rich showy designs that will be the "big sellers" of their class.

C1621—Feather, floral and peacock embossing, pearl, golden and florentine iridescent finishes. ½ doz. each:

9 in. bowl.	9 in. salad.	7 in. bonbon.
10 " vase.	7 " corn design vase.	6 " basket.
7 " deep nut bowl.	9 " nappy.	7 " jelly dish.
7 " high comport.	5 " rose bowl.	7 " rustic vase.
	6 doz. bbl., ——— lbs.	Doz. **85c**

Northwood's Corn vase in green. This example has the husk patterned base. Some examples have a plain base.

The Corn vase appears with good company in this Northwood assortment from the spring 1912 Butler Brothers catalog. With it are the Peacocks plate, Heart & Flowers bowl and compote, Nippon bowl, Daisy & Drape vase, Bushel Basket, Beaded Cable rosebowl, Fern compote, and Drapery candy dish, all offered here in marigold, amethyst, and white. This popular assortment appeared for several years in the Butler catalogs.

PATTERN: Corn Husk Vase

Make no mistake about it, the Corn Husk vase, or "Pulled Husk" as it is sometimes called, is one of the top Northwood carnival rarities. Standing about an inch taller than the standard Corn vase, with a much bulkier overall appearance, these impressive vases are masterpieces of mould-making. Unlike on their standard size cousins, the husks on these beauties are somewhat pulled and curled outward in much higher relief. They are signed with the Northwood trademark, and I have yet to see one with less than superb iridescent quality. Amethyst is the usual color, but a couple of green examples are also known.

Rarer still is the exciting find that surfaced just a few years ago. This example has the husks completely curled in a full loop, forming open handles on the sides. As these husk handles are moulded and not attached separately, this rare variant must surely have been made from a completely different mould. Only one example in amethyst has been documented, and it surfaced in California in 1995.

Shapes & Colors Known

Corn Husk vase: amethyst, green
Variant open husks: amethyst

One of the rarest and most highly treasured Northwood carnival vases: the Corn Husk vase in amethyst.

PATTERN: Daisy & Drape

Made only in a three-footed vase, Northwood's Daisy & Drape pattern is a popular and somewhat controversial design. Save for the addition of the draped effect on the body of the piece, it is virtually identical to a pattern called Vermont that was produced earlier in non-iridized form by the U.S. Glass Co. Could Northwood have purchased this mould from U.S. Glass and modified it by adding the Drapery pattern? That is one very distinct possibility, for Northwood is known to have purchased moulds from other firms. Another possibility is that Northwood could simply have copied the design. Few glasshouses filed for patents on their designs, and copying was quite rampant. We may never know the exact origins of Northwood's Daisy & Drape. Perhaps it is enough that we simply enjoy the design on its own merits.

The pattern first appeared in the wholesale catalogs in the spring of 1912, in company with another popular Northwood design, the Corn vase. It is interesting to note that like the Corn vase, Daisy & Drape vases seem to be most plentiful in white, a color that had been introduced earlier that year.

There are three slight shape variations known, all of which are confined to the row of daisies around the top edge. This edge may be flared outward, pointing straight up or slightly turned inward. The Northwood trademark is often present, but it is faintly moulded, deep inside the cone-shaped base and may be very difficult to see. As previously stated, white examples are far and away the most available, and a fair number of aqua opalescent ones turn up as well. Most of the other known colors will present a challenge. Marigold

Shapes & Colors Known

Footed vase: marigold, amethyst, green, blue, white, ice blue, ice green, aqua opalescent, aqua, ice blue opalescent

examples are surprisingly tough to find as are the blue vases. Amethyst examples are very scarce as are the non-opalized aqua ones. Ice blue is near the top of the rarity chain, just below the ice green examples. A couple of ice blue opalescent examples have also been reported. My vote for the top spot goes to the green Daisy & Drape vases. Only a relative handful is known.

Twenty to 30 years ago Daisy & Drape vases turned up on the market in pretty fair numbers. Not so today, as demand has far exceeded supply. Buy them now wherever you can. In a few years they will have all but vanished!

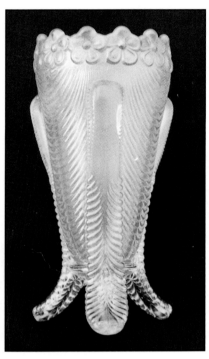 

Daisy & Drape vases in white, the most easily found color, and marigold, which is much harder to find. Note the cupped-in top on the white example.

PATTERN: DAISY & PLUME

Northwood and Dugan each made a version of this simple yet attractive design, and both versions made their appearance fairly early in the iridescent production era, circa 1909. They were both carry-over designs from earlier non-iridized opalescent production and rushed into carnival production in an effort to gain a share of the new market. While Dugan's version seems to be confined to the exterior of three-footed candy dishes with a plain, unpatterned interior, the Northwood examples of the design are found on four different shapes.

Three-footed rosebowls are the most popular and often seen shapes. Some have a plain interior while others are found with Northwood's Blackberry on the interior. Marigold, amethyst, and green examples are the most plentiful. The green ones are often found with

Northwood's Alaskan iridescent treatment of marigold iridescence over the green base glass color, but nice, rich emerald green examples with multicolor iridescence exist as well. Virtually all of the other known colors range from very scarce (cobalt blue, lavender, aqua) to very rare (white, ice blue, ice green). Topping the rarity list are the aqua opalescent rosebowls. From this, we know that the design was still in production during the 1912 – 1913 period, when this color was being made. Only three are known to date and have sold for five figure prices on the rare occasions when they have changed hands.

The same mould was used to fashion three-footed, ruffled candy dishes. These are found far less often than the rosebowls, and most are found with the Blackberry interior pattern. Marigold and green seem to be the most often found colors. Amethyst is much harder to find. White, ice blue, ice green, and lime green are all rarely seen.

The other known Daisy & Plume shapes are stemmed with a pedestal foot. The unique stemmed rosebowl with its crimped top is still quite available in marigold, amethyst, and green. A few scarce amber examples also exist and rarer still is a handful of cobalt blue examples. The same mould was also used to fashion ruffled compotes. Most are found with Northwood's Fern on the interior, but some are found with a plain interior. Here again, the most often seen colors are marigold, amethyst, and green, but a few cobalt

blue examples have been reported. (See Northwood's Fern for more information on these compotes.)

There is some confusion in distinguishing the Dugan version of the pattern from the Northwood, but there are ways to tell them apart. The Northwood three-footed pieces have a central, slightly raised rib on each foot. The Dugan version lacks this central rib. The Northwood version has 74 – 76 beads on the edge of each flower, while Dugan's has from 80 – 82. Dugan's version of the three-footed candy dish is known only in marigold, amethyst, and peach opalescent.

Shapes & Colors Known

Rosebowl, three-footed: marigold, amethyst, green, cobalt blue, aqua, lavender, white, ice blue, ice green, aqua opalescent

Candy dish, three-footed: marigold, amethyst, green, white, ice blue, ice green, lime green

Rosebowl stemmed: marigold, amethyst, green, cobalt blue, amber

Compote, stemmed, plain interior: marigold, amethyst, green

Compote, stemmed, Fern interior: see Northwood's Fern

Daisy & Plume footed rosebowl in marigold, stemmed compote in green, and the stemmed rosebowl in marigold.

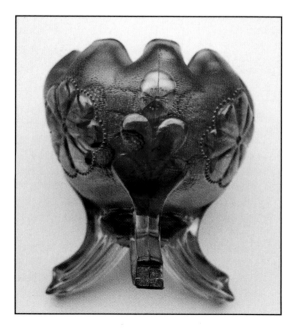

One of only two Northwood carnival patterns made in this shape, the Northwood Dandelion mug is a perennial favorite with collectors. It is distinctly different from the Northwood water set that bears the same name. The Dandelion mug actually depicts a representation of that pesky weed while the water set of the same name does not. From the colors known, we know that production of the Dandelion mug dates from the 1911 – 1912 period. It is not that easily found in any of them, but amethyst seems to be the most available followed by marigold and cobalt blue, in that order. Aqua opalescent, green, and horehound are scarcer, while the ice blue opalescent examples are rarely found.

Northwood also chose to use the Dandelion mug as the foundation for one of his most popular souvenir items. In May of 1912, the Knights Templar convention was held in Pittsburgh, Pennsylvania. A trade journal reports that "a Wheeling, West Virginia firm was given an order for 5,000 iridescent souvenir mugs." So, in this case, we not only know when these mugs were made, but we also know exactly how many, one of the few such instances of this. Of course only a percentage of these have survived, and they are eagerly sought by collectors. The mug is exactly the same as the standard Dandelion mug, with the exception of the Knights Templar emblem and the date "May 27,28,29 1912" moulded on the underside of the base. They are known in only three colors: marigold, ice blue, and ice green. Production of this Knights Templar souvenir coincides with Northwood's introduction of his new pastel colors, so it may well have been Harry Northwood's decision to produce this item in two of these newest color offerings. Definitely a good way to sow the seeds of popularity for these new colors and to promote them with the buying public.

Shapes & Colors Known

Dandelion mug: marigold, amethyst, green, cobalt blue, horehound, aqua opalescent, ice blue opalescent
Knights Templar souvenir: marigold, ice blue, ice green

The Dandelion mug in aqua opalescent.

The Knights Templar emblem on the mug's base.

PATTERN: DANDELION WATER SET

Marion Hartung named this pattern in her pioneer 10-volume series in the 1960s. The name has stuck even though this lovely design does not actually depict a dandelion. It is actually a sunflower and was advertised as such in a 1912 wholesale catalog. The pattern seems to have entered production in 1911 and is a perennial favorite with collectors today. The handsome, mould-blown tankard pitcher, with a separately applied handle, is considered by many to be one of Harry Northwood's finest efforts. The tumblers are pressed and usually bear the Northwood trademark while the pitchers are not signed.

These magnificent sets are in high demand, even in marigold (the most available color), so don't expect too many bargain finds with this one. Amethyst is the next most available color, but here again, prices will be high. Green sets are very scarce, and the cobalt blue sets definitely fall into the rare category, as do most Northwood carnival water sets in that color. When it comes to the pastel colors, white is probably the most often seen, particularly in the tumblers. The white pitchers are quite rare. Ice blue tumblers are rarely found, and the matching pitcher is extremely rare, often selling in the thousands of dollars. Ice green tops the rarity list here. Only one example of the ice green tumbler has sold at auction in recent memory. It brought several hundred dollars and had very poor iridescence. Only a couple examples of the ice green pitcher have been reported. Both have damage and neither one has changed hands in many years. I also know of at least one tankard pitcher in horehound, and I'm pleased to be able to show it here. Tumblers have also surfaced in lavender and in an odd smoky lavender combination with a slight slag effect in the base. This example may well be the result of a poorly mixed glass batch.

A variation of the tumbler with a ribbed interior is also known. They are much harder to find than the tumblers with a plain interior and have been reported in amethyst, white, ice blue, ice green, and lime green. The ice blue examples seem to turn up the most.

The Dandelion water set may also be found in non-iridized form in colors of emerald green and sapphire blue, usually with fired-on gold decoration. While quite handsome, these sets command nowhere near the value of their iridized counterparts.

Shapes & Colors Known

Water set: marigold, amethyst, green, cobalt blue, white, ice blue, ice green, horehound (tumblers only reported in lavender and smoky/lavender/slag)
Tumbler, ribbed interior: amethyst, white, ice blue, ice green, lime green

The Dandelion water set and the Oriental Poppy water set were truly sisters. They were nearly always marketed together as shown in this ad from the spring 1912 Butler Brothers catalog. Note that the Dandelion set, on the right, is marketed in the description as Sunflower.

C1967, "Florentine" Iridescent — 13½ in., ½ gal. blown tankard, 6 pressed tumblers, massive embossed poppy and sun flower panels, allover Florentine iridescent finish, 2 sets each golden, green and dark metallic. 6 sets bbl. 65 lbs. Set, **69c**

The Northwood Dandelion water set in amethyst.

To the best of my knowledge, this is the only known perfect example of the Dandelion tankard pitcher in horehound.

PATTERN: DIAMOND POINT BASKET

I'm probably going to stir up a hornet's nest of controversy here, but so be it. Sometimes a little controversy is healthy and stimulates thought. Most authorities place the Diamond Point basket firmly in the Northwood family of patterns. Well, I'm not 100 percent convinced of that; maybe just 90 percent. While there is a body of evidence to support a Northwood origin, we really have nothing absolutely conclusive to attribute it to Northwood. So, I will make no firm, final judgment here. I will present the evidence and let you, the jury, reach your own conclusions.

Resting on four stubby feet, the Diamond Point basket is roughly of the same basic size and configuration as the well known Northwood Bushel Basket and is known in marigold, amethyst, and cobalt blue carnival as well as non-iridized crystal, all colors that Northwood is known to have produced. A November 1915 trade journal describes Northwood's new #42 line as a line of "crystal footed novelties in a pressed diamond and ribbon effect," and that is a pretty fair description of this pattern. That pretty much sums up the existing evidence and also my 90 percent. Now, for my 10 percent of doubt. The impressed star design on the underside of the base is totally unlike any other found on known Northwood patterns. No example bearing the Northwood trademark has ever surfaced. The absence of any known examples in the pastel colors (white, ice blue, and ice green) also bothers me. Most Northwood carnival designs introduced during the 1912 – 1916 period are found in those colors; the Northwood Bushel Basket is found in all of them. Somehow it just does not seem logical to produce such a similarly configured item, during the same time frame, yet not in the same color production. So there you have the existing evidence and perhaps some additional food for thought as well. Perhaps one day we will have conclusive proof of a Northwood origin, but for now, the best we can give it is "likely" of Northwood manufacture.

Regardless of its origin, make no mistake. The

Diamond Point basket is extremely rare in any color, is in very high demand, and always brings top dollar when offered for sale. While all three known colors will bring healthy prices, there are probably a few more marigold examples than cobalt blue and amethyst. The iridescent quality on all colors is usually outstanding, often bordering on spectacular.

Shapes & Colors Known

Handled, footed basket; marigold, amethyst, cobalt blue

Northwood's Diamond Point Baskets in cobalt blue and marigold, always a rare and highly treasured find. This may well be Northwood's #42 line, somewhat vaguely described in a 1915 trade journal.

PATTERN: DIAMOND POINT VASE

Demand, popularity, and values on carnival glass vases have increased considerably in recent years, and Northwood's Diamond Point vases illustrate this trend well. Just a few years ago, examples of this vase in most colors could be purchased for between $25.00 to $100.00. Not so anymore. Many now sell in the hundreds of dollars and a couple are even closing in on the four figure price range! With a wide range of available colors and sizes ranging from the 6" squat vase to the 12" tall one, Diamond Point vases remain a favorite with collectors. All were fashioned from the same mould, which has a 3⅜" base diameter, and most bear the Northwood trademark. The tops of the bases usually are fashioned with 12 "flame" points, but some examples are found with only six flames.

The squat vases, ranging from 6" to 7½" in height, are especially popular. Green is the most often seen color here, followed by amethyst and marigold. White and cobalt blue examples are scarce, while aqua, ice green, and ice blue examples are rarely encountered. Other colors could well exist in this size, but have not yet been confirmed.

Examples in the 8" – 12" size range are generally called standard size, and the variety of known colors here is much broader. Marigold, amethyst, and green examples are still quite plentiful, and even the white vases still turn up with fair regularity. The other colors will present a challenge. Cobalt blue is the most available of these, followed by lavender, ice green, and horehound. Ice blue is harder to find and the beautiful aqua opalescent vases even more so. A few examples

Shapes & Colors Known

Squat vase: marigold, amethyst, green, cobalt blue, aqua, white, ice blue, ice green
Standard vase: marigold, amethyst, green, cobalt blue, white, ice blue, ice green, aqua opalescent, lavender, horehound, smoke, teal, sapphire blue, Renninger blue

in Renninger blue and smoke, always a rare color for Northwood, are also known. Topping the rarity list are the teal and sapphire blue vases. While probably about equal in rarity, the sapphire blue will generally beat out the teal when it comes to value, simply because most collectors want examples of that rare Northwood color in their collections. I only know of a couple of examples in each color.

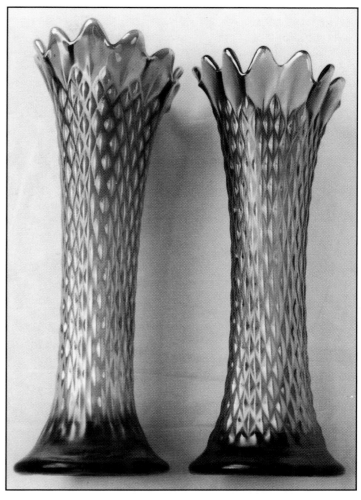

Northwood's Diamond Point squat vase in green, not too difficult to find. The other two examples are quite another story. Both are 12" tall. The one on the left is aqua opalescent and on the right is a very rare sapphire blue example.

PATTERN: DOUBLE LOOP

From the variety of known colors we know that this design was in production during the 1912 – 1915 period. Found most often in cobalt blue and aqua opalescent, the Double Loop creamer and open sugar are the only items found in this rather unimaginative pattern. While rarer examples do exist in marigold, green, and amethyst, the design is not all that popular with today's collectors, so values tend to be rather low, in any color. Still, the iridescent quality on most examples is superb and that's what carnival is really all about.

The pattern was also produced in custard glass in 1915 and a few non-iridized cobalt blue examples have been found as well. Most will bear the Northwood trademark.

Some collectors call this a chalice, but this aqua opalescent Double Loop piece is actually an open sugar.

Shapes & Colors Known

Creamer & open sugar: marigold, amethyst, green, cobalt blue, aqua opalescent

49

PATTERN: DRAPERY

What a shame that Northwood apparently chose to limit iridescent production of this popular design to so few shapes. Just prior to the carnival glass era, Northwood's Drapery underwent extensive opalescent glass production in a full line of functional shapes, including a berry set, table set, water set, rosebowls, and vases. All would have made stunning additions to the carnival glass family, but the majority of these shapes have never surfaced in iridescent form. To date, only the rosebowls, vases, tumblers, one small berry bowl, and a triangular shaped candy dish fashioned from the vase mould are known in carnival.

The rosebowl, available in a fairly extensive array of colors, is among the most popular of the known shapes. While Northwood's beautiful aqua opalescent color is rarely found in most patterns and shapes, here it is one of the most easily found colors. Amethyst is also quite available, and a fair number of cobalt blue rosebowls also surface. The rest of the colors will present much more of a challenge. White is rather scarce and marigold examples are surprisingly tough to find. Lavender and ice blue ones are rare and the ice green rosebowls extremely so. Topping the rarity list is the Renninger blue rosebowl, with only one example confirmed to date, but the green rosebowl puts up a good fight for the top spot as well. I personally have only heard of two examples, neither of which has changed hands for many years.

Drapery vases have gained a great deal in popularity over the last few years, and it's easy to see why.

The variety of known colors is even more extensive, and a display of them in combination with the matching rosebowls can be quite striking. Marigold, white, and ice green seem to be the most available, followed closely by ice blue. Cobalt blue examples are harder to find. Here again, green vases are very tough to find. The other colors could all be classified as rarely found, and these include aqua, teal, sapphire blue, aqua opalescent, and lime green. These vases may vary in height from 7" to 9", but a couple of rare 5" squat vases have also been reported. The little protruding "nub" feet on the bases are highly prone to nicks, chips, and slivers. Precious few are examples with absolutely perfect foot protrusions.

The Drapery candy dish, usually found in a roughly triangular shape, was fashioned from the vase mould. Ice blue and white seem to turn up the most. The other colors, including marigold, amethyst, cobalt blue, and ice green are much harder to find. Green again tops the list, with relatively few known. Here again, these pieces are likely to have nicks or chips on the protruding nub feet, so check them over carefully.

The only other shapes that have surfaced to date are two tumblers and one small berry dish, all three in white carnival. This certainly would tend to indicate that the matching water pitcher and master berry bowl must surely exist, but they have yet to be confirmed.

Shapes & Colors Known

Rosebowl: marigold, amethyst, green, cobalt blue, white, ice green, ice blue, Renninger blue, aqua opalescent, lavender

Vase: marigold, amethyst, green, cobalt blue, white, ice green, ice blue, aqua, teal, lime green, aqua opalescent, sapphire blue

Candy dish: marigold, amethyst, green, cobalt blue, white, ice green, ice blue

Tumbler: white

Small berry bowl: white

The Drapery rosebowl in aqua opalescent is one of the more easily found colors.

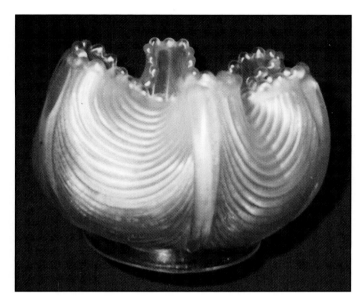

In contrast to the availability of the aqua opalescent rosebowl, this ice blue rose-bowl is very seldom found.

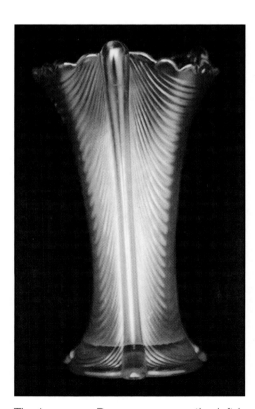
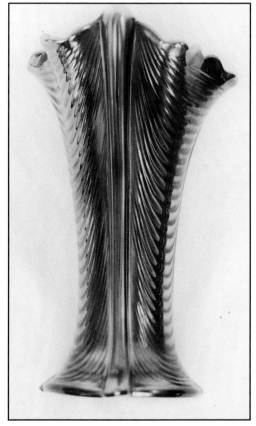

The ice green Drapery vase on the left is actually one of the more easily found colors, but the cobalt blue example on the right is much harder to find.

PATTERN: DRAPERY VARIANT

I've always had a personal theory regarding the production of the Drapery Variant vase, and recently uncovered information about the timeline of its production tends to reinforce that theory. The standard Drapery vase first appeared in the wholesale catalogs during the 1910 – 1911 period. The Drapery Variant vase is now known to have been in production during the 1912 – 1915 time frame. If you were a glassmaker and had a popular selling item in your line but it was highly prone to damage both during and after the manufacturing process, what would you do? The logical thing of course would be to correct the problem either by attempting to alter the mould or by replacing it with another one that eliminated the problem. I've always suspected that the Drapery Variant vase might have been the end result of just such a scenario. The standard Drapery vase must have been an extremely popular seller, as evidenced by its availability today and the wide variety of colors in which it is known. But, the small protruding "nub" feet on them were highly prone to damage. So many examples have this damage that I cannot help but wonder if a lot of it happened during the manufacturing process. And it's just possible that this problem was easily and inexpensively corrected by making a Drapery pattern vase without the problem "nub" feet. Making a new mould would have been expensive, but there was another alternative: Northwood simply started making Drapery vases "swung" from the existing Drapery tumbler mould, for that is exactly what the Drapery Variant vase is! Just a theory, but food for thought.

The Drapery Variant vase lacks the protruding "nub" feet of the standard Drapery vase. Both the Drapery pattern and the bordering vertical ribs do not extend all the way to the top edge, as on the standard Drapery vase. Most examples found are in the 8" – 10" height range are seen far less often than the standard Drapery vase, and the variety of known colors is very limited. Only marigold, amethyst, and cobalt blue have been confirmed to date, with the latter being the least often found. I have heard rumors of a green example, but have yet to confirm its existence. Still, it's very possible. Though none has ever surfaced, I would not be too surprised to learn of a white example, as the tumblers from which these vases were fashioned are known in that color.

Shapes & Colors Known

Vase, 8" – 10": marigold, amethyst, cobalt blue (green?)

Drapery Variant vases, all fashioned from the tumbler mould, in amethyst, marigold, and cobalt blue.

Let me state right away that I am not even close to being convinced that this very rare carnival pattern ever saw the inside of the Northwood factory, and I have included it here only as a possible Northwood creation, and with more than considerable reservations. Most collectors have always considered it to be a Northwood product, but I'm not even close to being convinced. In both shape and design characteristics it is virtually nothing like any other pattern, iridized or otherwise, known to have been made by Northwood. As far as I'm concerned, it has only two things going for it to possibly link it to Northwood. It is known in ice blue of which Northwood was the largest producer. The central medallion containing a lotus blossom design is very similar to that found on the Nippon pieces and the Lotus Land bonbon. But, that's about it!

The ice blue plate shown here measures 8⅝" in diameter and stands 1⅝" high at the edge. It rests on a hexag-onal-shaped dome foot measuring 3¼" in diameter. The edge of the plate has an ever so slight scallop. Only four examples of this pattern are known to exist at present. There are two known plates in ice blue, a ruffled bowl in ice blue, and an ice cream-shaped bowl in marigold.

So, if it's not a Northwood pattern, then who made it? The answer is simply that we really don't know. I've mulled this over considerably and that little voice in my head keeps bringing me back to two possibilities. Something about the design keeps saying "the U. S. Glass Company" to me, and that firm did make some carnival glass in ice blue. Then, a moment later, thoughts wander towards the possibility of European manufacture. But, these are just suspicions on my part, and I have no evidence for that any more than I have for a Northwood origin. So, for now, Elegance is included here as a possible Northwood pattern, with a rather strong emphasis on "possible."

Shapes & Colors Known

Bowl, 8" – 9", ruffled: ice blue
Bowl, 8" – 9", ice cream shape: marigold
Plate, 8" – 9": ice blue

One of only two known Elegance plates in ice blue. Northwood? Possibly, but I'm not 100 percent convinced.

PATTERN: EMBROIDERED MUMS

Dating from the boom years of Northwood's carnival production (1911 – 1912), Embroidered Mums is one of the most popular of Northwood's iridescent patterns. Strikingly similar to Hearts & Flowers, it was likely the artistic expression of the same mould designer. Patterns depicting a representation of delicate, embroidered lace designs must have been very popular sellers during the era of carnival production, as most major producers of the glass had some in their lines. Only three shapes were produced in this beautiful, intricate pattern. One was made in an extensive variety of colors, but mystery surrounds the apparently limited production of the other two.

Bowls, either broadly ruffled or with a pie crust edge, are perennial collector favorites and are known in a broad variety of iridescent colors. Cobalt blue and amethyst are the most often encountered of these, with marigold examples considerably harder to find. Virtually all of the others could rightfully be classified rare to extremely so. These include lavender, white, ice blue, ice green, sapphire blue, aqua, aqua opalescent, lime green opalescent, and ice blue opalescent. Which is truly the rarest? Tough call! White is surprisingly rare as is sapphire blue. Very few aqua opalescent examples are known and even fewer lime green opalescent. My vote for the top spot would be the ice blue opalescent, but it's awfully close to really choose. An example in green would be one of the all-time great finds, but none has been confirmed to date as far as I know. It's one of those things that surely must exist, but...

If one were to follow the usual scheme of things regarding most Northwood patterns, one would assume that the Embroidered Mums plate would be found in a near equal variety of colors. And one would be dead wrong! For here we have one of the great unsolved mysteries of Northwood's carnival production. Only three colors have ever been documented in this shape, and two of those have only surfaced in recent years. For many years, ice green was the only known color in the plate shape and of course, these examples were eagerly sought and highly treasured. In the last few years, single examples in cobalt blue

and white have been found, but to date, that's the whole story on the plates! There almost have to be other colors out there! Where are they?

The only other known shape in this pattern is a stemmed, two-handled bonbon, documented to date only in white. Here again, one would suspect that there must surely be other colors somewhere.

The exteriors of both the bowls and plates are usually ribbed, while the bonbon carries the Basketweave exterior design. Most examples of the pattern are unsigned, but a few have been found bearing the Northwood trademark.

The Embroidered Mums plate in ice green.

A gorgeous example of the Embroidered Mums ruffled bowl in amethyst.

Shapes & Colors Known

Bowl, 8" – 9": marigold, amethyst, cobalt blue, white, ice blue, ice green, lavender, aqua, aqua opalescent, sapphire blue, lime green opalescent, ice blue opalescent
Plate, 9": cobalt blue, white, ice green
Bonbon, stemmed: white

Probably one of the most often underrated pieces of Northwood Carnival: the Embroidered Mums bonbon in white, the only color reported in this shape, to date.

Found only on vases varying in height from 6" – 12", Feathers first appeared in non-iridized opalescent colors in 1904. The iridized version first appeared in 1909, offered in Northwood's Alaskan iridescent line, which was marigold iridescence on green base glass. The pattern remained in production at least through 1912 when the pastel colors were introduced.

The green examples with the Alaskan iridescent treatment are the most often encountered color, with marigold running a close second. Amethyst ones are really a lot harder to find than the usual asking price would indicate. Ice blue examples are rare and white even more so. Most examples bear the Northwood trademark.

Shapes & Colors Known

Vase, 6" – 12": marigold, amethyst, green, white, ice blue

Three Northwood Feathers vases. The green example, on the left, has the Alaskan iridescent treatment. It is quite easily found, as is the marigold example on the right. However, the ice blue squat vase shown here is very rare.

PATTERN: FERN

I suspect this pattern would generate a lot more interest were it to be found on the interior surface of bowls or plates, but it is confined only to the interior of some Daisy & Plume stemmed compotes. Still, they are not found all that often and by rights should bring a higher price than they usually do. The design dates circa 1911 – 1912, and only three colors, marigold, amethyst, and green, have been confirmed to date. However, a 1912 Butler Brothers catalog offers this compote in white! They must therefore exist in that color, but to my knowledge, none has ever been found. The 1911 – 1912 period was also when cobalt blue carnival began appearing in the wholesale catalogs. Here again, none has been reported in that color, but I would not be surprised if they may exist.

Shapes & Colors Known

Compote, Daisy & Plume exterior:
marigold, amethyst, green (white?)

The Northwood's Fern compote in green, another much underrated design. They are not that easily found in any color.

PATTERN: FINECUT & ROSES

How ironic that one of the most popular of Northwood's carnival rosebowl patterns was not even a Northwood creation! The design appears in opalescent form in several Jefferson Glass Co. assortments found in Butler Brothers catalogs from the 1904 – 1907 period, then suddenly appears in Northwood iridescent assortments in 1909. So, it becomes quite obvious that Finecut & Roses was one of several moulds that Northwood is known to have purchased from Jefferson in 1908. It was also obvious that this was a wise move on the part of Harry Northwood. Finecut & Rose must have been a popular seller, as it remained in iridescent production for a number of years, with a few slight mould modifications along the way. A footed rosebowl and ruffled candy dish, both fashioned from the same mould, are the only shapes known. Some examples are found with a delicate, embroidered interior pattern called Fancy, very similar in concept to Northwood's Hearts & Flowers and Embroidered Mums. Most have a plain interior. The Northwood trademark is often present, but not always.

The footed rosebowl is a collector's favorite, with a fairly wide range of available colors. Marigold, amethyst, green, and surprisingly, ice blue seem to be the most often found. Cobalt blue is actually quite rare, and the horehound and lavender examples always seem to pique interest as well. A few pearlized custard examples are known, but the ever popular aqua opalescent rosebowls come awfully close to winning the top spot. In popularity, they do, but in actuality the rarest honors go to the single known ice green rosebowl. An example in violet, a curious, pastel blueish/purple color has also been confirmed. All of these have a distinct raised ridge, or marie, encircling the exterior base inside the three feet. Examples without this marie have also turned up in amethyst and green, the result of a mould modification at some point. A few rare examples in amethyst have also been found with a round plain vertical top, rather than the usual crimped top. These may have been surviving test pieces for the newly acquired mould. Or, it's possible that these were made that way deliberately, perhaps as a footed violet vase.

The footed candy dish is also a popular item, available in a fairly extensive variety of colors, and still reasonably easy to find in most of them. With a plain interior, they are still readily available in marigold, amethyst, green, and white. Cobalt blue is rather hard to find. When found with the Fancy interior pattern, these candy dishes generate considerably more interest and higher prices and are not as easily found. They are known in amethyst, white, ice blue, ice green, cobalt blue, and aqua opalescent. White is probably the most often found with aqua opalescent and cobalt blue tied for the two rarest color here.

All of the Finecut & Roses pieces are highly prone to chips on the feet. Check them carefully before you buy.

Shapes & Colors Known

Rosebowl, plain interior: marigold, amethyst, green, cobalt blue, white, pearlized custard

Rosebowl, fancy interior: marigold, amethyst, white, ice blue, ice green, horehound, lavender, pearlized custard, violet, aqua opalescent

Candy dish, plain interior: marigold, amethyst, green, cobalt blue, white

Candy dish, fancy interior: amethyst, white, ice blue, ice green, cobalt blue, aqua opalescent

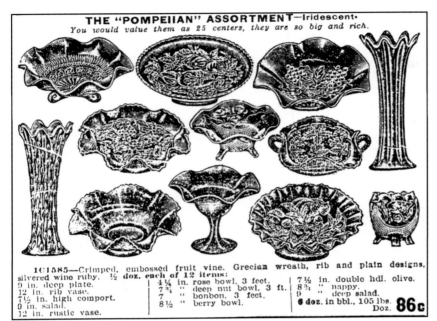

THE "POMPEIIAN" ASSORTMENT—Iridescent.
You would value them as 25 centers, they are so big and rich.

1C1585—Crimped, embossed fruit vine. Grecian wreath, rib and plain designs, silvered wine ruby. ½ doz. each of 12 items:
9 in. deep plate.
12 in. rib vase.
7½ in. high comport.
9 in. salad.
12 in. rustic vase.
4¼ in. rose bowl, 3 feet.
7¾ " deep nut bowl, 3 ft.
7 " bonbon, 3 feet.
8½ " berry bowl.
7½ in. double hdl. olive.
8¾ " nappy.
9 " deep salad.
6 doz. in bbl., 105 lbs.
Doz. **86c**

The Finecut & Roses rosebowl and candy dish both appear in this fall 1910 Butler Brothers assortment. Note the name "Pompeiian" used to market this assortment which appeared in the Butler catalogs for several years. Note also the price: 86 cents. That was the wholesale price for all 12 pieces.

Three Finecut & Roses rose-bowls: amethyst, ice blue, and marigold, all still readily available colors.

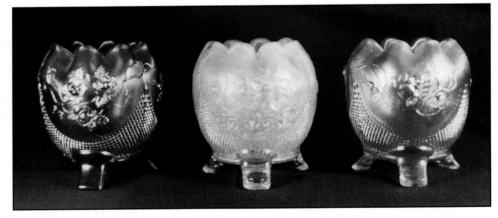

The aqua opalescent Finecut & Roses candy dish is rarely found.

PATTERN: FINE RIB

Just about every producer of old carnival glass made a version of the Fine Rib vase, and it can be confusing trying to distinguish one from the other. Fortunately that's not a problem here, for virtually every example I have ever seen of the Northwood version bore his famous trademark. Another way to distinguish Northwood from the Fenton version is in the manner in which the ribs end at the top of the vase. The vertical ribs on the Northwood version extend all the way to the top edge, while Fenton's end in broadly scalloped arches about one-quarter inch from the top.

Northwood's Fine Rib vases are found in heights ranging from a 6" squat version to as much as 18" tall. Most turn up in the 8" – 12" size, and all have a roughly 3½" base diameter. Marigold, amethyst, and

green examples are fairly abundant, with the green ones often found with the Alaskan iridescent treatment. The other known colors, including cobalt blue, white, ice green, and lime green, the latter often found with a marigold iridescent overlay, are all rather scarce. Topping the rarity list are a couple of sapphire blue examples that have surfaced only in the last few years.

Shapes & Colors Known

Vase, 6" – 18": marigold, amethyst, green, cobalt blue, white, ice green, lime green, sapphire blue

While the pattern itself does not command a great deal of collector interest, the Fine Rib squat vase shown here in white is actually quite rare.

PATTERN: FLUTE

Flute is one of Northwood's early iridescent efforts. The pattern had enjoyed a lengthy production run in non-iridized crystal and was rushed into carnival production early in 1909. It appears in early Northwood advertising as their #21 line, made in a wide variety of shapes, most of which can be found in iridized form. These include a berry set, table set, water set, breakfast size sugar and creamer, celery vase, stemmed sherbet, nut cup, and an unusual pedestal-footed salt set. There is also a swung vase that is generally categorized by most collectors as part of this line, even though it is really not part of the #21 line. Most examples bear the Northwood trademark and all, with the exception of the vase, have an octagonal-shaped marie (collar base). While the variety of known shapes is reasonably extensive, the colors are not. Most are found primarily in marigold, with a few pieces turning up in purple and green from time to time. The green Northwood Flute pieces tend to turn up with the Alaskan iridescent treatment. This is not surprising because 1909, the year the iridescent

production of this pattern began, was also the year that Northwood introduced this unusual treatment of marigold iridescent overlay on green base glass. The salt set, sherbet, and the vase are the only items found in a wider variety of colors.

The berry set has been reported to date only in marigold. The four-piece table set has been confirmed in both marigold and green. Oddly enough, the smaller breakfast size creamer and open sugar have been confirmed only in purple. The water pitcher is known in marigold and purple. The matching tumblers have also surfaced in green, but to date I know of no green pitchers; they must surely exist though. The celery vase is reported only in marigold. The nut set, or more correctly salt set, consists of a pedestal-footed 5" – 6" diameter flat master salt and six small 2" pedestal-footed salts. Colors reported to date include marigold, amethyst, vaseline, and sapphire blue. The nut cup was fashioned from the tiny individual salt and is known in marigold, amethyst, and vaseline. The stemmed sherbet is found mostly in marigold, although rare examples in amethyst, green, cobalt blue, white, and vaseline do exist.

The Flute vase is actually part of a different Northwood line, but as most collectors call it by the name Northwood's Flute, we include it here. This vase has a round marie, eight panels, and can generally be found in the 8" – 14" range. Marigold and green are the most often seen colors. The green examples often have the Alaskan iridescent treatment. Amethyst examples are much harder to find.

Shapes & Colors Known

Berry set: marigold
Butter dish & spooner: marigold
Creamer & covered sugar: marigold, green
Breakfast creamer & open sugar: purple
Water pitcher: marigold, purple
Tumbler: marigold, purple, green
Celery vase: marigold
Nut cup: marigold, amethyst, vaseline
Salt set: marigold, amethyst, vaseline, sapphire blue
Sherbet: marigold, amethyst, green, cobalt blue, white, vaseline
Vase, 8" – 14": marigold, amethyst, green

Northwood's Flute water pitcher and tumbler in marigold. Like most of the simpler designs, this one does not generate the popularity and collector interest that it rightfully should. Examples are not that easily found.

PATTERN: FOUR PILLARS

Sometimes called Four Columns, the Northwood Four Pillars vase had one of the longest and most varied production runs of any mould in the firm's history. The iridized version first appeared circa 1910. It was also produced in custard, circa 1914 – 1916. Examples with the "onionskin" effect of stretch iridescence, dating 1916 – 1920, have been documented. There are even examples in Northwood's "Chinese Coral," a line of opaque red glass dating from the firm's final year of operation in 1924 – 1925. Examples can also be found in non-iridized crystal and other non-iridized colors, all made at various times during this design's lengthy production. It must have been a very popular seller at the time, and it remains so today.

Most examples of this vase will be found in the 9" – 12" size range, but some very rare 5" – 7" squat vases are also known. Some examples are trademarked and some are not. As with the Northwood Drapery vase, these are highly prone to damage on the small, protruding "nub" feet, so always examine them very carefully.

There is a wide variety of colors to collect here, as far as the 9" – 12" sizes are concerned. Surprisingly, the aqua opalescent examples are one of the most often encountered, followed by amethyst, marigold, and green. A fair number of russet (olive green) vases also turn up. Ice blue examples are harder to find. The other colors will take some very persistent searching. Cobalt blue, white, and ice green are scarce. Sapphire blue, teal, and Renninger blue are quite rare, while the vaseline with marigold overlay, ice green opalescent, and lime green opalescent examples would be classed as very rare. The top spot would have to go to the marigold on custard vase. I only know of one, but others likely exist. Some of the green examples may be found with the advertising of a Delaware firm, "Howard's Furniture," molded on the underside of the base.

The squat 5" – 7" vase is very rare and to date has been confirmed only in amethyst and green. Amber has been reported, but I have yet to confirm that. Other colors will likely surface in this size, so keep your eyes peeled for them.

Shapes & Colors Known

Vase, 9" – 12": marigold, amethyst, green, cobalt blue, white, ice blue, ice green, russet, teal, aqua opalescent, ice green opalescent, lime green opalescent, sapphire blue, Renninger blue, vaseline/marigold overlay, marigold on custard

Squat vase, 5" – 7": amethyst, green

Advertising vase, "Howard's Furniture": green

The Four Pillars vase in aqua opalescent on the left is quite easily found. The sapphire blue example in the center is very rare. The vaseline example on the right has a marigold iridescent overlay. It is one of only two reported.

Only two things differ between this popular design and Northwood's Three Fruits pattern. Fruits & Flowers has small blossoms worked into the design, and it lacks the spray of cherries found in the center of the Three Fruits pieces. Aside from that, the two designs are identical and were in all probability part of the same pattern line. While Three Fruits is found only on bowls and plates, Fruits & Flowers is known in bowls of varying size, plates, handgrip plates, card trays, and stemmed, two-handled bonbons. Examples may be found both signed and unsigned. Most items are found with Northwood's distinctive Basketweave exterior pattern.

Large, ruffled 9" – 10" bowls are still quite available in marigold, amethyst, and green, but are quite scarce in ice green. I know of just one example in white and one in violet. The small, 5" – 6" ruffled sauces serve to make a most attractive berry set, when combined with the large bowls. They are known in the same colors. There are also intermediate sized bowls, roughly 7" in diameter, and these are known in a greater variety of colors. Here again, marigold, amethyst, and green are the most available. Cobalt blue examples are quite scarce. The other colors are all rare and include ice green, teal, sapphire blue, and at least one known amethyst opalescent example, which gets my vote for the top spot. A variation with a stippled background has also been reported, but only in marigold and green, to date. These stippled variants also differ in that they have a design of three inwardly pointing leaves in the center, a feature not found on the other Fruits & Flowers pieces.

There are two sizes of plates, an 8" – 9" size and a smaller, 7" – 7½" version. The large ones have been reported only in marigold and amethyst, but the smaller size is known in marigold, amethyst, green, cobalt blue, ice blue, and a very controversial example in marigold on custard. The same mould used for the smaller plate was also used to fashion a handgrip plate, with one edge curled up, and a card tray, sometimes called a banana dish, with two sides curled up. Both shapes have been reported only in marigold, amethyst, and green.

Perhaps the most popular shape in this design is that of the stemmed, two-handled bonbon, and it's easy to see why. They are found in a far more extensive variety of colors and can make a very impressive display. Marigold, amethyst, green, and cobalt blue examples are still quite easily found, but virtually all of the others will present a most interesting challenge. They are all rarely seen and assigning any one to the top spot is a really tough call. These include russet (olive green), clambroth, lavender, white, smoke, teal, ice blue, ice green, sapphire blue, aqua opalescent, and ice blue opalescent, so there's a lot to hunt for here. There are only a couple examples each known in smoke and teal, but my votes for the top spot would be a dead heat between the ice blue opalescent and the sapphire blue. Either one is a real treasure! Here again, there are also stippled variants known, but only

Shapes & Colors Known

Bowl, 9" – 10": marigold, amethyst, green, ice green, white, violet
Bowl, 5" – 6": marigold, amethyst, green, ice green
Bowl, 7": marigold, amethyst, green, cobalt blue, ice green, teal, sapphire blue, amethyst opalescent
Bowl, 7", stippled: marigold, green
Plate, 8" – 9": marigold, amethyst
Plate, 7" – 7½": marigold, amethyst, green, cobalt blue, ice blue, marigold on custard
Handgrip plate & card tray: marigold, amethyst, green
Bonbon, stemmed, two-handled: marigold, amethyst, green, cobalt blue, white, ice blue, ice green, russet, clambroth, lavender, smoke, teal, aqua opalescent, sapphire blue, ice blue opalescent
Bonbon, stemmed, two-handled, stippled: marigold, green, cobalt blue, Renninger blue

in marigold, green, cobalt blue, and Renninger blue, with the latter taking the top rarity honors. Production of the bonbon shape spanned a good many years. It was first made circa 1910 – 1911 and must have still enjoyed a least some limited production as late as 1919 – 1920, when the firm was making their exclusive russet color.

Fruits & Flowers bonbons are still easily found in amethyst, but an example with iridescence of this quality will always command a very respectable price.

A very rare Fruits & Flowers bonbon in sapphire.

Controversy surrounds this Fruits & Flowers 7" plate in marigold on custard. No one disputes the age of the piece itself, as these plates are known in non-iridized custard, but some feel this one may have been recently iridized.

One of the most popular and widely recognized of all Northwood carnival creations, this pattern is one of the few for which we may have some clues regarding its origin and evolution. It may well have been the end result of a mould re-tooling, done from one of Northwood's advertising pieces. Or, at the very least, the advertising piece in question no doubt inspired the Good Luck pattern.

Northwood made a variety of lettered or advertising pieces on commission from a number of purveyors of various products. Most of these date from the 1909 – 1910 period. Most feature the various companies' names or products in the center of the piece, surrounded by a simple design of mum-like flowers. They were relatively easy to make from just one, or very few moulds. Run off the requested number of pieces for one company, then simply re-tool the center portion of the same mould with the name of another and run those off. Thus, one mould suffices for all. However, unique among these items are the "Jockey Club" advertising pieces that feature a horseshoe and whip as the central design, with the "Jockey Club" name above it. Above this name is a tiny flower blossom with four small leaves, each at 90-degree angles to one another.

It would seem that the Jockey Club pieces were made from a mould other than the one Northwood used to make most of the other advertising pieces. Moulds were very expensive to make, even in 1910. So, what do you do with a mould when the production quota for such a highly specialized item such as a very limited production advertising piece has been filled? You could just scrap it, which is like throwing money out the window. You could just hold onto it in the hopes that the company for whom you made it might just request an additional quantity, which would seem the most logical thing to do with it. Unless, of course, the circumstances abruptly changed. And I am convinced that this is exactly what happened in this case: the circumstances abruptly changed!

In his excellent reference, *The Encyclopedia of Carnival Glass Lettered Pieces,* John D. Resnik uncovered solid evidence that the Jockey Club advertising pieces were made to promote a brand of perfume. The logo appears in advertising dating back into the 1850s. Mr. Resnik was able to track the company up into the early 1900s, to about the time of the production of the Jockey Club carnival pieces, but then all mention or trace of the firm abruptly vanished. Could it be that the Jockey Club advertising pieces were made to be given away as premiums by the perfume's manufacturer, distributors or retailers in an effort to boost sagging sales? And that this promotion was one of the manufacturer's last efforts before they went out of business? I am convinced that this is exactly what happened! And that the Northwood firm was now sitting on an expensive mould for which they had virtually no further use.

So, it was time for a little "mould re-tooling magic." The Jockey Club lettering was removed, and a few changes and additions in the flowers and leaves were added to the overall design. Presto! A new mould for an addition to Northwood's "standard" iridescent production line was born: the very rare Good Luck Variant bowl! Only three examples of this bowl are known: two with a pie crust edge and one ruffled. All are in marigold. All are likely surviving "test pieces" of the newly created mould. Perhaps others exist, but I doubt that very many were made, perhaps just enough to test the marketing waters of the new design. It was then decided that the pattern simply needed more to it to be acceptable for the mass market. At this point, a considerable reworking or re-tooling of the mould was undertaken. The design was embellished and enlarged to encompass a greater surface area of the finished piece, and the final result was the classic Good Luck pattern, as we know it.

I grant you that this is all theory. But it is theory based on hard fact. The Jockey Club pieces and the rare Good Luck Variant bowls are so similar in concept, right down to the tiny flower blossom with the four leaves above the logos, that it's a certainty that there is, at the very least, some kind of very close relationship between the two. The production timeline also falls right into place. The Jockey Club bowls, like nearly all of Northwood's advertising pieces, are known to have been produced fairly early in the iridescent glass era, circa 1909 – 1910. We know that the standard or classic Good Luck pieces are known in cobalt blue and the pastel colors, and these colors saw the heyday of their production two years later, so the classic Good Luck pattern was in heavy production two years after the Jockey Club pieces. The three known marigold Good Luck Variant bowls, which I believe to be surviving test pieces from the reworked Jockey Club moulds, fit nicely somewhere in the middle. It may just be theory, but I'm 99 percent convinced that it is indeed fact.

Regardless of the design's origins, it is safe to say that Good Luck is one of the most popular of all Northwood's iridescent efforts. Found only on the interior surface of bowls and plates, the pattern enjoyed a lengthy production, as evidenced by the wide variety of known colors. There is a lot to hunt for here, and that only adds to the design's popularity with collectors. The exterior surface may have Northwood's distinctive Basketweave pattern or may be ribbed. Some examples are signed with the Northwood trademark, but an equal number are not. The bowls may be ruffled or pie crust edged.

It is the "Eight Ruffled" bowl that is found in the widest variety of colors. Marigold, amethyst, green, and cobalt blue are far and away the most available. To say that all of the others will present a challenge is a considerable understatement. All are very rare at the least and some extremely so. These include lavender, aqua, teal, white, ice blue, ice green, horehound, lime green, sapphire blue, aqua opalescent, and ice blue opalescent. Ice green is probably the rarest of these, but ice blue and ice blue opalescent don't trail the leader by very much. Neither do the aqua opalescent and sapphire blue examples, but there are probably a few more of these known than there are of the other three. The pie crust edged bowls are somewhat more limited in colors known, but there is still a good variety. Here again, marigold, amethyst, green, and cobalt blue are most available. The others are all rare and include lavender, horehound, ice blue, Renninger blue, and aqua opalescent. Aqua opalescent wins the top spot here.

Like so many of Northwood's carnival patterns, there is also a version with a stippled background. These too may be either ruffled or pie crust edged and the variety of known colors limited to marigold, cobalt blue, and Renninger blue. All are found far less frequently than their non-stippled cousins.

Good Luck plates are much harder to find than the bowls, and the variety of known colors is far more limited. They are a collector's delight: highly treasured and eagerly sought! The most available colors here are marigold, amethyst, and green, with cobalt blue examples much harder to find. A few examples in horehound are also known. But the real treasures here are the ice blue and ice green plates. Only three are known in ice blue and two in ice green. Very serious money changes hands along with them, on the rare occasions when exchanges happen.

True to form, there are also rare stippled plates. Marigold, amethyst, and cobalt blue are the only reported colors to date and all are quite rare.

Shapes & Colors Known

Bowl, ruffled, 8" – 9": marigold, amethyst, green, cobalt blue, lavender, horehound, white, ice blue, ice green, aqua, teal, lime green, sapphire blue, aqua opalescent, ice blue opalescent

Bowl, pie crust edge, 8" – 9": marigold, amethyst, green, cobalt blue, lavender, horehound, ice blue, Renninger blue, aqua opalescent

Bowl, stippled: marigold, cobalt blue, Renninger blue

Plate, 9" – 9½": marigold, amethyst, green, cobalt blue, horehound, ice blue, ice green

Plate, 9" – 9½", stippled: marigold, amethyst, cobalt blue

Good Luck Variant bowl, 8" – 9": marigold

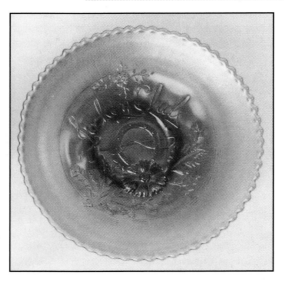

The Evolution of a Pattern
Step 1: The Jockey Club Advertising Plate, made circa 1909 – 1910 by Northwood, for a California based brand of perfume.

Step 2: The ultra-rare Northwood Good Luck Variant bowl, likely created from a slight re-tooling of the Jockey Club mould, circa 1910 – 1911. The Jockey Club logo was removed and the Good Luck lettering added, along with a few other minor changes, but essentially still very much like the Jockey Club pieces. Only three of these bowls are presently known.

Step 3: A second re-tooling around 1911 resulted in the classic Good Luck pattern, as we know it. More was added to the design, filling out the empty space and a real winner was born!

A Good Luck ruffled bowl with ribbed exterior in ice blue, an extremely rare color for this pattern. This one is a real beauty.

One of the most misused terms in carnival glass is "electric" iridescence. Well, no mistakes here: this stunning electric blue pie crust edged Good Luck bowl has *real* electric iridescence!

The Good Luck 9" plate in green.

PATTERN: GRACEFUL

One of Northwood's early carnival efforts, dating circa 1908 – 1910, Graceful was actually a revival of an earlier Northwood line called Spool, that was made in mosaic (slag) and non-iridized opalescent colors from 1903 – 1906. In iridescent form it is known only in the shape shown here. Some call it a vase while others refer to it as a compote. Marigold, amethyst, and green are the usual colors with only the amethyst a little tough to find. However, there are a couple rarities in this often overlooked pattern. It was apparently in production at least through 1912, as evidenced by single known examples in white and ice blue. Most bear the Northwood trademark. Some have an impressed star on the underside of the base, while others are plain.

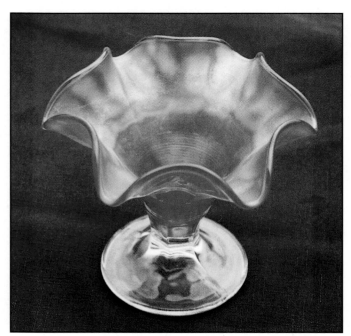

Northwood's Graceful vase in marigold.

Shapes & Colors Known

Compote/vase: marigold, amethyst, green, white, ice blue

No other pattern has become more synonymous with the name Northwood, or with carnival glass itself, than has Grape & Cable. Sometimes called Northwood's Grape, it was created by Harry Northwood specifically for iridescent production and introduced to the trade in 1910. It is far and away the most widely known and recognized design of any ever made in iridescent form by any manufacturer. It is also one of the most consistently popular patterns with collectors today. Within the broad field of carnival glass collecting, fads come and go. Plates may be a hot item for awhile and then water sets take over. Pastels then become all the rage only to give way to red pieces. So it goes. Through it all, over the last 35 years, Grape & Cable has maintained a constant, steady level of popularity and collectibility. Entire collections comprised solely of Grape & Cable have been built.

Harry Northwood introduced this new pattern line in January of 1910, and it quickly became one of his greatest successes. Production of it continued for a number of years, in both iridized and non-iridescent forms. New shapes were constantly being added to the line, and when all was said and done, an astounding variety of over 70 different Grape & Cable shapes were produced, making it one of the most extensive pattern glass lines ever produced by any American glasshouse. It was so popular with the buying public that Fenton eventually produced a version of it as well, but nowhere near the scope of Northwood's line. Carnival glass examples of Grape & Cable are known in nearly every iridescent color produced by the Northwood firm, though not all shapes are known in every color. There were "whimsey" items made and several pattern variations exist, including both stippled and non-stippled items in many shapes. It was also produced in many non-iridized forms including custard glass, color stained crystal, cobalt blue, emerald green, and even acid treated satin glass. The field is a vast one indeed, and an entire book could easily be devoted to Grape & Cable.

With that thought in mind, we will take a slightly different approach in format here. It is simply far too complex an area to present in the same manner as we have the other Northwood carnival patterns. In order to give some sense of perspective on this, I have presented all the known Grape & Cable shapes and variations along with brief notes concerning known colors and rarity. This, combined with the values given at the back of this book, should give the reader a clear picture of the tremendous variety that collecting Grape & Cable offers. Not every known color for each shape listed is presented in this text. Additional colors may be found listed in the value guide, with prices giving a good indication of rarity and desirability.

Shapes & Colors Known

Banana bowl, large, oval, footed: Measures 12" – 13" in length. These are curiously never trademarked. Most often seen in amethyst, marigold, and green, in that order. Scarce in white, ice blue, ice green, and pearlized custard. Rarely found in cobalt blue.

Banana bowl, stippled: Sometimes called "banded," these are often found with a roughly ½" wide raised band running around the top portion. Harder to find than the non-stippled version. Known in marigold, green, cobalt blue, Renninger blue, and aqua.

Berry set, thumbprint version: Easily recognized by the large raised thumbprints encircling the lower portion. Pattern is on the exterior surface. Large bowl measures 10" – 10½"; small bowl about 5" – 6". Most often found in amethyst and marigold. Green is tougher, cobalt blue very scarce, pearlized custard rare, and ice green very rare.

Berry set, ruffled: Pattern is on the interior. Shaped from the same mould used for the ice cream set. No thumbprints. Has the Basketweave exterior. Large bowl measures 11" – 12"; small bowl 5 – 6". Seen most often in amethyst and marigold. Tougher in green, scarce in cobalt blue. Rare in white, ice blue, and ice green.

Bonbon, two-handled: Basketweave exterior. Easily found in marigold, amethyst, green, and cobalt blue. White is scarce. Pearlized custard is rare, and aqua opalescent extremely so. A single known example in peach opalescent exists.

Bonbon, two-handled, stippled: Seen less often than non-stippled version. Known in marigold, amethyst, green, cobalt blue, white, aqua, and black amethyst. Single known examples in marigold on custard and violet.

Bowl, salad, 10" – 12": Fashioned from the master ice cream bowl, these are deep in shape, sometimes with straight sides and a few known with pie crust edge. Rare shape reported only in marigold and green to date.

Bowl, 7" – 7½" ruffled, collar base: Pattern on the interior with Basketweave exterior. Easily found in marigold, amethyst, and green. Rare in ice blue. Extremely rare in aqua opalescent with only a few known.

Bowl, 8" – 9", ruffled, collar base: Pattern on interior with Basketweave exterior or plain exterior. Easily found in marigold, amethyst or green. Very scarce in lavender, olive green or cobalt blue. Rare in white, ice blue or ice green. Extremely rare in aqua opalescent.

Bowl, 8" – 9", collar base, pie crust edge: Pattern on interior with Basketweave or plain exterior. Known in the same colors as the ruffled bowls as well as a couple known examples in sapphire blue.

Bowl, 8" – 9", collar base, ruffled, stippled: Has a stippled background and is often found with a band of three raised lines encircling the pattern. Exterior is usually ribbed. Harder to find than the non-stippled version. Marigold and amethyst most available. Cobalt blue and green are scarce. White, ice blue, aqua, teal, and aqua opalescent very rare. Ice green extremely rare.

Bowl, 8" – 9", collar base, pie crust, stippled: Reported in the same colors as the ruffled version.

Bowl, 8" – 9", collar base, "tendril" variant: Made from a different mould, on this version the tendrils from the leaves extend into the center of the bowl. Known in both ruffled or pie crust edged, stippled or non-stippled. Most have a plain exterior; some with Basketweave. Most available in non-stippled version in marigold, amethyst, and green. Scarce in blue and lavender. Rare in aqua and ice blue; extremely so in aqua opalescent. Stippled version usually has ribbed exterior. Rarely found. Reported in marigold, green, cobalt blue, and aqua opalescent.

Bowl, 8" – 9", collar base, "leaf" variant: Has a single leaf in the center. Most often seen in marigold, amethyst, and green. Also reported in cobalt blue and lavender.

Bowl, 8" – 9", spatula footed: Has the meander exterior pattern and broad, spade-like feet. Reported only in marigold, amethyst, green, cobalt blue, and ice green, to date.

Breakfast creamer & open sugar: Smaller than the full-size table set pieces with no thumbprints around the base. Known only in marigold, amethyst, and green.

Candlestick: Roughly 6" tall and known only in marigold, amethyst, and green.

Candle lamp: Comprised of the 6" candlestick with matching, round shade and metal attachment fittings. Very scarce in any color but seen most often in green. Marigold and amethyst harder to find.

Card tray, 6" – 8": Fashioned from the 6" – 7" plate mould with two sides turned up. Basketweave exterior. Known in marigold, amethyst, green, and lavender.

Centerpiece bowl, large, footed: Rests on three scrolled feet. Fashioned from the mould for the shallow fruit bowl. The "flame" edge points may be cupped inwards, like a rosebowl, or pointing straight up, all in an even line. Tough piece to find in any color. Most often seen in amethyst or marigold. Green, white, ice green, and cobalt blue are scarce. Ice blue is rare. One example reported in pearlized custard.

Chop plate, footed: Flattened out from large, shallow fruit bowl. Only two examples reported, and both are in white.

Cologne bottle: Marketed as part of the six-piece dresser set and also as a liquor decanter with six tiny shot glasses. Two of these stoppered bottles came with the dresser set. Most often seen in marigold and amethyst. Green is scarce and ice blue rare. No complete white example has yet been confirmed, but I have held a white stopper in my own hands, so I know there must be a bottle out there somewhere. Like the dresser tray, a stippled, banded version has also been reported, but only in marigold.

Compote, large, covered: Not too difficult to find in amethyst, but very rare in marigold.

Compote, large, open: Most often seen in amethyst. Marigold is scarce, and green is rare.

Compote whimsey: Fashioned from the covered sweetmeat base and ruffled or flared out. Reported only in marigold and amethyst.

Cracker jar, covered: Has two handles. Marigold and amethyst still quite available. All others are rare, including cobalt blue, white, smoke, ice green, and the ultra-rare aqua opalescent. None yet reported in green or ice blue.

Cracker jar, covered, stippled: Rarely seen and reported only in marigold, to date.

Cup & saucer: Comprised of a punch cup combined with a 5" – 6" saucer. The true saucer is easily identified by the sharply defined, circular recess in the center to accommodate the cup. They are rare in any color. Reported in marigold, amethyst, green, and white.

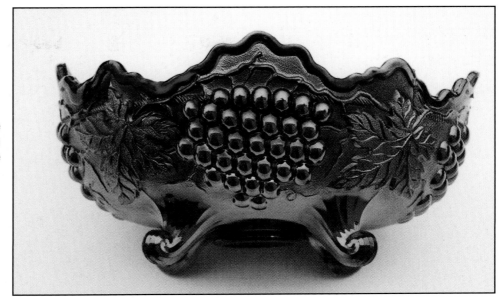

If you look closely, you can see the stippled background on this beautiful Grape & Cable banana bowl in blue.

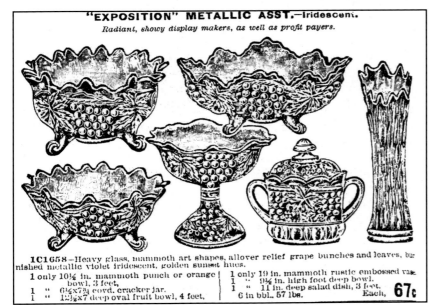

The Grape & Cable banana bowl appears in this assortment of large Grape & Cable pieces from the fall 1910 Butler Brothers catalog. Along with it are the shallow and deep versions of the footed fruit bowl, the large open compote, the cracker jar and curiously, the large tree trunk funeral vase. With a wholesale price of 67 cents each, they likely retailed for about $1.00. That may seem cheap, but in reality that was close to half a day's pay for the average wage earner.

The Grape & Cable centerpiece bowl in ice green. This one has the points straight up.

Dresser tray: Oval, flat, and measures roughly 11" – 12" long. Marketed as part of the six-piece dresser set. There are two versions. The most often seen has a scalloped edge. Marigold and amethyst are the most available, green is scarce. Ice blue is rarely seen and at least one white example is known. The second version is usually stippled, has a smooth edge and a roughly ½" wide raised band encircling the edge. Reported only in marigold, to date.

Fernery, footed: Round and rests on three scrolled feet. Has straight, vertical sides, a smooth edge, and originally came with a metal liner. Very scarce item in any color. Known in marigold, amethyst, white, ice blue, ice green, and pearlized custard.

Fruit bowl, large, footed, shallow: Roughly 11" wide, resting on three scrolled feet and about 4" – 4½" high. Easier to find than the deeper version. Known in marigold, amethyst, green, cobalt blue, white, ice blue, and ice green. Two known examples in ice blue have been reported.

Fruit bowl, large, footed, deep: Sometimes called an "orange bowl." Much harder to find than the shallow version, these bowls stand roughly 6" – 7" high. Colors known include marigold, amethyst, green, cobalt blue, white, russet (olive), and ice green.

Fruit bowl, large, footed, banded: This deep shape variation has a raised, ½" wide band replacing the cable. Rarely seen and reported only in marigold and cobalt blue, to date.

Hatpin holder: Marketed both individually and as part of the six-piece dresser set. Footed, standing roughly 7" tall. Found in a wide variety of colors. Marigold, amethyst, and green are most available. Cobalt blue and black amethyst are very scarce. All others are rare including lavender, white, ice blue, ice green, and lime green. Two ultra-rare examples in aqua opalescent are known. Beware of numerous reproductions coming from Taiwan!

Hatpin holder, banded: On this version, there is no cable. It is replaced by a roughly ½" wide raised band. Rarely seen and reported only in marigold, amethyst, and cobalt blue.

Hat shape, ruffled: Fashioned from the tumbler mould and reported only in marigold, amethyst, and green.

Humidor: Sometimes called a tobacco jar. No handles and the underside of the lid has three prongs to hold a moistening sponge. Most often seen in marigold and amethyst. Cobalt blue is scarce. Two ultra-rare aqua opalescent examples are known.

Humidor, stippled: Most often seen in cobalt blue. Marigold examples are harder to find.

Ice cream bowl, large, 10" – 11": Collar based with Basketweave exterior. Round, almost flat and plate-like, but with the edge turned up 1" – 2" all the way around. Very desirable and popular shape. Found most often in marigold, amethyst, and surprisingly, white. Hard to find in green or lavender and rare in cobalt blue. Very rare in ice blue and ice green.

Ice cream bowl, small, 5" – 6": Same pattern and shape characteristics as the matching large bowl. Painfully difficult to find in any color, but known in marigold, amethyst, green, cobalt blue, white, ice blue, and ice green.

Nappy, one-handled: These were fashioned from the punch cup, flattened out and somewhat "scoop" shaped. Sometimes called a pin dish. Easy to find in marigold, amethyst, and green. Very rare in ice blue.

Pin tray: Tiny, oval-shaped, about 4" – 4½" long with a scalloped edge. Marketed as part of the six-piece dresser set. Hard to find. Known in marigold, amethyst, green, white, ice blue, and pearlized custard.

Pin tray, banded: Usually stippled and has a wide raised band around the outer, smooth edge. Reported only in marigold, amethyst, and pearlized custard.

Powder jar, covered: Marketed both individually and as part of the six-piece dresser set. Perfect lids are very difficult to find. Most often found in marigold, amethyst or green. Cobalt blue and lavender are rare. Extremely rare in white, ice blue, and ice green. Two known aqua opalescent examples exist.

Plate, collar base, 6" – 6½": Flattened out from the small ice cream bowl and rare in any color. Reported in marigold, amethyst, and green.

Plate, collar base, 7" – 7½": Basketweave exterior. An intermediate size, most often found in amethyst or green. Marigold is surprisingly rare in this size. Also reported in horehound and a couple of rare marigold on custard examples.

Plate, 7" – 8", handgrip: Has one edge turned up. Known only in marigold, amethyst, and green.

Grape & Cable 9" ruffled bowl in amethyst and a pie crust edge 9" bowl in marigold. Note the tendrils of the leaves running into the center on the marigold example which is sometimes called Grape & Cable variant. Note also how the bunches of grapes are more triangular on the amethyst bowl than they are on the marigold one.

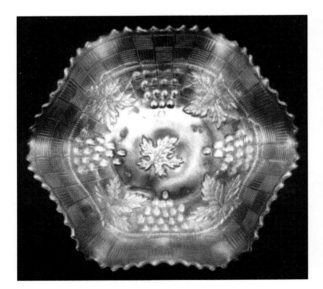 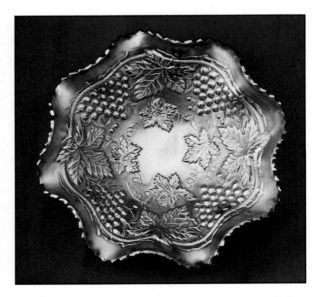

This rare ice blue Grape & Cable 7½" ruffled bowl at left has a single leaf center, yet a third pattern variation found on Grape & Cable bowls. The amethyst bowl on the right measures 11" in diameter. This is the master berry bowl to the ruffled berry set, fashioned from the same mould used for the master ice cream bowl.

Plate, 8" – 9", collar base: May be found with Basketweave or plain exterior. Known in marigold, amethyst, green, clambroth, lavender, and very rare ice blue examples.

Plate, 8" – 9", collar base, stippled: Usually has a ribbed exterior. Has the band of three raised lines encircling the pattern. Known in marigold, amethyst, green, cobalt blue, smoke, and sapphire blue. Much harder to find than the non-stippled version.

Plate, 9", spatula-footed: Rests on three spade-like feet. Has the meander exterior pattern. Seen most often in marigold and amethyst. A little harder to find in green, very scarce in cobalt blue, and rare in ice green.

Punch bowl & base, small size: Measures roughly 11" – 12½" in diameter. Most often found in marigold or amethyst. Green is rarely found. White is extremely rare, but ice blue and ice green far more so, with only a few known. The single known example in aqua opalescent is a rarity of the highest possible order!

Punch bowl & base, small size, stippled: Rarely seen and reported only in marigold and cobalt blue, to date.

Punch bowl & base, mid-size: Sometimes called "table size," measures roughly 13" – 14½" in diameter. Most often seen in amethyst. Very scarce in marigold. Rare in cobalt blue, or green. Extremely rare in teal, white, ice blue, and ice green.

Punch bowl & base, mid-size, stippled: Rare in any color. Confirmed in marigold, amethyst, and cobalt blue. Reported, but not confirmed in green.

Punch bowl & base, banquet size: Huge! Measures 16½" – 18" in diameter. Most available in amethyst. Much harder to find in marigold. Very rare in green, cobalt blue, and white. Extremely rare in ice green and ultra-rare in ice blue with only one example known.

Punch cup: Found in all the colors known in the three sizes of punch bowls, both stippled and non-stippled.

Sherbet, small, pedestal-footed: Has thumbprints on the exterior. Measures roughly 5" in diameter. Known only in marigold, amethyst, and green. Easily found.

Shot glass: Tiny, just roughly 2½" tall, looking like a miniature of the tumbler. They were marketed as a part of a whiskey set with the tall, handled Grape & Cable whiskey decanter and also as part of a liquor set in combination with the cologne bottle and the Holiday flat tray. Known only in marigold and amethyst and tough to find in either color.

Spittoon whimsey: Fashioned from the base of the covered powder jar. Extremely rare. Few examples known in marigold or amethyst. One green example known.

Sweetmeat compote, covered: Has a "pagoda-like" shaped lid. Not too difficult to find in amethyst, but extremely rare in marigold with few known examples.

Table set, four-piece: Comprised of covered butter dish, covered sugar, creamer, and spooner. Has the thumbprints around the base. Most often found in marigold and amethyst. Green a little harder to find. Extremely rare in ice blue. BEWARE OF REPRODUCTIONS, particularly on the butter dish. The old butter dish has a sawtooth-like edge around the base. The new ones have a broadly scalloped base.

Triangular whimsey, footed: Fashioned from the large fruit bowl, but in a three-sided shape. Only one example, in amethyst, known.

Vase, footed whimsey: Fashioned from the hatpin holder. Has tiny fluted edge points rather than the large "flame" points, and the edge is flared outwards. Extremely rare! Reported only in amethyst and green. Few known.

Water pitcher, standard size: Stands roughly 8" – 8½" tall. Most often seen in marigold and amethyst. Green is scarcer. Extremely rare in ice green. One example in smoke is known and one in a most unusual "smoke opalescent."

Tumbler, standard size: Roughly 4" tall. Easy to find in marigold or amethyst with green a bit tougher. Rare in lavender, horehound, ice green, and lime green.

Water pitcher, tankard size: Stands roughly 10½" tall. Seldom seen even in marigold or amethyst, the two most available colors. Extremely rare in green and even more so in ice green.

Tumbler, tankard size: Stands roughly 4¼" tall with a more widely flared top edge. Known in marigold, amethyst, green, and ice green. Harder to find than the standard size.

Tumbler, stippled: Curious! No stippled pitchers known, but tumblers are known in marigold and amethyst.

Whiskey decanter, handled: Stands roughly 10½" tall, with a cruet-like neck and spout. The stopper is flat-topped. Known only in marigold and amethyst. Very hard to find with the stopper intact.

Grape & Cable hatpin holder in amethyst, standard size water pitcher in marigold, tumbler in green, cracker jar in marigold, and the stippled humidor in cobalt blue. All of these pieces are still reasonably available in these colors.

I'm very pleased to be able to show this extremely rare piece of Grape & Cable. This is the large, deep fruit bowl in ice green, one of only four or five examples known in this color.

The ad for the fernery is from the special Christmas 1910 Butler Brothers wholesale catalog. It was offered complete with gift box, ready for Christmas giving, at 72 cents each wholesale. Note the reference to the "white enamel removable lining" that came with it.

This ad from the spring 1912 Butler Brothers catalog offers the complete Grape Cable dresser set in amethyst, and it was a regular fixture in the catalogs for several years thereafter. The set includes the dresser tray, hatpin holder, pin tray, covered powder jar, and two cologne bottles. You will note that there is no small perfume bottle. The so-called Grape &

DECORATED BUREAU SETS.

C1141, Florentine Iridescent—Grape cluster and leaf embossed, dark metallic iridescent finish, rainbow hues, 29½ in. bottles, 3½x3¾ covered puff box, 7¼ in. hat pin holder, 11 in. comb and brush tray, 5¾ in. pin tray. 1 set corrugated case. Set, **75c**

Cable perfume bottle was not part of the dresser set. In fact, it is not even the Grape & Cable pattern and was not a Northwood product. It has been misidentified as Grape & Cable for 30 years, and it's high time we corrected this. This perfume bottle was actually made by Dugan, and it is an identical pattern match to Dugan's Vintage Grape covered powder jar.

1C834—**Covd. Puff Box, 3½x3¾**, relief embossed grape bunches and leaves, beaded base, allover rich golden metallic violet iridescent. 1 doz. in box. **Doz. 96c**

1C835—**Hatpin holder, 7¼ in., 3** rib embossed feet spaced open top As 1C834, 1 doz. in box.,...**Doz. 92c**

Northwood's production of the hatpin holder and covered powder jar pre-dates production of the full dresser set, and for well over a year these two items were offered separately, as shown in this ad from a 1911 Butler Brothers catalog. This would certainly explain why these two items are much more easily found today than are the other pieces in the dresser set.

Grape & Cable dresser tray and covered powder jar, both in marigold.

While the Grape & Cable covered sweetmeat compote is easily found in amethyst, only a few of the extremely rare marigold examples, like the one shown here, are known. Also shown is the complete Grape & Cable candlelamp in marigold, a scarce item in any color.

"VINELAND" DINING SET ASST—(Iridescent)

Rich enough to call gorgeous. Good sellers.

1C1679 — Large pcs., scalloped, grapevine embossing, allover iridescent amethyst and green. 2 only 7 pc. water sets—half gal. jug, six 4x3 tapered tumblers. 2 only 7 pc. berry sets — 9¼ in. bowl, six 5 in. nappies. 2 only 4 pc. table sets —

covered butter and sugar, spoonholder, creamer.

6 sets in bbl., 59 lbs.   Set, **59c**

Both of these ads are from the fall 1910 Butler Brothers catalog. One offers the Grape & Cable berry set, water set, and table set. Note the name "Vineland," used to market these sets. The other ad offers the Grape & Cable tankard water set. Note the taller, more elongated shape of the tankard pitcher as compared to the standard size pitcher.

METALLIC IRIDESCENT 7 PIECE WATER SET.

An unusually rich one to retail at $1.00

1C1950 — 9¾ in. ½ gal. tankard, 6 belled tumblers, relief grape bunches and leaf wreath, allover golden sunset, metallic violet iridescent. 6 sets in bbl. 67 lbs.   Set, **65c**

The Grape & Cable small breakfast creamer in marigold. Part of a two-piece set, it came with a matching, two-handled open sugar.

Here it is! The ultimate Grape & Cable rarity! This is the small size Grape & Cable complete punch set in aqua opalescent. It is the only known complete set in this color, and it surfaced in upstate New York a little over three years ago. We knew that such a set must surely exist as a handful of punch cups in aqua opalescent were in collections scattered about the country, but no matching punch bowl or base had ever surfaced.

For nearly 40 years of carnival collecting, we assumed that the scarce Grape & Cable shot glasses came with the tall, handled whiskey decanter. You can imagine my surprise when I found this ad in a newly discovered 1912 Butler Brothers wholesale catalog. Shown here is an ad for a Grape & Cable whiskey set, but it certainly does not include the tall, handled whiskey decanter! In its place is a Grape & Cable cologne bottle from the dresser set. Of particular note is the heading "new design." Grape & Cable had been in production since January of 1910. Is it mere coincidence that the Grape & Cable complete dresser set also first appeared in 1912, the date of this ad? While it's only theory, the following scenario is certainly "food for thought." The Grape & Cable tall, handled whiskey decanter must have been an expensive item to produce. Perhaps it was a poor seller because of this and by 1912 had already been dropped from the line. It would also explain why the tall, handled whiskey decanter is so difficult to find today. Note also that this ad contains a second surprise. Included in the set is a Northwood Holiday undertray shown elsewhere in this book! So we can now also confirm at least one of the functions for which the Holiday tray was marketed.

Grapes were one of the most popular motifs with the glass buying public during the early part of the 1900s. This is one of several Northwood iridescent creations that incorporated them, dating circa 1909 – 1910. It was apparently a successful seller (as were most grape patterns), enjoying a production run that spanned at least six years. The moulds were also used for custard glass production during 1914 – 1915, and examples in non-iridized crystal and emerald green were made throughout the 1909 – 1915 time frame as well.

In iridescent form, berry sets, table sets, and water sets are the only shapes known, and all are still quite available in marigold. Amethyst and cobalt blue pieces are harder to find. Grape & Gothic Arches may also be found in custard glass with a delicate, pastel iridescence, usually with fired-on gold trim around the top edges. Most collectors refer to these pieces as "pearlized custard." Examples of this unique form are quite scarce, but still do turn up from time to time. The top honors here go to the green carnival examples. Virtually any Grape & Gothic Arches item is rarely found in green.

Most items in this line are not signed, but a few examples of the water pitcher have been found with the Northwood (N) trademark.

Shapes & Colors Known

Berry set, table set, water set: marigold, amethyst, green, cobalt blue, iridized custard

Any piece of Grape & Gothic Arches in green, like this beautiful tumbler, is very difficult to find.

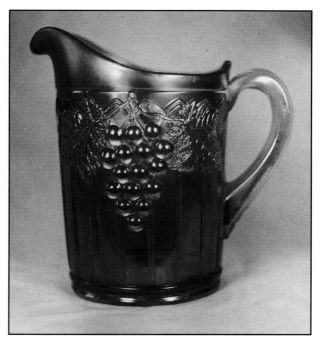

The Grape & Gothic Arches water pitcher in marigold.

PATTERN: GRAPE ARBOR

There seem to be two schools of thought regarding the Northwood Grape Arbor water set: You either love it or you don't! Some feel the design and shape to be a bit "grotesque," but I admit to being an avid admirer of this pattern. The combination of pattern and shape on these mould-blown, tankard pitchers was no doubt inspired by classical Greek antiquities, and one cannot help but marvel at the fact that any of these delicate beauties has survived the years. The Northwood version of the pattern was in production during the 1911 – 1914 period and is found on water sets and a ruffled hat shape, fashioned from the tumbler mould.

The tankard water pitchers are mould-blown, with a separately applied handle and are not trademarked. Marigold is by far the most available color, although being highly prone to damage due to their delicacy and the unusually high relief of the pattern, perfect examples are really not all that easily found. In my opinion, they are still grossly undervalued. Amethyst is next in line, followed by white and ice blue. At present, the top honors go to the cobalt blue tankards. Only three are known and have brought very serious prices on the rare occasion when they have changed

hands. To date, I have not been able to confirm a single example of the pitcher in ice green, but as tumblers are known in that color, they must surely exist out there somewhere. A pearlized custard tankard would also be a great find. Here again, tumblers are known, but no matching pitcher has yet surfaced. The same holds true for aqua and lavender, both colors now confirmed in the tumbler, but as yet, no matching pitchers are known. I have always thought it very strange that virtually no examples of this pattern have ever surfaced in green. Could they still be lurking out there, undiscovered as yet? Entirely possible! One thing I learned many years ago is "never say never," when it comes to carnival glass.

The only other Northwood-made shape in this pattern is that of a ruffled hat, fashioned from the tumbler mould. Marigold and cobalt blue are the most available colors here. White is harder to find, and the ice green examples are quite scarce.

The Dugan/Diamond Glass Co. of Indiana, Pennsylvania also produced a version of the Grape Arbor pattern, but only in a large, footed fruit bowl with the Feather Scroll (inverted Fan & Feather) exterior pattern.

Shapes & Colors Known

Tankard pitcher: marigold, amethyst, cobalt blue, white, ice blue
Tumbler: marigold, amethyst, cobalt blue, white, ice blue, ice green, lavender, aqua, pearlized custard
Hat shape: marigold, cobalt blue, white, ice green

In my opinion this handsome Grape Arbor water pitcher and tumbler in marigold is one of the most undervalued and underappreciated of all Northwood water set patterns.

Three Grape Arbor tumblers in amethyst, marigold, and ice blue. The ice blue may take some patient searching, but all three colors are still reasonably available.

The iridized version of this pattern dates from the time of Northwood's brief revival of custard glass, circa 1914 – 1915. It was originally part of Northwood's "Verre D'Orr" line and appears in the 1906 Northwood Factory catalog. "Verre D'Orr" means "glass of gold." Most of the items in this line, found on amethyst, cobalt blue, and emerald green base glass, had lavish, fired-on gold decoration.

Pearlized custard is the only iridescent color known on this large 10" – 11" three-footed ice cream-shaped bowl. There are only about seven or eight examples known, and all have been found with remnants of fired-on gold decoration on the edges. The exterior surface is plain, and the Northwood trademark is usually present.

Shapes & Colors Known

Bowl, 10" – 11", footed: pearlized custard

Trying to capture on film the delicate, pastel iridescence on this pearlized custard Grape Frieze bowl is almost impossible, but this rare bowl is indeed iridized.

PATTERN: Grape Leaves

This design first appears, in iridized form, late in a 1909 Butler Brothers wholesale catalog, thus making it one of Northwood's earliest carnival patterns to feature a grape motif. Production of the design lasted through 1912. It is found only on the interior surface of 8" – 9" bowls, usually with the Blossoms & Palms exterior design. The Northwood trademark is always present on a raised "button" directly in the center of the pattern. Examples are known with six broad ruffles, eight ruffles, or with the "three in one" crimped edge.

There has been a myth circulating for several years concerning the examples found with the three in one crimped edge. Some have speculated that Northwood never made carnival glass (or any other form of glass) using this edge treatment. It is time to dispel this myth right here and now! Some have speculated

that the examples with the three in one edge treatment must surely be Dugan products, even though they bear the Northwood trademark, made in a mould left behind by Northwood when he left that firm in 1901. This is virtually impossible! First, the Grape Leaves pattern did not even exist in 1901 when Northwood left Pennsylvania for West Virginia. Secondly, the Northwood N in a circle trademark did not exist in 1901. It was first registered by Northwood in 1905, four full years after he moved to Wheeling. So, he could not possibly have "left behind" a mould that contained it. Thirdly, Northwood did indeed make a variety of pieces incorporating the three in one edge crimping. The 1906 Northwood factory catalog shows many examples in opalescent glass. Butler Brothers wholesale catalogs from the 1907 – 1910 period feature many Northwood assortments of both carnival and other glass, all offered with the three in one edge crimping. Carnival assortments in 1909 – 1910 Butler Brothers catalogs offer bowls in the Grape Leaves, Bullseye and Leaves, Netted Roses, and Greek Key dome-footed patterns, all with a three in one edge. Rest assured that the Grape Leaves bowls with the three in one edge are definitely Northwood products.

The examples with the three in one edge treatment have been documented in marigold, amethyst, green, and cobalt blue. Marigold and amethyst are the most available of these. Green is scarce and the cobalt blue quite rare. The ruffled bowls have been found in a wider variety of colors, with marigold, amethyst, and green the most often found. Cobalt blue examples are scarce, and examples in lavender and amber are rarely seen. There is also a handful of known examples in what appears to be a true clambroth or "ginger ale" coloring, with a spectacular pastel, multicolor iridescence. The top spot goes to the ice blue examples. I only know of two, but others surely exist.

Shapes & Colors Known

Bowl 8" – 9", three in one edge: marigold, amethyst, green, cobalt blue
Bowl 8" – 9", ruffled: marigold, amethyst, green, cobalt blue, lavender, clambroth, amber, ice blue

You shouldn't have too much trouble finding a Northwood Grape Leaves bowl in amethyst like the one shown here. It is perhaps the most often found color in this pattern. The ice blue example is at the other end of the rarity spectrum. Only a few of these are known, and they command great interest and very serious prices on the rare occasion they change hands.

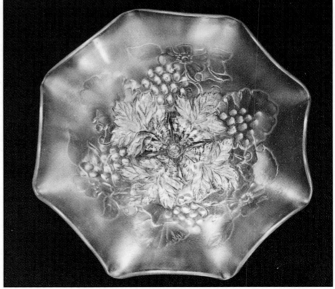

There are really three distinct versions of this popular Northwood pattern. The design was initially introduced as an exterior pattern on dome-footed bowls that first appeared in iridescent form circa 1909. The design was expanded in 1911 to include collar-based bowls, plates, and a handsome water set. Production of the line was apparently short-lived as pieces are difficult to find today. A single known example of a bowl in ice green does indicate production through at least early 1912.

There are actually two versions of the dome-footed Greek Key bowl. They are a carry-over from earlier opalescent production, appearing in that form in the 1906 Northwood factory catalog. The Greek Key design is on the exterior surface, combined with a pattern of Scales. Some are found with a plain interior while others have a Stippled Rays interior design. The edge may be broadly ruffled, octagonal or have the three in one crimping. Of these, the three in one crimped bowls are the least often seen. Marigold, amethyst, and green are the only reported colors, with amethyst being the most difficult to find. Most of these will bear the Northwood trademark.

The collar-based bowls and plates are very popular items, found in a slightly wider variety of colors. The design here is on the interior surface. Most examples will carry the Basketweave exterior pattern, but a couple of rare examples with a ribbed exterior are known. The bowls may be either ruffled or have the pie crust edge. Some examples are signed while others are not. They are found primarily in marigold, amethyst, and green, but cobalt blue examples are also found on rare occasion. Topping the rarity list is the single known ice green bowl. The plates are extremely popular items and will not come cheap in any color. Most often seen are marigold and amethyst. Green is tougher to find, and cobalt blue examples are rare. Topping the rarity list here are the marigold plates with the ribbed exterior. I know of only two examples, to date.

The Greek Key water sets are perhaps the most eagerly sought and highly treasured of all the shapes in this design. Combining the Greek Key design with a shape highly reminiscent of classical Greek form, the mould-blown tankard pitchers with their separately applied handles are a handsome sight to behold. On both the pitcher and tumblers, which are pressed, the Greek Key band encircling the center is bordered on the top by fan-shaped designs and below by hanging prisms. Marigold, amethyst, and green are the only reported colors. Marigold is the most often found, but a set in any color is really a rare find. They just don't turn up very often. The tumblers usually bear the Northwood trademark, but the pitchers are never signed.

Shapes & Colors Known

Bowl, 7" – 9", dome-footed, and water set: marigold, amethyst, green
Bowl, 8" – 9", collar-based: marigold, amethyst, green, cobalt blue, ice green
Plate, 9", collar-based: marigold, amethyst, green, cobalt blue

The Greek Key 9" ruffled bowl in green and a pie crust edge 9" bowl in amethyst.

Plates in the Greek Key pattern, like this beautiful marigold example, are very difficult to find. The water pitchers are very seldom found and highly treasured. The tumblers are getting scarce, but still turn up from time to time.

PATTERN: HEARTS & FLOWERS

You could write volumes about this beautiful and extremely popular Northwood creation and still not do it justice. Most of the major producers of carnival glass made similar designs in imitation of delicate embroidery, but Northwood's Hearts & Flowers seems to be far and away the most eagerly sought and highly treasured of all of them. Found in a dazzling array of colors, entire collections have been built around this masterpiece of the mould-maker's art. The design first appeared in the wholesale catalogs early in 1912 and holds the distinction of being among the first to be produced in Northwood's new pastel colors that were introduced in January of that year. The pattern is found on the interior surface of bowls, plates, compotes, and a rare, stemmed whimsey plate, fashioned from the compote mould. Some examples bear the Northwood trademark, but unsigned examples far outnumber these.

The 8" – 9" bowls may be found ruffled or with the pie crust edge. Most have a ribbed exterior, but a few rare examples with Northwood's distinctive Basketweave exterior pattern are known. In the ruffled shape, white and ice blue are by far the most available colors, a testament to the initial popularity of those two colors when introduced to the buying public in 1912. Amethyst and lavender are next in line. Cobalt blue,

marigold, lime green, and ice green examples are much harder to find. All the other known colors would be classed as rare to extremely so, and these include Renninger blue, aqua, aqua opalescent, and green. Green gets my vote for the top rarity spot, but aqua opalescent is not far behind. The pie crust edged bowls are much more difficult to find in any color. Ice blue and marigold seem to be the most often found, but even they are scarce. Amethyst, cobalt blue, and white are next in line, in that order. Ice green, lime green, and green are near evenly tied for the top ranking, but here again, my vote goes to the green examples.

The 9" flat plates are really very rare in any color and in very high demand. Even the marigold examples, the most available color, will generally sell in excess of a thousand dollars! Amethyst and ice blue are next, followed by ice green, lime green, cobalt blue, white, green, and sapphire blue. All are extremely rare, but there's no contest for the top ranking. It goes to the vaseline examples; only two are known! Both have damage but would still surely sell for a staggering price if they are ever offered for sale. What a perfect one would bring, should it ever turn up, would be nearly incomprehensible!

The lovely, stemmed Hearts & Flowers compotes

are found in the greatest variety of colors of any of the known shapes in this pattern, and that makes them a real delight for collectors. The Hearts & Flowers pattern is carried over to the exterior of the stem. The exterior of the top portion may be either ribbed or plain, with most examples having the ribbed exterior. White is by far the most often found color, followed closely by marigold. Aqua opalescent and ice blue examples are quite plentiful too, but will often bring higher prices than the slightly scarcer amethyst, cobalt blue, and clambroth compotes. Eveyone just seems to want an aqua opalescent and an ice blue one. Ice green, lime green, and lavender are next in this long line of colors. Green is next followed closely by Renninger blue. All of the other colors are extremely rare. These include ice blue opalescent, powder blue opalescent, sapphire blue, sapphire blue opalescent, cobalt blue opalescent, and marigold on custard. Which is the top color? That's a nearly impossible call. There is only one known example in cobalt blue opalescent, but it is damaged. The marigold on custard will usually bring the highest price, but there are probably fewer known actual examples of most of the others in that group. Any one of them is a top

rarity. I have heard rumors of the existence of an iridized vaseline opalescent compote for many years. It was allegedly seen and examined in the state of Pennsylvania nearly 30 years ago by a very reliable and knowledgeable collector, one very well known and respected in carnival glass collecting circles. However, all efforts on my part (and they have been extensive) to confirm this piece have led to a dead end. Still, non-iridized vaseline opalescent Hearts & Flowers compotes do exist, so the possibility of an iridized one remains tantalizing, but as yet unconfirmed.

The only other reported shape is a unique stemmed whimsey plate, fashioned from the compote mould, with the top portion flattened out. Only one example, in white, is known to date.

Shapes & Colors Known

Bowl, 8" – 9", ruffled: marigold, amethyst, green, cobalt blue, white, ice blue, ice green, aqua, aqua opalescent, lime green, Renninger blue

Bowl, 8" – 9", pie crust edge: marigold, amethyst, green, cobalt blue, white, ice blue, ice green, lime green

Plate, 9": marigold, amethyst, green, cobalt blue, white, ice blue, ice green, lime green, sapphire blue, vaseline

Compote: marigold, amethyst, green, cobalt blue, white, ice blue, ice green, lime green, aqua opalescent, lavender, clambroth, Renninger blue, ice blue opalescent, powder blue opalescent, sapphire blue, sapphire blue opalescent, cobalt blue opalescent, marigold on custard

Stemmed whimsey plate: white

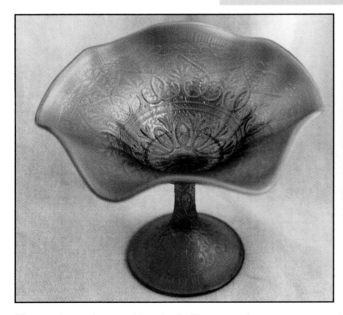 

Two extremely rare Hearts & Flowers pieces: a compote in sapphire blue opalescent and a pie crust edge 9" bowl in cobalt blue. Only two or three of each are known.

PATTERN: HOLIDAY

Known only in a large, round, flat tray, Holiday is another carry-over pattern from Northwood's pre-iridescent production. Collectors have traditionally called this a cake tray, but that was not its original purpose. It was marketed in crystal as an undertray for both wine sets and water sets during the pre-carnival era, and we can now confirm that the same purpose was carried over into the iridescent production years. The tray appears in company with a Grape & Cable wine set in a spring 1912 Butler Brothers wholesale catalog. Marigold is the only reported color to date, and most examples bear the Northwood trademark. They may not sell for big bucks, but carnival examples of the Holiday tray are really quite rare in actual numbers known.

Shapes & Colors Known

Large round tray: marigold

Northwood's Holiday tray was often marketed as an undertray for both water sets and liquor sets.

PATTERN: INTAGLIO LINE

There are actually three distinct patterns in this line: Strawberry Intaglio, Cherry Intaglio and Peach & Pear Intaglio. All were carried over from pre-iridescent production from Northwood's Intaglio line, circa 1905 – 1907. This Intaglio line was comprised of heavy crystal pieces, decorated with painted gold and red colors. The items in this line have the pattern deeply impressed on the underside, rather than raised in relief on the inner surface. Collectors today call these items "goofus glass." Three of these patterns were rushed into iridescent production, circa 1908 – 1909, in order to gain a quick share of the new market until other designs more appropriate to iridescent production could be created. All are seldom found today, indicating a very short production run in iridized form.

These three patterns are all found in berry sets, comprised of a large, 10" master bowl and six small, 4¾" bowls. The glass is nearly ½" thick on these very heavy pieces. These patterns quite obviously were the inspiration leading to three well-known carnival designs that entered production at later dates. Peach & Pear Intaglio and Strawberry Intaglio are strikingly similar in concept to Three Fruits and Northwood's Strawberry. Cherry Intaglio is virtually an intaglio version of Northwood's Cherry & Cable, right down to the cable encircling the design! An occasional example is found with the Northwood trademark, but most are unsigned. Marigold is the only reported color for all three patterns.

Shapes & Colors Known

Master berry, 10", ice cream shape: marigold
Small berry, 4¾", ice cream shape: marigold

Two views of the Intaglio Peach & Pear large ice cream-shaped bowl, showing how the pattern is impressed on the underside rather than having the usual relief molding found on most carnival designs.

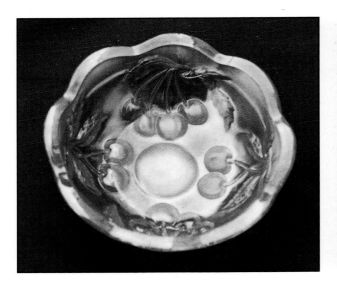

These two views show an Intaglio Cherry small 4¾" ice cream-shaped bowl. Aside from the Intaglio molding, note the amazing similarity to Northwood's Cherry & Cable, right down to the cable encircling the pattern.

18   H. NORTHWOOD CO., GLASS MANUFACTURERS.

"Intaglio"

SOME very choice pieces are shown here, but like the "Verre D'or" we have to depend on description as it is impossible to show the designs and coloring on plates.

We do not show quite all of the pieces contained in the Assortment as the plate is too small. The glass is the very best fire polished Crystal and the designs graceful and artistic. The large dishes at the top of the plate are very heavy and the design is cut in very deep on the underside, then treated in color and gold effects. The edge of the dishes are fired Bright Gold and we particularly recommend these to your attention, as they are very high class. The 4½ inch Nappies are of the same grade but are made only in the two round shapes. These are made in Strawberry and Apple and Pear Designs. The Apple and Pear Pattern is not shown on the plate, but it is a beauty.

The other pieces are lighter in weight, more delicate and patterned after the expensive Import Goods of this character. The design is Scroll and Poppy, very graceful and artistic. You will be delighted with these goods as they are Holiday Trade Makers and you will duplicate your order more than once. These also are treated with pretty shadings of color on the leaves and flowers, and then the whole design is filled with a Matt Gold Effect. The edges of all the pieces are fired Bright Gold.

The assortment consists of :—

1—10	inch	Round Fruit	"Strawberry"		$12 00	$ 1 00
6— 4½	"	"	"	"	3 50	1 75
1—10	"	"	"	"Apple and Pears"	12 00	1 00
6— 4½	"	"	"	"	3 50	1 75
1—11	"	Cake Plate	"	"	12 00	1 00
6— 5	"	"	"	"	4 00	2 00
2— 9	"	Comports, Scroll and Poppy..			8 00	1 33
2— 6	"	Berry Dish.	"	"	6 00	1 00
3— 6	"	Comports,	"	"	5 00	1 25
6— 6	"	Sweets,	"	"	4 50	2 25

$14 33

35

$14 68

Bbl.........

Even though this is a pre-carnival, non-iridized assortment, I thought you might enjoy seeing this grouping of Northwood's Intaglio line from the 1906 Northwood factory catalog. The Strawberry Intaglio bowl, which is known as marigold, is shown in the top row center.

PATTERN: JESTER CAP

Here we have a classic example of why patterns should never be named based solely on shape. The name originated with Marion Hartung way back in the early 1960s, but we should in no way fault her for the choice of names. At that point in time, she was pioneering the cataloging of carnival glass patterns, with virtually nothing to go on, and likely had only seen this pattern in the Jester Cap or Jack-in-the-Pulpit shape. Since then, numerous other shape variations of these ribbed vases have surfaced, but the name has stuck. We are apparently stuck with it too, although some collectors are starting to refer to this design as Fine Rib Footed which is much more appropriate. I include it here by the original name, if for no other reason than that of convenience.

To date, I have been able to document these vases, all of which stand from 5½" to 7½" tall depending upon shape, in four different shapes and an equal number of colors. Some examples are signed, while others are not. The Jester Cap shape is the most familiar of these and is most often found in marigold. Amethyst is harder to find, green is very scarce, and cobalt blue quite rare. Perfectly round, non-ruffled, cone-shaped vases are seen on occasion, but have only been documented in marigold. Examples with a four-ruffled top are known in marigold, amethyst, and cobalt blue. Vases with six ruffles have been documented in all four of the aforementioned colors. The cobalt blue and green examples seem to be the least often found in any shape.

Fenton made a nearly identical vase, but it is easily distinguished from the Northwood version. The Fenton vase has a raised, bulging ring around the stem where it joins the pedastel foot. On the Northwood vase the stem flows smoothly into the pedestal foot, with no ring.

Northwood's Jester Cap vase in green.

Shapes & Colors Known

Vase, jester cap: marigold, amethyst, green, cobalt blue
Vase, cone shape: marigold
Vase, four-ruffled: marigold, amethyst, cobalt blue
Vase, six-ruffled: marigold, amethyst, green, cobalt blue

PATTERN: LEAF & BEADS

A favorite with collectors, Leaf & Beads enjoyed a lengthy production run in a wide variety of categories. It first appeared in non-iridized opalescent colors in the 1906 Northwood factory catalog. Iridized production of the pattern began circa 1908 – 1909, and the moulds were revived for custard glass during 1914 – 1916. The pattern is also found in iridized and non-iridized colors that Northwood did not introduce until the 1919 – 1920 period, so this design was a very popular seller in its day, and the firm certainly got a lot of mileage out of the Leaf & Beads moulds.

The earliest iridized form in which this pattern appeared was a dome-footed 7" – 9" bowl, usually with a plain interior. Most examples bear the Northwood trademark. The edges of these bowls may be ruffled or in a smooth, octagonal shape. Marigold, amethyst, and green are the only reported colors. The green examples seem to be most often found, and

they usually have Northwood's Alaskan iridescent treatment. A single known dome-footed plate in green, fashioned from this mould, is also known.

The three-footed rosebowls and ruffled bowls, the most popular shapes in this design, entered production about a year later, and a classic was born. The rosebowls are particularly popular and are found in a wide variety of colors and variations. The interior of the rosebowls may be plain, rayed or patterned with a stylized sunflower design. There are also three styles of edge shaping known: scalloped, the most often found; beaded, which is extremely rare; and completely smooth, also rarely found. These edge effects were achieved quite easily by simply changing the top ring in the mould. With a scalloped top and plain or rayed interior, the rosebowl is found in the widest variety of colors. Marigold, amethyst, green, and cobalt blue are still found in fair supply. Aqua opalescent examples are not terribly difficult to find either, but still bring respectable prices since everybody wants one. Russet, Northwood's version of olive green, is harder to find but still turns up from time to time. Most of the remaining colors will present a challenge as all are rarely found. These include aqua, white, ice blue, ice green, sapphire blue, teal, smoke, lavender, ice blue opalescent, ice green opalescent, Renninger blue, and lime green opalescent. Any of these is a real find, but my vote for the top ranking goes to the ice green opalescent. I know of only a couple examples, but there's enough to hunt for to keep any collector happy.

The scalloped top rosebowl with the stylized sunflower interior is found in a far more limited variety of colors. Once suspected to be a Dugan product, we now have proof that it is indeed Northwood. It is pictured right alongside the plain interior version among an assortment of Northwood items in a Butler Brothers wholesale catalog. Marigold, amethyst, and green are the most easily found colors here. Russet is scarce, while teal and sapphire blue are very rare.

The beaded top rosebowl is very rare. Only two colors, marigold and oddly enough cobalt blue, have been reported to date. The smooth top rosebowl is also very rare and has been reported in marigold, amethyst, and pearlized custard, sometimes with nutmeg stain on the latter.

The footed nutbowl, fashioned from the same mould as the scalloped top rosebowl, is also known in a fair range of colors. The scalloped top on the nutbowl does not turn inward as on the rosebowl. The top points straight up or is flared outward. The nutbowl is actually much harder to find than the rosebowl. Nutbowls have been reported in marigold, amethyst, green, cobalt blue, white, and aqua opalescent. While aqua opalescent Leaf & Beads rosebowls are still quite available, the nutbowl is very rare in that color. Another shape fashioned from the same mould is a footed, ruffled bowl, often found in a triangular shape. The interior on these is usually rayed, but some examples with the Sunflower interior are known. Colors reported here include marigold, amethyst, green, cobalt blue, and white.

The only other shape on which the Leaf & Beads pattern is found is as an exterior design on the rare Northwood Lovely pattern bowls, shown on page 92.

Three Northwood Leaf & Beads rosebowls in cobalt blue, aqua opalescent and pearlized custard. Note the nutmeg stain and smooth top variation on the pearlized custard example.

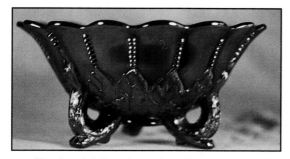

The Leaf & Beads nutbowl in amethyst.

Shapes & Colors Known

Bowl, 7" – 8", dome-footed: marigold, amethyst, green
Plate 9", dome-footed: green
Rosebowl, scalloped top, plan or rayed interior: marigold, amethyst, green, aqua, cobalt blue, white, ice blue, ice green, aqua opalescent, russet, sapphire blue, teal, smoke, lavender, Renninger blue, ice blue opalescent, ice green opalescent, lime green opalescent
Rosebowl, sunflower interior: marigold, amethyst, green, russet, sapphire blue, teal
Rosebowl, beaded top: marigold, cobalt blue
Rosebowl, smooth top: marigold, amethyst, pearlized custard
Nutbowl, footed: marigold, amethyst, green, cobalt blue, white, aqua opalescent
Bowl, footed, ruffled: marigold, amethyst, green, cobalt blue, white

PATTERN: LEAF COLUMNS

Leaf Columns vases are among the harder to find of any of Northwood's numerous vase patterns. They have never been plentiful, even in the early days of carnival collecting and are rarely found today in any color. The pattern dates from the 1911 – 1912 period. Sizes can range from the 6" squat version up to about 12" in height. Most examples turn up in the 9" – 12" size range. Marigold and amethyst seem to be the most available colors, but even they are not often found. All the others are rare and include green, white, ice blue, ice green, teal, and sapphire blue, the latter being the rarest. A Leaf Columns vase in any color is really a nice find. They just don't turn up very often and bring respectable prices when they do. A cobalt blue Leaf Columns vase would be a real find. None is yet known, to the best of my knowledge, but I wouldn't be surprised if one exists somewhere.

Shapes & Colors Known

Vase, 6" – 12": marigold, amethyst, green, white, ice blue, ice green, teal, sapphire blue

This stunning ice blue Leaf Columns squat vase stands just 6¾" tall and is one of only a few known in this size and color.

PATTERN: LINN'S MUMS

After nearly 40 years as a popular collectible, previously unreported Northwood carnival patterns are not strongly anticipated. However, some still are discovered on very rare occasions, and this is one of those occasions. The first known example of this Northwood carnival creation, found by collector Linn Lewis, hence the name Linn's Mums, came to light only a few years ago. It has been a kind of unwritten law and tradition in the innermost circles of carnival collecting that when something previously undocumented is discovered, like this bowl, the honor of naming it goes to its discoverer. I guess we are rather like explorers and archaeologists in that respect.

This elaborate floral pattern is found on the interior

of 8" – 9" three-footed bowls. The exterior carries the Ruffles & Rings design, one of the moulds Northwood purchased from Jefferson around 1908. Note the similarity of the mums in this pattern to the ones used on some of Northwood's advertising pieces shown elsewhere in this book. In fact, from the positioning of one of the mums on this bowl, I cannot help but wonder if Linn's Mums came to be as the result of a re-tooling of an advertising mould. It would certainly make economic sense. These moulds were expensive to make, even in the 1910 era. After the orders for the various advertising pieces were completed, it would make perfect sense to find another use for a mould rather than just scrap it.

Amethyst is the only reported color for Linn's Mums and only two examples are known. The second surfaced less than two years after the first, and oddly, in the same general area: the Pacific Northwest. Perhaps these were made for a specific customer somewhere in that area. Perhaps more examples in other colors will one day surface. I would not be too surprised if they might be found in marigold or green.

Shapes & Colors Known

Bowl, 8" – 9", footed: amethyst

The ultra-rare Linn's Mums bowl in amethyst, one of only two examples of the pattern known to exist.

PATTERN: LOTUS LAND

If a contest is ever held to determine the rarest Northwood carnival pattern, you can bet that Lotus Land will be one of the top contenders. Fewer than 10 examples of this pattern are known to exist at this time! It is found only on the interior of large 8" – 8½" diameter, collar-based, two-handled bonbons. All but one of the known examples are in amethyst. The other is marigold and is fashioned like a card tray shape, with the handled sides pulled up. As these are the only known colors, a production time frame of 1909 – 1910 seems likely. Those were two of the three Northwood primary iridescent production colors at that time. The other is green, and I'm surprised a Lotus Land bonbon has not surfaced in that color, but they could well exist. Needless to say, Lotus Land bonbons command a great deal of excitement and hefty prices on the rare occasion when one changes hands.

Shapes & Colors Known

Bonbon, two-handled: marigold, amethyst

Lotus Land bonbons in marigold and amethyst. There are only about six amethyst examples known, and the marigold one shown here is the only example known, not only in that color, but in the card tray shape, with two sides pulled up.

PATTERN: Lovely

Here's another very rare and seldom seen Northwood carnival pattern. Northwood's Lovely is found only on the interior of three-footed bowls, all having the Leaf & Beads exterior pattern. The pattern is actually an unusual one for Northwood in that the design radiates outward from the center. Very few Northwood bowl patterns have that design characteristic. Most either encircle the center (like Grape & Cable, Strawberry, and Three Fruits), or have no real discernible central point (like Peacocks). There is also some controversy as to whether this pattern ever saw the inside of the Northwood factory. The overall design characteristics do resemble many Dugan patterns, and the outward radiating effect of the design and the fan-like leaf clusters bordering the pattern are indeed very typical of Dugan. The late William Heacock also reported that shards of Leaf & Beads (the exterior pattern here) were unearthed at the Dugan site in Pennsylvania. Let me say right from the top that I held, and still do hold, Bill's research efforts in the highest esteem. His work has added more knowledge to the field of glass study than any other researcher in history. However, by his own admission, he was at the time the now-famous Dugan shards were brought to light very much a novice in the field of carnival glass. By his own later admission, he did misidentify several other shards from those diggings. With regards to this pattern, I would have to say any evidence for a Dugan attribution is at best circumstantial. Another thing that bothers me about crediting this design to Dugan is the existence of green examples. Dugan made precious little green carnival. I'm including this pattern here as a "likely" Northwood creation, until such time as concrete evidence surfaces.

Most of the known examples of Lovely are of the round, flared shape, but on rare occasion a triangular-shaped example is found. Marigold, amethyst, and green are the only confirmed colors known, with amethyst being the most often found; I personally know of only one marigold example. Regardless of a Northwood or Dugan origin, the colors known would indicate a production of around 1910 for this rare pattern.

Shapes & Colors Known

Bowl, round, flared: marigold, amethyst, green,
Bowl, triangular shape: amethyst

Two views of the rare Northwood's Lovely triangular-shaped footed bowl. The exterior carries the Leaf & Beads pattern.

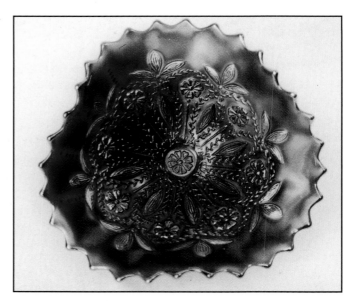

PATTERN: LUSTRE FLUTE

One of Northwood's early carnival efforts, iridescent Lustre Flute dates circa 1909. It was one of the lines carried over from earlier non-iridescent production in opalescent, crystal, and colored ware. In those forms, it was produced in a full line that included a berry set, table set, water set, custard cup, and breakfast size creamer and open sugar. Of those items, only the custard cup and breakfast sugar and creamer are known in iridized form. The custard cup is often called a punch cup by collectors, however no matching punch bowl is known to have been made. The cups were marketed individually as custard cups. Other known iridized shapes include a ruffled hat shape, fashioned from the tumbler mould; small, ruffled 5" – 6" bowls; and a two-handled bonbon fashioned from the breakfast sugar mould. Marigold, amethyst, and green are the only reported colors on all known shapes. The green examples are usually found with the Alaskan iridescent treatment. Amethyst examples of this simple design are actually quite difficult to find, but the pattern does not really generate a lot of collector interest, so prices remain low on most items. Most examples bear the Northwood trademark.

Why Northwood chose to eliminate the berry set, table set, and water set from iridescent production remains a mystery. All of these items are quite striking in non-iridized blue opalescent. No carnival examples of these pieces have ever surfaced.

Lustre Flute breakfast creamer in marigold.

Shapes & Colors Known

Breakfast creamer & sugar, hat shape, bowl, custard cup, bonbon: marigold, amethyst, green

PATTERN: MEANDER

One of the moulds that Northwood purchased from Jefferson in 1908, Meander enjoyed a lengthy production history in the hands of its former owner. Jefferson produced it in non-iridized opalescent colors for a number of years. Northwood used it solely as an exterior design, primarily on Three Fruits spatula-footed bowls. I know of no iridized examples without an accompanying interior pattern, but it's always possible that such a piece exists.

Shapes & Colors Known

Exterior design used primarily on Three Fruits spatula-footed bowls

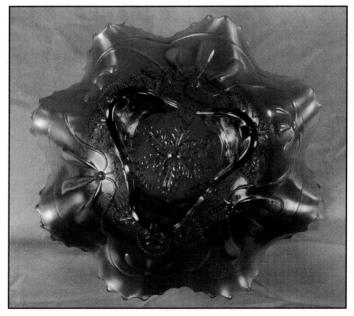

Northwood's Meander pattern, one of the moulds purchased from Jefferson, on the exterior of a Three Fruits spatula-footed bowl.

PATTERN: MEMPHIS

One of the very few geometric or nearcut type designs found in Northwood Carnival, Memphis was originally Northwood's #19 line and was in production in non-iridized crystal and colored ware in 1908 when the iridescent craze hit the market. In non-iridized form, this line was an extensive one indeed, made in a wide array of shapes that included a berry set, table set, water set, punch set, wine decanter, fruit bowl and base, large stemmed compote, salt and pepper shakers, and even a covered mustard pot. However, only a handful of these items is known in iridized form which is a shame. This design was made to order for carnival production and is absolutely stunning in iridized form. Why the bulk of the pattern line was apparently not carried over into iridescent production remains one of the great mysteries of Northwood's production. In recent years some tantalizing Memphis finds have surfaced to suggest the possibility of a more extensive iridescent production than was previously thought.

Carnival shapes known include the berry set, punch set, fruit bowl and base, and the large stemmed compote. The berry set has been documented only in marigold and amethyst. It is a rather odd one, as Northwood berry sets go, in that the master berry bowl is exceptionally large, measuring from 11" – 13" in diameter and resting on an octagonal collar base. In contrast, the small berry bowls are quite tiny, often only about 4" in diameter. The true punch bowl is quite deep in shape and has a round marie (collar base) that fits into the matching stand. They are still reasonably available in marigold and amethyst, but the other colors will present a challenge. Green is very scarce while white, ice blue, and ice green are all extremely rare.

The two-piece fruit bowl and base differs in several aspects. It is shallower and has an octagonal collar base. There is a slight recession or circular slot on the underside of this collar base, and the top ridge of the matching stand fits into this slot. It is known in the same colors as the punch bowl and also lime green. Both the punch bowl and fruit bowl use the same base. The punch bowl/fruit bowl base has also been documented in cobalt blue, so the matching cups and bowl must be out there somewhere. To date, none has surfaced, that I know of. The large, stemmed compote is known only in amethyst to date, and I have heard of only two examples.

A few years ago an exciting Memphis find was made, a covered sugar in amethyst. This is quite significant in that it would tend to indicate that the four-piece table set was produced in carnival glass. However, to date, no other table set pieces have surfaced.

The most exciting Memphis find of recent years is also one of the most important Northwood carnival finds of all time. In the early spring of 2000, a collar-based Memphis fruit bowl, shaped from the master berry bowl, surfaced for sale on an eBay Internet auction site in aqua opalescent, the first piece of the Memphis pattern ever documented in that color. The bowl was positively gorgeous with rich aqua color, beautiful pastel, multicolor iridescence, and extremely heavy opalescence. The only downside to its appearance was that it was badly cracked. Still, it just goes to show how significant this piece really is: even in that condition, it went to a new home for a winning bid of $6,000.00!

Shapes & Colors Known

Berry set: marigold, amethyst (aqua opalescent master bowl only known)
Punch bowl & base: marigold, amethyst, green, white, ice blue, ice green, cobalt blue (base only known in cobalt blue)
Fruit bowl & base: marigold, amethyst, green, white, ice blue, ice green, lime green, cobalt blue (base only known in cobalt blue)
Punch cups: marigold, amethyst, green, cobalt blue, white, ice blue, ice green, lime green
Large stemmed compote: amethyst
Covered sugar: amethyst

The Memphis two-piece fruit bowl and base in ice green, a very rare color for this.

94

Just about every major producer of carnival glass had variations of the Peacock Tail pattern, and this is Northwood's version of the design. It can be easily distinguished from the others by the central medallion of a stylized lotus blossom, a likeness of the Imperial Crest of the Empress of Japan. (Nippon, pronounced "Nee-Hon" by the Japanese people, is the true name of that nation. The word "Japan" is actually an American invention.) Production of the pattern dates from the 1911 – 1912 period, and Nippon was one of the first Northwood patterns to be offered in the pastel colors. It is found only on the interior of 8" – 9" bowls and 9" plates. The exterior may be plain, ribbed or have the Basketweave pattern. Some examples are signed, others are not. The bowls may be broadly ruffled or have a pie crust edge.

The ruffled bowls are most often found in marigold, white, and amethyst. Green, ice blue, and ice green are harder to find. Cobalt blue is the rarest color here, by far. Only about a half dozen examples are known. The pie crust edged bowls are known in a greater variety of colors and are actually seen more often than the ruffled version. White and ice blue are by far the most available, with marigold and amethyst examples much harder to find. Green is scarce and lime green and ice green even more so. A few very rare teal examples are known as well, but aqua opalescent tops the rarity list here. Only one example is known! I have yet to see or hear of a cobalt blue pie crust edged example, but you never know.

Nippon plates are rare to extremely rare in any color. Marigold and green probably turn up most but are still rarely seen. All others are extremely rare. These include white (three known), ice blue (one known), and aqua opalescent (one known). A Nippon plate is a great find in any color! None has yet surfaced in ice green or cobalt blue, but here again, they could well exist.

Shapes & Colors Known

Bowl, ruffled, 8" – 9": marigold, amethyst, green, cobalt blue, white, ice blue, ice green
Bowl, pie crust edge, 8" – 9": marigold, amethyst, green, white, ice blue, ice green, teal, lime green, aqua opalescent
Plate, 9": marigold, amethyst, green, white, ice blue, aqua opalescent

Northwood's Nippon 9" plate in green, a scarce and popular color for this.

This stunning ice green Nippon ruffled bowl belongs to my wife, Marsha, and I simply must relate the story behind it. When we were first married in 1996, she knew nothing about carnival glass but soon got the bug. One day she returned from a business meeting in a town about 65 miles from our home, walked in the door with a paper bag in her hand, announced she had stopped in a small roadside antique shop on her way home, bought her first piece of carnival, without my presence or advice, and hoped she hadn't paid too much. She unwrapped the magnificent piece you see here and asked if the $27 she paid for it had been too much. I just stood there with my lower jaw resting on the floor. When I told her what she had and what it was worth, the sight of her dancing with glee kept me amused for a long time. What a find for someone's first-ever purchase of carnival glass.

PATTERN: NORTHWOOD'S NEARCUT

Originally marketed during 1904 – 1906 as Northwood's #12 semi-cut crystal, this pattern in non-iridized form was one of the most extensive lines ever produced by Harry Northwood. A full seven pages of the 1906 Northwood factory catalog are devoted to it, showing 34 different items in the line. It must have been an extremely popular seller to undergo such production. Yet, in iridized form, only four different items in this pattern are known. Strangely enough, three of these are not listed as available in the 1906 Northwood catalog. Where are the iridescent examples of the other 33 items known to have been made in this line? In crystal, the 1906 Northwood catalog lists two styles of water sets, table set, berry set, salt and peppers, cruet, celery tray, mayonnaise bowl and underplate, several sizes of bowls, handled nappies, handled baskets, two-handled bonbons, a punch set, plates, several sizes of vases, and the list just goes on. There is even a tea set listed! This line was apparently so popular that Northwood advertised it as an open stock line. That means that it was in near constant production, with huge quantities warehoused at the factory, and the customer could order any item, any time, with certainty of availability.

In carnival, the only items known to date are the water pitcher, tumbler, goblet, and compote. That's it! The carnival version of the water pitcher is very different from the two styles of crystal pitchers shown in the 1906 catalog. It is somewhat cone-shaped, resting on a domed base, and very similar in basic configuration to the Northwood Raspberry water pitcher. Marigold is the only color reported to date, and very few examples are known. This only deepens the mystery surrounding the limited iridescent production of this pattern. Why go to the expense of making a mould for yet a third style of pitcher, to be used specifically for iridescent production, and then not produce the rest of the line? The matching tumblers have ground bases. They are known in marigold and amethyst, so there must be an amethyst pitcher somewhere. The stemmed goblet and compote, both fashioned from the same mould, are also very rare, and both are known in marigold and amethyst. A single known example of the compote in green has also been confirmed. Most known examples of Northwood's Nearcut bear the Northwood trademark.

Shapes & Colors Known

Water pitcher: marigold
Tumbler: marigold, amethyst
Goblet: marigold, amethyst
Compote: marigold, amethyst, green

This pattern is absolutely stunning in iridized form, so the lack of any other known carnival shapes is most puzzling indeed. It would seem to have been a natural for more extensive iridescent production. With so many different items known in non-iridized crystal, the alert collector should keep his eyes open on this one. The carnival possibilities are great, and you might just be the lucky one to find a previously unreported piece.

Northwood's Nearcut Goblet in amethyst, at left, and water pitcher and tumbler in marigold, above. The goblets are scarce, but do turn up from time to time. The pitcher and tumbler are extremely rare, with only a few examples of each known.

PATTERN: OCTET

The simplicity of this design combined with the limited range of known colors probably accounts for the fact that Octet bowls don't usually generate a lot of collector interest or high prices. By rights, they should bring much more than they usually do, for Octet is a very seldom found Northwood carnival pattern. It is found only on the interior of dome-footed 7" – 9" bowls with the Vintage Grape exterior design, one of the moulds Northwood purchased from Jefferson in 1908. The bulk of production likely dates around 1910, but as a few pastel examples are known, it was carried over at least through 1912. Green and amethyst seem to be the most available colors, and marigold is seen less often. A few very rare white and ice green examples are also known. Most examples bear the Northwood trademark.

Shapes & Colors Known

Bowl, 7" – 9", dome-footed: marigold, amethyst, green, white, ice green

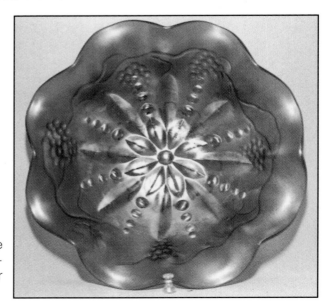

Northwood's Octet dome-footed bowl in green. The Vintage Grape exterior pattern, one of the moulds Northwood purchased from Jefferson, can be clearly seen from the exterior surface.

PATTERN: ORIENTAL POPPY

Yet another of the many iridescent creations to emerge from the Northwood factory during the pattern boom years of the 1911 – 1912 period, Oriental Poppy water sets were frequently advertised and sold in company with Northwood's Dandelion water sets. They were, in effect, sister patterns and likely the creation of the same mould artist.

The impressive mould-blown tankard pitchers have a separately applied handle and are not trademarked. The matching tumblers are pressed and usually are signed with the underlined N in a circle. Marigold and amethyst seem to be the most frequently found colors, with green, white, and cobalt blue next in line. Ice blue is quite rare, but the top ranking goes to the ice green water sets. Tumblers have also been reported in lime green. It should be noted that this ranking varies somewhat between pitchers and tumblers. While ice blue and white pitchers are rare, the tumblers in those two colors do turn up in fair numbers. Personally, I feel the cobalt blue examples are quite underrated.

These sets were also produced in non-iridized crystal, emerald green, and sapphire blue, usually with fired-on gold decoration. They are far more available than the carnival examples.

In 1991, a large marigold ruffled bowl surfaced that was immediately identified as Oriental Poppy. This is really an iridized example of Northwood's Intaglio Poppy design, carried over from a non-iridized Intaglio line, circa 1906. Still, most collectors will continue to refer to this one-of-a-kind rarity as Oriental Poppy.

The Oriental Poppy tankard pitcher and tumbler in white, an extremely rare color for these pieces.

Shapes & Colors Known

Water pitcher: marigold, amethyst, green, cobalt blue, white, ice blue, ice green
Tumbler: marigold, amethyst, green, cobalt blue, white, ice blue, ice green, lime green
Bowl, 11", ruffled: marigold (one known – actually an iridized example of Northwood's Intaglio Poppy)

This pattern dates from right about the time of Northwood's earliest carnival production, circa 1908, and is yet another of the many unsolved mysteries involving Harry Northwood. In non-iridized form, Paneled Holly underwent extensive production. A full line, including berry set, table set, and water set, was produced in crystal, emerald green, and opalescent colors, usually with fired-on gold decoration. Only bits and pieces of this line are known in carnival. There is only one known amethyst water pitcher, one creamer, only one covered sugar in amethyst, and a single spooner in marigold. No matching tumbler, butter dish or any of the pieces from the berry set have yet surfaced in iridized form. However, a two-handled bonbon fashioned from the spooner mould is known, and these are surprisingly plentiful. They surface more often than not in green, usually with the Alaskan iridescent treatment. Marigold and amethyst examples are harder to find, but do turn up from time to time. Needless to say, any iridized piece of Paneled Holly, aside from the bonbon, is an extremely rare find! The water pitcher is ranked among the very highest of Northwood carnival rarities. At the very least, the tumbler and the butter dish must surely exist, but remain unconfirmed to date. All known examples of Paneled Holly bear the Northwood trademark.

Shapes & Colors Known

Water pitcher: amethyst
Covered sugar: amethyst
Creamer: amethyst
Spooner: marigold
Bonbon, two-handled: marigold, amethyst, green

The green bonbon, shaped from the spooner mould, is actually quite plentiful.

PATTERN: PEACH

Dating from the 1911 – 1912 period, Northwood's Peach was made in a full line including berry set, table set, and water set. However, this pattern is yet another example of the mysteries and inconsistencies that still plague research efforts involving Harry Northwood. The variety of colors known in Northwood's Peach is extremely limited, and not all the items from these three sets have yet been documented in all the colors known for each set. Again, bits and pieces are all that have surfaced in some colors which can be a bit confusing, so bear with me.

The water set is known in cobalt blue and white; either one is a rare find. The cobalt blue sets often exhibit stunning electric iridescence, and the white sets frequently are found with fired-on gold decoration on the peaches, leaves, and cable that encircle the piece. A handful of rare tumblers is also known in marigold, but to date, I know of no matching water pitcher.

The full, four-piece table set is known primarily in white, usually with the fired-on gold decoration. Only the spooner and creamer have been confirmed in cobalt blue, and a spooner has also been confirmed in marigold. The butter dish and covered sugar have yet to be confirmed in cobalt blue or marigold, but must surely exist.

The berry set is known in cobalt blue and white, and a single known small berry bowl and one master bowl in sapphire blue have also been reported. I have also received a report of a small berry bowl in marigold, but it remains unconfirmed.

Most items in this line have the Northwood trademark.

Northwood's Peach water pitcher and tumbler in cobalt blue, always a popular item and not easily found.

The Peach water set in white is often found with fired-on gold trim, like the set shown here. These are actually not as rare as the cobalt blue sets.

100

This is not only one of the most popular patterns with today's collectors but was surely one of the most popular with the buying public at the time of its manufacture. Three companies, Northwood, Millersburg, and Fenton, all produced a version of Peacock & Urn. It seems highly probable that Millersburg's version was the first to be produced. Fenton's version appears in the wholesale catalogs during the mid teens. Northwood's version underwent extensive production in the pastel colors, including aqua opalescent, the peak years for which were 1912 – 1914. Since Millersburg was only in business from 1909 to 1912, it seems logical to credit that firm with the design's origin.

Northwood's Peacock & Urn is quite distinctive from the other two versions. First, look for the Northwood trademark on the underside of the base. Most examples have it. On the Northwood version the center area on the underside of the marie (collar base) is always plain. There are three rows of beads on the urn and a bee in front of the peacock's beak. The Millersburg pieces will have an impressed star design on the underside of the marie. Most examples (but not all) will have no beads on the urn and will lack the bee as well. The Fenton version of the Peacock & Urn bowls will always carry an exterior pattern called Bearded Berry and is thus easily distinguished from the other two. Fenton and Millersburg also produced the design in a stemmed compote, and Northwood did not.

Without a doubt, the most popular of the Northwood shapes are the ice cream sets, consisting of a large, 9" – 10½" master ice cream bowl and the companion 5" – 6" bowls. They are found in an extensive array of colors and make a most impressive display. The master bowl seems to be most available in marigold, amethyst, and white. Examples in cobalt blue, clambroth, and horehound seem to be next in line, followed by ice blue and ice green. Green examples are rarely found, and lime green and honey amber bowls are rarer still. Virtually all of the other known colors fall into the extremely rare category. These include Renninger blue, aqua opalescent (8 – 10 known), sapphire blue (two known), and vaseline (one known). The vaseline example is a brilliant, all-over canary yellow color with a beautiful, pastel iridescence. The matching small bowls have been documented in marigold, amethyst, green, cobalt blue, white, ice blue, ice green, and aqua opalescent, the latter topping the rarity list with only 6 – 8 examples known to date.

Like so many of Northwood's iridescent efforts, there is also a stippled version of this ice cream set. The stippled background effect extends almost all the way to the edge of the pieces. These sets are known in a more limited range of colors, and all are harder to find than the non-stippled versions. Marigold is the only color that could be called reasonably available, but even they are hard to find. Cobalt blue is next in line, followed by ice blue. All others, including Renninger blue, honey amber, horehound, smoke, and sapphire blue, fall into the extremely rare category. Oddly, the matching stippled small bowls have to date been documented only in marigold, cobalt blue, and Renninger blue.

Large, 9½" – 10½" ruffled bowls, fashioned from the same mould used for the non-stippled master ice cream bowls, are also known. These are actually very rare and have been reported only in marigold, amethyst, and green. The same mould was used yet again to fashion the very rare chop plates, measuring 10½" – 12" in diameter. Amethyst is the common color here, but extremely rare examples in marigold, white, and ice green are also confirmed.

Small, 6" – 7" flat plates, fashioned from the small ice cream bowl mould, are known in marigold, amethyst, and cobalt blue. All are extremely rare. A couple of rare stippled 6" plates are also known in cobalt blue.

There is certainly a lot to hunt for here, but don't expect too many bargain finds in this pattern. Demand is rapidly exceeding supply, and none of these pieces come cheap anymore.

Shapes & Colors Known

Master ice cream: marigold, amethyst, green, cobalt blue, white, ice blue, ice green, lime green, horehound, honey amber, clambroth, Renninger blue, aqua opalescent, sapphire blue, vaseline

Small ice cream: marigold, amethyst, green, cobalt blue, white, ice blue, ice green, aqua opalescent

Master ice cream, stippled: marigold, cobalt blue, ice blue, horehound, honey amber, smoke, Renninger blue, sapphire blue

Small ice cream, stippled: marigold, cobalt blue, Renninger blue

Bowl, large ruffled: marigold, amethyst, green

Chop plate, 10½" – 12": marigold, amethyst, white, ice green

Plate, 6" – 7": marigold, amethyst, cobalt blue

Plate, 6" – 7", stippled: cobalt blue

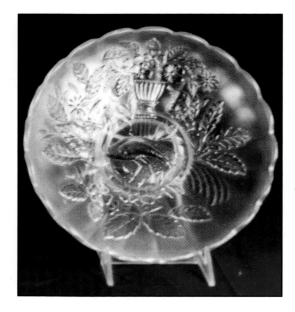

Peacock & Urn master ice cream bowl in ice blue, an extremely popular item, one becoming very difficult to find.

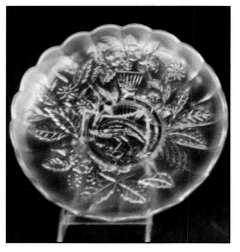

Peacock & Urn master ice cream bowl in a vivid shade of ice green that many collectors have come to call lime green.

PATTERN: PEACOCK AT THE FOUNTAIN

Another of "Harry's Birds," Peacock at the Fountain was introduced in 1912 and has become one of the most popular iridescent creations ever produced by the Northwood firm. It is the only carnival pattern for which Harry Northwood is known to have filed a patent, in February of 1914. The patent was granted in July 1914. This may well have been done as an attempt by Northwood to halt production of a copy of the design that was being produced by the Diamond Glass Co. By 1914 Thomas Dugan had sold his interest in the Dugan Glass Co., and it became the Diamond Glass Co. So, it seems likely that Diamond was the copycat culprit here and not Thomas Dugan. I have often wondered if perhaps the battle over the production of this pattern was in part responsible for Thomas Dugan's departure from the company. After all, he and Harry Northwood were cousins.

Northwood's Peacock at the Fountain was made as a full line including a berry set, table set, water set, and punch set. In addition, a large, footed fruit bowl, stemmed compote, and a whimsey spittoon were also made. Most items will bear the Northwood trademark.

The berry set is most often seen in marigold and amethyst. Cobalt blue and white are scarce. Ice blue and ice green are seldom seen. Like nearly all shapes in this pattern, green is one of the rarest colors. The same rarity ranking can also be applied to both the

Shapes & Colors Known

Berry set: marigold, amethyst, green, cobalt blue, white, ice blue, ice green
Table set: marigold, amethyst, green, cobalt blue, white, ice blue
Water set: marigold, amethyst, green, cobalt blue, white, ice blue, ice green
Punch set: marigold, amethyst, green, cobalt blue, white, ice blue, ice green, aqua opalescent, Renninger blue (punch bowl only in Renninger blue)
Punch set, points in line: marigold, amethyst, white
Fruit bowl: marigold, amethyst, green, cobalt blue, white, ice green, horehound, aqua opalescent
Fruit bowl, points in line: marigold, amethyst
Fruit bowl, points turned inward: amethyst
Stemmed compote: marigold, amethyst, green, cobalt blue, white, ice blue, ice green, aqua opalescent
Whimsey spittoon: amethyst, green

water set and table set, with one notable exception. Strangely, no table set pieces have yet been found in ice green. The punch sets are particularly popular with collectors and are most often found in marigold and amethyst, but even these are becoming scarce now. Only the marigold can still be purchased under the four-figure level. Cobalt blue sets are very seldom seen. White, ice blue, and ice green are very rare and green punch sets extremely so, all selling in the multi-thousands of dollars. Topping the rarity list are the aqua opalescent punch sets. I know of four complete ones, a few bases, and a scattering of punch cups in various collections. Mention should also be made of a single known punch bowl in Renninger blue, but no matching base or cups have yet surfaced. Most of the punch bowls are shaped with alternating inward and outward flared "flame" points on the edge. On rare occasion an example with the flame points all in a straight line will surface. I know of a few examples of these in marigold, amethyst, and white; all are rare.

The large, footed fruit bowl, or orange bowl as it is sometimes called, is most often seen in marigold. Surprisingly, cobalt blue examples seem to turn up with reasonable frequency as well. Amethyst examples are seen less often than the cobalt blue. All other known colors are very rare, including white, green, and horehound. I know of one example in ice green, but it is damaged, and I have yet to confirm an ice blue example in any condition. Topping the rarity list here is the aqua opalescent fruit bowl. Only two are known, and neither has changed hands for many years but would surely bring a staggering sum if either was ever offered at auction. Like the punch set, an occasional example of the fruit bowl will surface with the flame points all in an even line. I have heard of these in marigold and amethyst. Also, an example in amethyst is known with the flame points turned inward, much in the fashion of a rosebowl.

The stemmed compote was made from the same base mould (Northwood's #637) as the Hearts & Flowers compote and, in fact, does carry the Hearts & Flowers pattern on the stem. They are seldom seen in any color, but white, amethyst, and marigold, in that order, seem to turn up the most. Cobalt blue and ice blue are much harder to find, and ice green examples are considered rare. Here again, aqua opalescent tops the rarity list with relatively few examples known.

The only other known shape is a rare "bird" indeed! It is a whimsey spittoon fashioned from the base to the covered sugar. Only two are known, one in

Peacock at the Fountain water pitcher and tumbler in green, always a rare color for this pattern.

green and one in amethyst. Both have garnished five-figure price tags at auction!

The only pieces in this pattern known to have been copied by the Diamond Glass Co. are the water pitcher and tumbler, and only in marigold, amethyst, and cobalt blue. There have been numerous and lengthy diatribes written on how to tell the differences between them, covering everything from the position of the mould seams to the number of berries on cer-tain branches in the design. You don't need to go through all that — there are some quick ways to tell them apart. The Northwood water pitcher is always signed with the Northwood trademark; the Diamond examples are unsigned. The Northwood tumblers have four mould seams while the Diamond version has only three. Simple enough!

This stunning green Peacock at the Fountain fruit bowl is second in rarity only to the aqua opalescent examples. Only a few are known in green.

This ad from the spring 1912 Butler Brothers catalog offers the Peacock at the Fountain berry, table, and water sets. This same ad continued to appear with an ever-increasing wholesale price through 1917, so this must have been a very popular seller.

If a contest were ever held to determine which Northwood carnival pattern most clearly defines the mystique and popularity of that firm's iridescent creations, you can bet that Northwood's Peacocks would most certainly be a top contender for the honor. Sometimes called Peacocks on the Fence, this design personifies what Northwood carnival is all about. Though confined to only two shapes, bowls and plates, the aesthetics of the design itself combined with the astounding variety of available colors have made this pattern one of the all-time collector favorites. The pattern was one of those introduced during Northwood's iridescent pattern boom years, circa 1911 – 1912, and was among the first to be made in the new pastel colors unveiled in early 1912. The ruffled bowls were also produced in non-iridized blue opalescent and custard glass, so the production of the design was quite extensive.

The bowls usually measure in the 8" – 9" size range, resting on a collar base (marie), and the edge may be either broadly ruffled or pie crust. The exterior may be either plain, ribbed or carry the Basketweave pattern, with the ribbed exteriors most often found. Some examples bear the Northwood trademark, and some do not. In the ruffled version, marigold, amethyst, and cobalt blue are the most available colors. Green is much harder to find as is lavender. White, ice blue, ice green, horehound, honey amber, clambroth, aqua and aqua opalescent examples are considered very scarce, but perhaps the aqua opalescent bowls are most available of these. They do turn up in fair numbers but always bring good prices — everybody wants one. Virtually all of the remaining colors range from rare to extremely rare. These include smoke, ice blue opalescent, lime green opalescent, pearlized custard, and a most unusual powder blue opalescent. Topping the rarity list here

are the iridized blue slag examples with only three known to date. The ruffled bowl may also be found with a stippled background, but only four colors are documented to date. Marigold and cobalt blue are the usual colors here. A single known example in aqua opalescent exists. I am also pleased to be able to show here the first reported, ruffled, stippled example in Renninger blue. The pie crust edged bowls are known in a somewhat more limited variety of colors, but there is still a lot to collect. Again, marigold, amethyst, and cobalt blue seem to be the most available with green, lavender, and white much harder to find. Ice blue and Renninger blue are very scarce and ice green and smoke quite rare. Topping the rarity list are single known examples in aqua opalescent and lime green. Stippled examples are seldom seen in any color, and here again, the variety is quite limited. They are known in marigold, amethyst, cobalt blue, and Renninger blue.

The plates generally measure 9" – 9½" in diameter and may be found with plain, ribbed or Basketweave exteriors. As with the bowls, the ribbed exterior seems to be the most often found in most colors. Marigold, amethyst, cobalt blue, white, and ice green examples are more available with ice green probably the most available. Lavender and green are quite scarce, and ice blue examples are very scarce. Rarer still are the smoke, horehound, and Renninger blue plates. Rarest of all is the single known sapphire blue plate. Stippled versions have been documented in only three colors to date: marigold, cobalt blue, and Renninger blue, but I would not be surprised if an amethyst one turned up, as the bowls exist in that color. Strangely, no plates, either plain or stippled, have yet surfaced in aqua opalescent. Most collectors dream of being the first to find one.

Shapes & Colors Known

Bowl, 8" – 9": marigold, amethyst, green, cobalt blue, white, ice blue, ice green, aqua opalescent, lavender, horehound, aqua, clambroth, honey amber, smoke, ice blue opalescent, lime green opalescent, powder blue opalescent, pearlized custard, iridized blue slag

Bowl, 8" – 9", ruffled, stippled: marigold, cobalt blue, Renninger blue, aqua opalescent

Bowl, 8" – 9", pie crust edge: marigold, amethyst, green, cobalt blue, white, ice blue, ice green, lavender, Renninger blue, smoke, lime green, aqua opalescent

Bowl, 8" – 9", pie crust edge, stippled: marigold, amethyst, cobalt blue, Renninger blue

Plate, 9" – 9½": marigold, amethyst, green, cobalt blue, white, ice blue, ice green, lavender, smoke, horehound, Renninger blue, sapphire blue

Plate, 9" – 9½", stippled: marigold, cobalt blue, Renninger blue

Three examples of Northwood's Peacocks ruffled bowls, each with its own distinctive appeal. The amethyst example above exhibits a brilliant, rich multi-color iridescence. The aqua opalescent bowl (below) has an exceptionally nice pastel aqua coloring and unusually heavy opalescence. The third example (right) has been backlighted to show the base color. If you have ever wondered just what the much talked-about color Renninger blue looks like, this is it! This bowl is unique in that it is the only known Renninger blue example that is both stippled and ruffled. All the other known examples in this color have the pie crust edge.

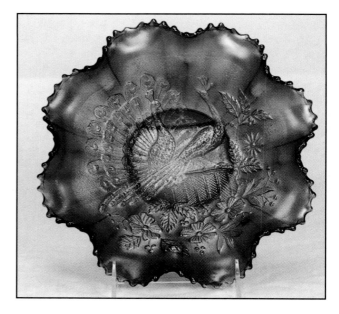

Two versions of the Northwood Peacocks plate: a green non-stippled example and a stippled one in cobalt blue with outstanding iridescence. Both are very hard to find in these colors.

Last, but far from least, is this one-of-a-kind decorated Peacocks plate in white. While we may never be 100 percent sure, we presently have no reason to suspect that this unusual painted decoration was not done at the Northwood factory. The quality of the work, as well as the choice of colors used, certainly suggests the work of a professional artist.

BEWARE OF BOWL REPRODUCTIONS
The Peacocks ruffled bowls are being reproduced, probably in Taiwan. The pattern on these fakes covers nearly the entire inner surface, extending almost to the edge, and the iridescence is very shiny, mirror-like, and gaudy. The bowls rest on a flat, solid disk of glass, rather than the usual style marie. They have an "N" mark on the base which is two to three times larger than the original Northwood mark, with no circle around it. They have been confirmed in marigold, cobalt blue, and green. No reproduction plates have been confirmed.

PATTERN: PETALS

This simple design is found only on the interior surface of rather short stemmed, ruffled compotes. The exterior is plain, and the Northwood trademark is often present. The pattern first appeared in the wholesale catalogs in 1909, but was apparently produced through at least 1912. Marigold is the most often found color, followed by amethyst and green. A few very rare ice blue examples are also known, and at least one cobalt blue example has now been confirmed. Keep your eyes peeled for examples in white and ice green. None have been reported to date, but they could well exist.

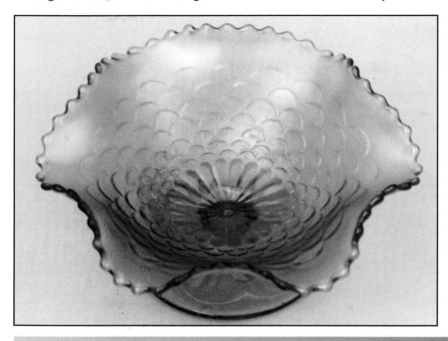

The Petals compote is not too difficult to find in marigold, amethyst or green, but examples like this ice blue one are very rare.

PATTERN: PLUMS & CHERRIES

The Plums & Cherries tumbler in cobalt blue. The reverse side has a spray of cherries nearly identical to the one found on Cherry & Cable.

Only three examples of this pattern are known in iridized form: a tumbler and a spooner in cobalt blue, and an amethyst single sugar, missing the lid. The design is more often seen in non-iridized, color stained crystal, in which a full line (berry set, table set, water set, and an unusual large, covered serving bowl) was made. The concept of the pattern is quite similar to Northwood's Cherry & Cable with a few notable differences. The cable is replaced by a band of three lines encircling the piece. While one side has a spray of cherries, identical to that found on the Cherry & Cable pattern, the other side has two plums. All known examples bear the Northwood trademark. The color stained crystal examples date circa 1907 – 1909, so one might assume the iridized production would date from the same time frame. However, two examples of the pattern are known in cobalt blue carnival, a color which Northwood is not believed to have produced until the 1911 – 1912 period. The extremely limited iridized production of this pattern remains shrouded in mystery. There must surely be other iridized examples of Plums & Cherries, so be on the alert for them.

Shapes & Colors Known

Covered sugar: amethyst (missing lid)
Spooner: cobalt blue
Tumbler: cobalt blue

Many consider this beautiful pattern to be one of Northwood's best iridescent efforts. The design dates circa 1912 – 1914 and in iridized form is found only on the interior surface of 8" – 9" three-footed bowls, with a ribbed exterior. I have yet to see a signed, iridized example. The range of known colors is somewhat limited, and none of them is easily found. Examples in cobalt blue and amethyst seem to turn up most often. Marigold bowls are surprisingly scarce. All others range from rare to extremely rare. Ice blue examples qualify as rare, as does horehound. I know of only four examples in aqua opalescent. We have a two-way tie for the top rarity honors, only one example in green and one in white.

Poinsettia Lattice bowls were also produced in non-iridized opalescent white, blue, and canary yellow, as well as color-stained custard glass. A single known custard glass plate exists, but to date, no plate in carnival has surfaced. If one were to be found, it would be at the very highest level of carnival rarities.

Shapes & Colors Known

Bowl, 8" – 9", footed: marigold, amethyst, green, cobalt blue, white, ice blue, horehound, aqua opalescent

Poinsettia Lattice ruffled bowl in cobalt blue at left, the most often found color, below, and a positively stunning ice blue example below, an extremely rare color for this pattern.

PATTERN: Poppy

The existence of the aqua opalescent and pastel examples of Northwood's Poppy tells us that this pattern was in production during the 1912 – 1914 period. Found in only one shape, a ruffled, oval bowl often called a pickle dish, the design is often confused with Imperial's Pansy pattern, which is found in a very similar shape. Some examples of Northwood's Poppy are signed, but most are not. It is not all that easily found today, in any color, so I suspect the production was not all that extensive.

Marigold and cobalt blue are probably the most often seen colors, followed by amethyst and green.

Most of the others range from the scarce ice blue, lavender, black amethyst, and white to the rare aqua, amber, and rarer still aqua opalescent. Topping the rarity list are the few known marigold on custard examples. These no doubt date from the 1914 – 1915 period when Northwood attempted a brief revival of custard glass and decided to iridize a few examples. Strange that no ice green examples have yet surfaced, but they could well exist. The Northwood Poppy pickle dish may also be found in non-iridized custard.

Shapes & Colors Known

Oval pickle dish: marigold, amethyst, green, cobalt blue, white, ice blue, lavender, black amethyst, aqua, amber, aqua opalescent, marigold on custard

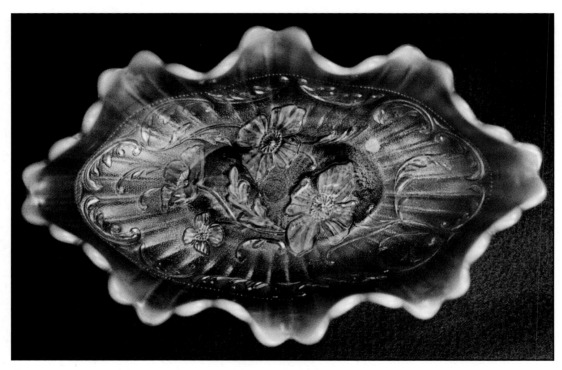

For its sheer beauty and appeal, this Poppy pickle dish in aqua opalescent is one of my personal favorites among all the pieces shown in this book.

A masterpiece of the mould-maker's art, Poppy Show, along with its sister pattern Rose Show, truly defines the very best of Northwood's iridescent production. The three-dimensional effect of the pattern, often combined with lavish, spectacular iridescence, jumps right out at you. Found only on ruffled bowls and flat plates, Poppy Show dates from the 1912 – 1914 period. There is considerable evidence to indicate that this pattern was the brainchild of George Mortimer, owner of the Mortimer Glass Co. Mortimer was an independent jobber. The firm manufactured no glass but had glass made for them by various glasshouses, often in moulds owned by Mortimer. They would then market the wares as their own product. No wholesale catalog assortments featuring this pattern have ever surfaced nor has any advertising associating it with Northwood. Yet, the known colors follow the Northwood scheme of things precisely, and there is little doubt that the pattern was molded and iridized by Harry Northwood. Poppy Show is never trademarked.

The ruffled bowls are most often found in white. In fact, there seems to be an overabundance of white examples, so it must have been one of the most popular colors with the buying public at the time of production. Cobalt blue, amethyst, and marigold line up next. A few scarce true clambroth examples with a beautiful ginger-ale coloring are also known, but seldom found. Ice blue, lime green, and ice green examples are eagerly sought, with ice green being the hardest to find. Green examples are considered rare and rightly so. Aqua opalescent tops the rarity chain, with only a couple known examples.

The same order of rarity can generally be applied to the plates as well, with a couple of notable exceptions. Marigold examples, particularly those with dark, rich marigold color, are surprisingly rare. They are much harder to find than most of the other known colors. No lime green or clambroth plates have yet been confirmed, but likely do exist. Here again, aqua opalescent examples top the rarity list. I only know of one, but others likely exist.

This is one of the most popular of all Northwood carnival bowl and plate shapes. Everybody wants examples in their collections and demand exceeds supply. Even in white, the most common color, pieces still sell in the $350 – $500 range, so be prepared to part with some cash if you plan to specialize in this pattern.

Shapes & Colors Known

Bowl, 8" – 9", ruffled: marigold, amethyst, green, cobalt blue, white, ice blue, ice green, lime green, clambroth, aqua opalescent
Plate, 9" – 9½": marigold, amethyst, green, cobalt blue, white, ice blue, ice green, aqua opalescent

Is it any wonder that Poppy Show is an all-time collector favorite? Just look at the dazzling iridescence on this cobalt blue Poppy Show bowl.

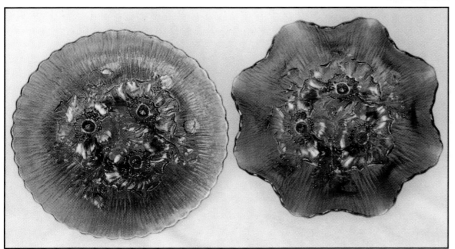

Green is a very scarce and desirable color for Poppy Show plates and bowls.

PATTERN: Poppy Variant

Although the name implies it, this pattern is really not a variation of the pattern found on the Northwood Poppy pickle dish. It is a separate entity and a much earlier Northwood design, dating from the 1909 period. It is found only on the exterior surface of small, 6" – 7" ruffled bowls. The interior is usually plain, but on occasion an example surfaces with a single, multi-petalled flower on the interior center. These are fairly common bowls, known in marigold, amethyst, and green. The green ones often have the Alaskan iridescent treatment. Most examples bear the Northwood trademark.

Poppy Variant on the exterior of a 7" ruffled bowl with a plain interior.

Shapes & Colors Known

Bowl, 6" – 7": marigold, amethyst, green

PATTERN: Raspberry

This popular Northwood pattern is found primarily on water sets and dates from the 1911 period. It is one of the more easily found Northwood carnival water sets today, at least in the vivid colors. This is primarily due to an unusually large production of the design by Northwood, and we now know the reason. This pattern was produced in huge quantities by Northwood for several large distributors and wholesalers for the purpose of promotional give-away. I have seen numerous circa 1911 – 1912 advertisements from various firms offering the Northwood Raspberry water sets and milk pitchers as premiums, items included free with a minimum order of certain quantities of other products. This would certainly explain the abundance of these sets today, particularly in marigold and amethyst, the two colors always mentioned in these promotional ads. Nearly all examples of the Raspberry pattern are signed with the Northwood trademark.

The water sets are most often found in marigold and amethyst. Green is a little harder to find, particularly with regards to the tumblers. However, these are the only three colors that are reasonably available today. White and ice blue sets are rare and the ice green extremely so. The cobalt blue water sets also fall into the extremely rare category, with only a few known. Some tumblers are also known in horehound and lavender, but I have yet to hear of a matching pitcher in either color. The water pitcher will usually measure 8½" to 9" tall at the spout.

The milk pitchers stand 7½" tall. Colors follow the same order of rarity here as the water set, although no cobalt blue milk pitchers have yet surfaced.

The handled, footed occasional piece is identical in configuration to the Dugan Fan occasional piece. This too was offered as a premium piece. Some call this a gravy boat, but period advertising confirms its intended purpose as a breakfast creamer. They are known in only four colors: marigold, amethyst, green and teal, the latter being by far the rarest. However, these occasional pieces are available in far less abundance than the water sets.

Here's a most unusual Northwood Raspberry water pitcher. While it may technically fall into the ice green category, it is actually a most unusual shade of green — much lighter than the normal green, yet darker and far more vivid than ice green. It could best be described as vivid lime green.

This ad for the Raspberry water set in green, marigold, and amethyst from the spring 1911 Butler Brothers catalog gives us a clear insight into why this set is so easily found in these colors today. Most Northwood carnival water sets wholesaled at from 59 to 89 cents per set. This would result in a retail price of from $1 to $1.35 on average. But with a wholesale of just 42 cents per set, this would enable the retailer to sell these at 70 to 75 cents per set. These must have been a big volume seller for Harry Northwood, the wholesaler, and the retailer as well. No wonder they are so abundant in those colors today.

IRIDESCENT WATER SET ASST.
Better value never offered. Attractive new art designs.

1C1960 —9 in., tankard pitcher, embossed blackberries, blossoms and leaves, six 4½ in. table tumblers to match. 4 sets each golden, green and amethyst iridescent finish.

12 sets in bbl.   Set, **42c**

Raspberry milk pitcher and water pitcher in marigold with amethyst tumbler, all still readily available.

PATTERN: Ribbed

Ribbed exteriors seem to have gradually replaced Northwood's Basketweave exteriors starting around 1911 – 1912. The reason for this becomes clear when you consider the timeline for the production of Northwood's iridescent colors. Prior to 1912, most items were produced in vivid colors of marigold, amethyst, green, etc., and the Basketweave pattern was a perfectly acceptable choice as an exterior pattern for those colors. However, by 1912, the era of the pastels

(white, ice blue, ice green, etc.) had begun. The Basketweave exterior was no longer a practical choice. The design showed through, distracting from and distorting the detail of the primary interior pattern. Thus, use of the more simple, less distracting Ribbed exterior came into more widespread use. This also explains why pastel pieces are much harder to find with the Basketweave exterior, especially on bowls and plates.

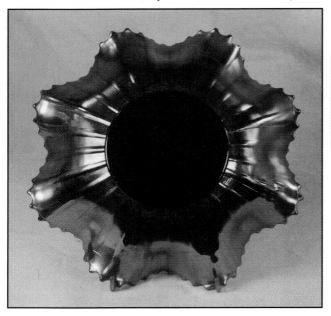

Shapes & Colors Known

Exterior design used on bowls, plates, compotes, bonbons, etc.

This Ribbed pattern began replacing Northwood's Basketweave as the primary exterior design on bowls and plates around 1912.

PATTERN: Rose Show

Like its companion pattern Poppy Show, Rose Show dates from the 1912 – 1914 period and is believed to be another item made by Northwood for George Mortimer. The general concept of the design is quite similar to Poppy Show, but the background and exterior are different. While Poppy Show carries a bark-like exterior pattern, Rose Show has an exterior design based on an earlier Northwood pattern called Woven Wonder which was made in opalescent glass during the 1904 – 1908 period. Again, the high relief, three-dimensional effect of the pattern jumps right out at you, and the iridescence is usually top quality. Found on ruffled 8" – 9" bowls and 9" – 9½" plates, Rose Show is known in a far greater variety of colors than its sister pattern and is an even more popular favorite with collectors.

Rose Show serves as an excellent illustration of how value and true rarity do not necessarily go hand in hand. Examples are not particularly rare in many of the

Shapes & Colors Known

Bowl, 8" – 9", ruffled: marigold, amethyst, green, cobalt blue, white, ice blue, ice green, aqua opalescent, lime green, ice blue opalescent, ice green opalescent, horehound, aqua, sapphire blue, powder blue opalescent, marigold on custard

Plate, 9" – 9½": marigold, amethyst, green, cobalt blue, white, ice blue, ice green, lavender, lime green, ice green opalescent, vaseline, marigold on custard

known colors. They turn up with reasonable frequency. Yet they always command very respectable prices. There are just so many collectors that want them. So, prices remain high on these pieces, even in the more available colors.

The bowls are really quite available in several colors. White is by far the most commonly seen, but examples in marigold, amethyst, cobalt blue, and even aqua opalescent turn up in surprising numbers as well. Even the ice blue and ice green bowls are reasonably available, with a little patient searching and the right amount of cash. But from here on, things may tend to strain the budget a bit. Virtually all of the other known colors could well be classified as rare to extremely rare. Falling into the rare category are aqua, lime green, ice blue opalescent, and green. The very rare category includes horehound, ice green opalescent, and sapphire blue. Topping the rarity list at the extreme level are the two known marigold on custard examples and a single known bowl in powder blue opalescent.

The plates follow quite close to the bowls in rarity order, with a few notable exceptions. The green and ice green opalescent plates rank higher on the rarity list than do the bowls. Amethyst plates are much harder to find than the bowls as well. Here again, marigold on custard ranks near the top of the list, surpassed only by a single known vaseline example. I know of no existing examples in sapphire blue, powder blue opalescent or ice blue opalescent, to date. It is also curious that while aqua opalescent Rose Show bowls are quite available, no plates have yet surfaced in that color.

Rose Show bowls may also be found in non-iridized blue opalescent and custard glass. The plates have also been reported in non-iridized custard as well. Most puzzling is the existence of at least two known Rose Show bowls that are not glass. They are made of brass and are identical in every detail to the glass examples and even have a light iridescence to them, and were surely made in the original moulds. But by whom and when? There have been several theories regarding them. First is that they were made to test the mould. That reasoning makes no sense to me because if you are going to test a mould for glass production, why would you test it in another material? Second, these pieces made of brass were carried by the salesmen in their travels because brass would not be prone to breakage. I suppose that's possible, but it still seems a little far-fetched to me. It would be very difficult for a prospective buyer to judge the beauty of the iridescent

Rose Show bowls and plates, like their Poppy Show counterparts, are very desirable in green.

quality and base glass color combination by looking at a metal sample. The third theory is the one that I favor and think makes the most sense, that these brass Rose Show bowls were made in the original moulds, but by someone else at a later date. Which leads to the distinct possibility that the original Rose Show moulds still exist somewhere, perhaps in the hands of a foundry or metal worker. If so, who has them?

The crisp, high relief molding and outstanding iridescence on this rare lavender Rose Show bowl make this a highly desirable example of the mould-maker's art.

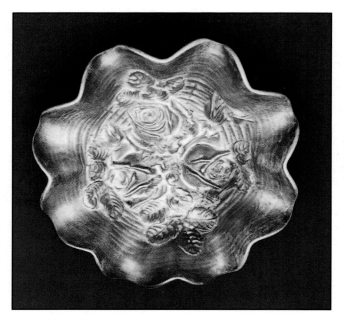

The origins of this mysterious brass Rose Show bowl remain uncertain. I know of only two of these.

Just why this variation of the Rose Show pattern was made and why it is found in so few colors has long been a topic of controversy and speculation. It was undoubtedly made in a different mould, as there are considerable differences between it and the standard Rose Show design. There are minor differences in the pattern detail, but the most obvious ones concern the edge, exterior design, and the collar base (marie). Unlike the broadly scalloped edge found on Rose Show, the variant has a fluted, or serrated, edge with distinct points, much like the edge style found on most other Northwood bowl and plate patterns. While the Woven Wonder design is retained here as an interior background, the exterior is ribbed. These pieces also have a more standard style of marie, with a solid fill of glass rather than the hollowed-out or intaglio moulded base of the standard Rose Show pieces. These pieces are also somewhat lighter in weight, and the relief molding of the roses is not quite as dramatic. Perhaps after the contract was completed for the standard Rose Show pieces made for George Mortimer, Northwood decided to make and market a version of the design himself. Pattern copying was rampant during the early 1900s, as few companies ever filed patents on their designs. We will likely never know the exact circumstances. Regardless, Rose Show Variant pieces must have undergone an extremely limited production. They are much harder to find than the standard Rose Show pieces, and the range of known colors is very limited.

Like the standard Rose Show pattern, Rose Show Variant is found on the interior of 8" – 9" ruffled bowls and 9" – 9½" plates. Only three colors, marigold, cobalt blue, and Renninger blue, are known in either shape. All are rarely found. The plate is particularly rare in Renninger blue.

Shapes & Colors Known

Bowl or plate: marigold, cobalt blue, Renninger blue

The Rose Show Variant plate in cobalt blue, always easily distinguished from Rose Show by the fluted edge points and a ribbed exterior. These are much harder to find than the standard Rose Show pattern.

PATTERN: ROSETTE

Not considered by most collectors to be one of Harry Northwood's best iridescent efforts, Rosette dates fairly early in the carnival era, circa 1909 – 1910. It is found only on the interior surface of three-footed, ruffled 7" – 8½" bowls, often rather deep in shape. The exterior carries the Ruffles & Rings pattern, one of the moulds Northwood purchased from Jefferson. Most examples are trademarked. Marigold, amethyst, and green are the only reported colors, with amethyst being the most often encountered. Marigold is much harder to find and green even more so. The iridescent quality often tends toward the rather "dull" side, but some beautifully iridized examples turn up on occasion.

Shapes & Colors Known

Bowl, 7" – 8½", footed: marigold, amethyst, green

Not the most appealing of designs, the Rosette bowls are most often found in amethyst, like this one. Green and marigold examples are actually quite scarce.

PATTERN: RUFFLES & RINGS

The Jefferson Glass Co. of Follansbee, West Virginia, produced this pattern in a variety of non-iridized opalescent colors and shapes. Harry Northwood purchased this mould from them in 1908, and the design saw considerable use in his hands. It was used as an exterior design on footed bowls and plates with the Wishbone and Rosette interior patterns. On rare occasion it surfaces as a primary pattern with no accompanying interior design. Such is the case on the single known Ruffles & Rings bowl in peach opalescent. It is ice cream-shaped and measures roughly 8½" in diameter. The interior is plain. It is the only iridized example of the pattern that I know of with no accompanying interior design.

Shapes & Colors Known

Bowl, 8½", footed: peach opalescent
Also used as an exterior design on Wishbone and Rosette footed bowls

Ruffles & Rings, one of the pattern moulds that Northwood purchased from Jefferson in 1908.

One of the most well-known patterns to emerge from the Northwood factory iridescent production of Singing Birds dates circa 1911. The moulds were revived during the 1915 – 1916 period for production in non-iridized crystal, often found with an unusual vivid blue stain on the birds. Northwood called this type of ware his Bluebird line. This was a full line pattern and carnival shapes include berry set, table set, water set, mugs, and a pedestal-footed sherbet. Other shapes were added to the line for the 1915 crystal production including covered compotes, stemmed goblets, and a most unusual large, covered serving bowl. None of these items has ever been reported in iridescent form. Most pieces will bear the Northwood trademark.

The full berry sets, table sets, and water sets are known in only three colors: marigold, amethyst, and green. These items serve as an excellent illustration of just how regional the original distribution and current availability of some carnival patterns can be. In the northeastern U.S., green Singing Birds pieces are so abundant it borders on the ridiculous, particularly with regard to the water sets and berry sets, so much so that here in Maine, where I live, we have a standing joke. If you go into an antique shop or antique mall and don't see at least one or two green Singing Birds pitchers, tumblers or berry bowls, then something is wrong! Amethyst Singing Birds pieces are not found here often, and marigold examples are almost non-existent! In other parts of the country collectors rarely see green Singing Birds pieces, and they are considered very desirable while marigold and amethyst pieces are far more abundant. Apparently, most of the green Singing Birds pieces were originally shipped to retail outlets here in the Northeast, while the marigold and amethyst pieces went elsewhere. Availability depends on where you are. It should be noted that tumblers are also known in olive green, horehound, and smoke, but no matching pitchers have yet surfaced in those colors. The small berry bowl is also confirmed in cobalt blue, but I have heard of no master berry bowl to match, as of this writing. It should also be noted that the correct base for the butter dish is the same one used on Peacock at the Fountain and Springtime, apparently a cost-saving move by Harry Northwood.

The Singing Birds mugs are a collector's delight and known in a wide variety of colors. Marigold, amethyst, cobalt blue, and green examples are all fairly abundant. Lavender and horehound examples are scarce and ice blue, white, pearlized custard, and teal mugs even more so. Aqua opalescent mugs and ice blue opalescent examples top the list, value wise, but in actuality fewer smoke examples are known. On occasion, amethyst mugs are found with souvenir lettering around the top edge, usually from a city, town, hotel or resort. This lettering was stenciled on with ink, and care should be taken in cleaning. The stenciling will wash right off when wet. For many years, as long as I can remember, collectors have eagerly awaited

Shapes & Colors Known

Berry set, table set, water set: marigold, amethyst, green (tumblers also known in olive green, horehound, smoke; small berry bowl known in cobalt blue)

Mug: marigold, amethyst, green, cobalt blue, white, ice blue, smoke, lavender, horehound, teal, pearlized custard, aqua opalescent, ice blue opalescent

Mug, stippled: marigold, amethyst, green, cobalt blue, Renninger blue

Sherbet, pedestal-footed: marigold

This Singing Birds mug in marigold is one of the most easily found colors in this shape.

the first reported Singing Birds mug in ice green. We are still waiting! None has ever been confirmed. A stippled version of the mug also exists, but in a more limited range of colors. They are most available in marigold, quite scarce in cobalt blue, scarcer still in green, rare in amethyst, and extremely rare in Renninger blue. Singing Birds mugs may also be found in non-iridized blue opalescent, custard glass, usually with nutmeg stain, and an unusual shade of green we used to call sea foam. Collectors today tend to call it Coke bottle green, as it is very similar in color to the old glass Coca-Cola bottles.

The only other carnival shape reported to date is a small, pedestal-footed sherbet, very similar in configuration to the Northwood Grape & Cable sherbet. Marigold is the only color reported, and only a few examples are known.

BEWARE OF TUMBLER REPRODUCTION
There are new Singing Birds tumblers in aqua opalescent and ice blue opalescent, neither of which is known in the originals. They are unmarked as to maker, but are believed to have been made by Summit Art Glass Co. There are also new tumblers in amethyst with a bright, rather gaudy iridescence.

Near the opposite end of the rarity scale from the marigold mug is this beautiful aqua opalescent Singing Birds mug.

Rarer still is this stippled Singing Birds mug in Renninger blue. Only a handful of these is known.

Northwood, Dugan, Fenton, Imperial, and Westmoreland all made iridized versions of this simple design. Distinguishing the Northwood version from the others is very simple. Look for the Northwood trademark. Virtually every Northwood example I have ever seen has it. It is one of Northwood's earliest iridescent offerings, dating circa 1908 – 1910. In fact, it appears in the very earliest known Northwood iridescent assortments in the Butler Brothers catalogs.

Northwood's Smooth Rays is known in ruffled berry sets, compotes, bonbons, hat shapes, and small plates. All of these have been documented in marigold, amethyst, and green. The compote and bonbon are also known in cobalt blue and lime green. Cobalt blue examples are really quite rare. The green examples are often found with the Alaskan iridescent treatment. The pattern often receives little attention from collectors, but a little tip here: I have seen a few amethyst examples of the ruffled berry set that exhibited positively astounding iridescence! And, these are not all that easily found in amethyst. This actually seems to be the case with most of the shapes in Smooth Rays. Marigold and green examples abound, but amethyst pieces with top quality iridescence are seldom found.

Shapes & Colors Known

Berry bowl, 9" – 10", ruffled: marigold, amethyst, green
Berry bowl, 5" – 6", ruffled: marigold, amethyst, green
Bonbon, two-handled: marigold, amethyst, green, cobalt blue, lime green
Compote: marigold, amethyst, green, cobalt blue, lime green
Hat shape: marigold, amethyst, green
Plate, 6": marigold, amethyst, green

Northwood's Smooth Rays compote in green.

PATTERN: Springtime

This is another of Northwood's full line patterns, dating from 1910 – 1911, that was used exclusively for iridescent production. It is not known in any other form of glass, and the production must have been very limited, for it is not easily found today. Berry sets, table sets, and water sets are the known shapes, and all pieces usually bear the Northwood trademark. The water set is identical in configuration to the Singing Birds set. The butter dish has an unusual, pagoda-shaped lid but uses the same base as the Singing Birds and Peacock at the Fountain butter dishes. Marigold, amethyst and green are the only colors reported for all items in this pattern. There really is no one color rarer than the others. All are very difficult to find, much in demand, and highly treasured by collectors.

Shapes & Colors Known

Berry set, table set, water set: marigold, amethyst, green

Northwood's Springtime water pitcher in green. This is one of the more difficult to find patterns.

PATTERN: STAR OF DAVID

Many collectors refer to this early Northwood carnival effort as Star of David & Bows so as not to confuse it with Imperial's carnival pattern of the same name. The iridescent version dates circa 1909 – 1910 and has an interesting history. It was a design rushed into early iridescent production and was created by re-tooling an existing mould from Northwood's Verre D'Orr line, which was in production circa 1905 – 1908. Verre D'Orr was a non-iridized line of pressed patterns in emerald green, amethyst, and cobalt blue, all with heavy, fired-on gold decoration. Star of David was re-tooled from a pattern in this line called Ribbons and Overlapping Squares. That pattern has a central design of two overlapping squares but is oth-

erwise virtually identical. It was a simple job to re-tool the center portion into the Star of David, and a new pattern was born.

Star of David is found only on the interior surface of dome-footed, ruffled 7" – 8½" bowls, often fairly deep in shape. The exterior carries the Vintage Grape design, one of the moulds Northwood purchased from Jefferson in 1908. Like the Northwood's Rosette bowls, Star of David is often found with somewhat less than spectacular iridescence, but some very nicely iridized examples turn up on rare occasion. Amethyst is the most available color. Green examples are quite scarce, and I would go so far as to call the marigold ones rare, as I only know of a few of them.

Shapes & Colors Known

Bowl, 7" – 8½", dome-footed: marigold, amethyst, green

Northwood's Star of David, sometimes called Star of David & Bows, was created by re-tooling an earlier Northwood pattern called Ribbons & Overlapping Squares.

PATTERN: STIPPLED RAYS

All of the major carnival glass producers made a version of this simple, yet effective design, so it must have been very popular with the buying public. Northwood's version was made in huge quantities starting around 1909, remaining in the line for several years. Virtually all known examples are trademarked, so it is easily distinguished from other makers' versions of the design. While most collectors tend to associate this pattern only with 8" – 9" common ruffled or pie crust edged bowls, it was actually made in a variety of shapes, and there are some true rarities to hunt for here.

Collar based ruffled or pie crust edged bowls, usually 8" – 9" in diameter, are probably the most commonly found shape. The exterior may be plain or have the Basketweave pattern. Marigold and

amethyst examples abound, and green ones turn up in fair numbers as well. Cobalt blue examples are actually quite scarce, and the white bowls are rarely found. Ice blue bowls are very rare and for many years actually topped the rarity list here. But that is no longer the case. In the late fall of 2000, the first known ice green Stippled Rays bowl surfaced and now resides in Australia.

A second bowl shape is also known. This version is dome footed and carries the Greek Key exterior pattern. Found in marigold, amethyst, and green, it is seen far less often than the collar-based bowls.

A collar-based, two-handled bonbon and a stemmed compote also exist. Both have been reported in marigold, amethyst, green, and cobalt blue, the latter color being rather hard to find.

Topping the rarity list shape-wise are the Stippled Rays flat plates. These are collar-based and measure roughly 6½" in diameter with a plain exterior. They have surfaced only in the past couple years, and I know of only three examples, two in amethyst, and one in marigold. All three turned up for sale on the Internet. I would not be surprised if green ones also exist, but none have yet been reported.

Shapes & Colors Known

Bowl, 8" – 9", collar base: marigold, amethyst, green, cobalt blue, white, ice blue, ice green
Bowl, dome-footed, Greek Key exterior: marigold, amethyst, green
Compote: marigold, amethyst, green, cobalt blue
Bonbon, two-handled: marigold, amethyst, green, cobalt blue
Plate, 6½": marigold, amethyst

Northwood's Stippled Rays pie crust edged bowl in amethyst, one of the most easily found Northwood carnival patterns.

PATTERN: STRAWBERRY

A very popular design both when it was made and with collectors today, Northwood's Strawberry first appeared in wholesale catalogs in the fall of 1910 and apparently remained a staple in Northwood's iridescent lines through the 1912 – 1914 period. Although only found on collar-based 8" – 9" bowls, 9" plates, and a 6" – 7" handgrip plate, there is still a lot to collect. The variety of known colors is fairly extensive, there are both plain and stippled versions, and three different exteriors: plain, ribbed or Basketweave. All of this combines to make Northwood's Strawberry a collector's favorite. While many examples bear the Northwood trademark, a near equal number are unsigned.

Ruffled bowls are still frequently found in marigold, amethyst, and green. The others are far more challenging and include clambroth, horehound, lime green, ice green, and smoke. Topping the rarity list are the white examples with only a couple known. Stippled examples of the ruffled bowl are much harder to find. The stippled version has a band of three slightly raised lines encircling the outer edge of the patterned area. Marigold is about the only color that is reasonably available here. Amethyst, lavender, and cobalt blue examples are much harder to find. Lime green, ice green, and Renninger blue examples are rare, but aqua opalescent tops the charts, with just one confirmed example known.

Pie crust edged bowls are also readily available in marigold, amethyst, and green. They have also surfaced in smoke, always a rare color for Northwood, and an unusual shade that is known variously as wisteria, violet or lilac. It is a unique blend of pastel purple and blue, known only in a very few pieces of Northwood carnival. Personally, I prefer the name violet which most accurately describes the color. The stippled version of the pie crust edge bowl is rarely found in any color. They are known in marigold, amethyst, green, cobalt blue, and horehound, and the green examples are the rarest.

Like the bowls, the 9" plates are still quite available in marigold, amethyst or green, but rather scarce in lavender. The only other color known here is a rare one indeed: true peach opalescent, always an *extremely* rare color for Northwood. The opalescence is very light on all three known examples, confined to just the fluted edge points, but it is definitely there! Even the most available color on the stippled version of the plate, amethyst, is not easily found. They are very rare in green, cobalt blue or marigold. Top honors go to a single known ice blue example which sold for a staggering sum in 1995. Odd that no white or ice green Strawberry plates, either plain or stippled, have ever been confirmed.

The only other known shape is that of a 6" – 7" handgrip plate, with one edge turned up. They are not considered rare in any color and have been reported in marigold, amethyst, and green.

In general, Northwood's Strawberry bowls and plates are found most often with a Basketweave exterior in marigold, amethyst or green. Most stippled examples in any color have a ribbed exterior. Plain exteriors may be found in just about all known colors on the unstippled version.

A gorgeous example of a Northwood Strawberry plate.

Shapes & Colors Known

Bowl, 8" – 9", ruffled: marigold, amethyst, green, white, ice green, horehound, lime green, smoke, clambroth

Bowl, 8" – 9", ruffled, stippled: marigold, amethyst, cobalt blue, lavender, ice green, lime green, Renninger blue, aqua opalescent

Bowl, 8" – 9", pie crust edge: marigold, amethyst, green, smoke, violet

Bowl, 8" – 9", pie crust edge, stippled: marigold, amethyst, green, cobalt blue, horehound

Plate, 9": marigold, amethyst, green, lavender, peach opalescent

Plate, 9", stippled: marigold, amethyst, green, cobalt blue, ice blue

Handgrip plate, 6" – 7": marigold, amethyst, green

An extremely rare Stippled Strawberry bowl in ice green. Note the band of three slightly raised ribs that encircles the pattern. Many of Northwood's stippled pieces have this curious feature.

The Northwood Strawberry bowl appears in the bottom row of this assortment from a 1911 Butler Bothers catalog.

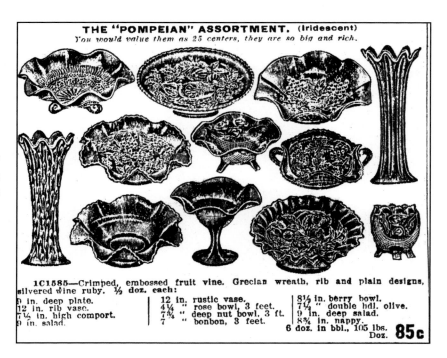

125

PATTERN: SUNFLOWER

A simple yet highly effective design, Sunflower is found almost exclusively on the interior of 8" – 9" spatula-footed bowls. It can be positively stunning when found with a dazzling electric iridescence. The exterior has the Meander pattern, one of the moulds Northwood purchased from Jefferson in 1908. Initial production of the design likely dates from the 1909 – 1910 period, with at least some production carried through 1912. Marigold, amethyst, and green are the most available colors. Cobalt blue is very scarce, while Renninger blue and teal examples are quite rare. But the top honors go to the ice blue bowls with just a few examples known.

You will note that I stated this design was "almost" exclusively confined to bowls. Almost, but not quite! I can personally vouch for the existence of one marigold spatula-footed 9" flat plate. Though it was nearly 30 years ago, I held this piece in my hands, so I know it exists. The owner of it, at that time, has long since passed away. When his glass was sold at auction, in the mid 1980s, the plate was *not* among the pieces sold! I have no idea as to its fate or current whereabouts, but I assure you it existed in the early 1970s. I have also had a report of an amethyst one, but it remains unconfirmed.

Shapes & Colors Known

Bowl, spatula-footed: marigold, amethyst, green, cobalt blue, Renninger blue, teal, ice blue
Plate, 9", spatula-footed: marigold (amethyst?)

Two rare Sunflower bowls in two distinctly different shapes: the Renninger blue example (left) is seldom found and the stunning ice blue bowl (right) is very rare.

PATTERN: SWIRL RIB & INTERIOR SWIRL & PANEL

In my first book on Northwood's carnival glass, published in 1994, I reported on the existence of six different shapes and variations of this Northwood water set pattern. In recent months, two more styles of Swirl Rib water pitchers have surfaced, making this the most extensive line of iridescent water sets ever produced by Harry Northwood. The wholesale catalogs bear out that all of them were in production during the 1909 – 1910 time frame so, although this pattern remains only moderately popular with today's collectors, it must have been a very popular design with the buying public of the day. Seven of the eight known pitcher shapes are mould-blown, with separately applied, clear handles. The other, often referred to as Interior Swirl & Panel, is a pressed pitcher, virtually identical in size and configuration to the North-wood Raspberry water pitcher. None of the mould-blown pitchers is ever signed. The pressed Interior Swirl & Panel pitcher is always trademarked. The same tumbler was marketed with all eight pitchers. They are mould-blown, have factory ground bases, and most examples are signed. The Swirl Rib pattern is found on the interior surface of both the pitchers and tumblers.

I have always detested the overuse of the term "variant" with regards to similar glass patterns, but in this case it becomes a necessity. We have eight water pitchers, all of widely varying shape, but all definitely part of the same Northwood pattern line, so we really have little choice but to use the term variant, numbers 1 through 8. They may be identified as follows:

VARIANT #1: A tall, 12" – 13" tankard shape, easily identified by two to three bulging rings around the base. Most often found in marigold, very scarce in green (usually with the Alaskan iridescent treatment), and extremely rare in amethyst, with only two examples reported to date.

VARIANT #2: This is the most easily found of the eight known shapes, also a tall, 12" – 13" tankard, identical in basic configuration to Variant #1, but this version lacks the bulging rings around the base. It is known only in marigold.

VARIANT #3: Yet another tall, tankard shape, this pitcher is identical in configuration to the Northwood Dandelion pitcher shown elsewhere in this book. This is perhaps the second rarest of the eight pitcher shapes and is known only in marigold.

VARIANT #4: This pitcher is more bulbous in shape, but not truly round. It is more of a tear-drop shape, similar to Dugan's Vineyard water pitcher. It is usually found with a crimped top and known only in marigold. This too is rarely found and only in marigold.

Shapes & Colors Known

Water pitcher variant #1: marigold, amethyst, green

Water pitchers, variants #2 through #7: marigold

Water pitcher, variant #8: marigold, green

Tumblers: marigold, amethyst, green

Offered here in this spring 1909 Butler Brothers ad are three different Northwood Swirl Rib water sets. They are, left to right, variants #4, #1, and #5. Note that the same tumbler accompanied all three styles. This is also, to date, the earliest documented appearance in the wholesale catalogs of any Northwood carnival water sets.

VARIANT #5: Slightly taller than Variant #4, yet shorter than the tankards, this style is of a cylindrical shape, with a defined shoulder where the body joins the neck and a crimped top. Here again, marigold is the only reported color.

VARIANT #6: This version of the Swirl Rib water pitcher surfaced for the first time in the late fall of the year 2000. This is a true, round cannonball shape. Only one example, in marigold, is confirmed at this time, so it wins the top rarity spot at present.

VARIANT #7: This is the pressed version of the pattern, usually referred to as Interior Swirl & Panel. It is identical in size and configuration to the Northwood's Raspberry water pitcher. Marigold is the only reported color, and these are quite scarce.

VARIANT #8: Similar in configuration to Variant #3, but shorter, more squat in appearance, and with a rounded, bowl-shaped base. Usually with a tightly crimped top, this version is known in marigold and green.

One other interesting fact should be mentioned here concerning Variants #3 and #7. Variant #3 is identical in size and configuration to the Northwood Dandelion pitcher, while #7 is identical to the Northwood Raspberry pitcher. As the production of all of these Swirl Rib variations definitely pre-dates the production of both Dandelion and Raspberry, it seems probable that both of these patterns came about as a result of a mould re-tooling of these two Swirl Rib variants.

The marigold variant #7 pitcher on the left is often called Interior Swirl & Panel. It is the only variation of this pattern that is pressed rather than mold-blown. Note that it is virtually identical in configuration and size to Northwood's Raspberry water pitcher. I would not be surprised to learn that the Raspberry water pitcher was created by re-tooling this mould. The green pitcher on the right is variant #8, a very scarce one, and has the Alaskan iridescent treatment.

This very scarce green Swirl Rib Variant #1 tankard pitcher with the Alaskan iridescent treatment has two distinct bulging rings around the base. The marigold tankard set at right is Variant #2, which is the most often seen of all variations, and it lacks these two base rings.

PATTERN: THIN RIB

I've always preferred the name Wide Rib for this Northwood vase pattern as I feel it is more descriptive of the wide, unpatterned area between the ribs, but thin rib has always been the generally accepted name. So be it. Found only on vases, comprising nine vertical ribs, and in three different size classifications, Thin Rib enjoyed one of the lengthiest production runs in the entire Northwood arsenal of patterns. The pattern first appeared in the wholesale catalogs in 1909 and continued as part of the line in both iridescent and non-iridescent forms right up until the Northwood factory closed in 1925. Some examples bear the Northwood trademark, but an unusually large number is unsigned. Some of the known iridized colors, like vaseline, russet, and sapphire blue, may be found with a stretch effect to the iridescence.

The standard size swung vases have a base diameter of roughly 3" to 3½" and can vary in height from a 5" – 7" squat version to about 12" tall. There is a wide variety of colors to hunt for here. The 5" – 7" squat vases are a little tough to find in any color, but turn up most often in marigold, amethyst, and green. The cobalt blue examples are harder to find, while examples in white, ice blue, ice green, teal, and russet (olive) are seldom found. Vases in the 8" – 12" range

are generally more easily found. They are known in all of the previously mentioned colors as well as rare examples in aqua, sapphire blue, vaseline, and smoke. Jack in the Pulpit-shaped examples, often called jester caps and made from this size base mould, also exist but are rarely found in any color. They have been reported in marigold, amethyst, green, cobalt blue, and teal, with the marigold and teal examples probably the least often found.

The midsize vases have a base diameter of from 4¼" to 4½" and can vary in height from a rare 6½" tall size, often called a jardiniere, to as much as 15" tall. Most are found in the 12" to 14" height range. Marigold, amethyst, and green examples are reasonably available, and cobalt blue and white vases turn up in fair numbers. All others are quite rare and include ice blue, ice green, lime green, sapphire blue, vaseline, amber, and aqua opalescent, the latter two colors topping the rarity list. The 6½" jardiniere has been reported only in amethyst, to date, and is very rare.

The true funeral vase has a 4¾" to 5" base diameter with heights ranging from 16" to as much as 21". They are very rare in any color and have been reported in marigold, amethyst, green, cobalt blue, white,

Three Thin Rib midsize vases in white (scarce), sapphire blue (rare), and vaseline (very rare). All of these have the 4¼" to 4½" size base.

sapphire blue, and vaseline, but are topped-off by a single known example in aqua opalescent.

Thin Rib vases may also be found in non-iridized crystal, emerald green, sapphire blue, custard glass, and an opaque red color that Northwood made in 1924 called Chinese coral, which is very similar to Fenton's mandarin color.

Shapes & Colors Known

Vase, 3" – 3½" base, 5" – 7" height: marigold, amethyst, green, cobalt blue, white, ice blue, ice green, teal, russet

Vase, 3" – 3½" base, 8" – 12" height: marigold, amethyst, green, cobalt blue, white, ice blue, ice green, teal, russet, aqua, sapphire blue, vaseline, smoke

Vase, 3" – 3½" base, jester cap (Jack in the Pulpit): marigold, amethyst, green, cobalt blue, teal

Vase, 4¼" – 4½" base, jardiniere 6½" height: amethyst

Vase, 4¼" – 4½" base, midsize, 11" – 15" height: marigold, amethyst, green, cobalt blue, white, ice blue, ice green, lime green, sapphire blue, vase line, amber, aqua opalescent

Funeral vase, 4¾" – 5" base, 16" – 21" height: marigold, amethyst, green, cobalt blue, white, sapphire blue, vase line, aqua opalescent

Thin Rib Jack in the Pulpit-shaped vases in green and marigold, each with a distinctly different shaping to the top.

Introduced in 1910, Three Fruits underwent a massive production run, remaining a staple of the line throughout the entire span of Northwood's carnival production. Even after 40 years of buying pressure by collectors, it is still readily available in many colors. The design was no doubt produced in huge quantities. It is nearly identical to Northwood's Fruits & Flowers, differing only in its lack of flower blossoms. In fact, the two designs were likely all part of the same pattern line. Though it is found only on the interior surface of bowls and plates, there are a number of variations and a wide range of colors, making Three Fruits one of the all-time collector favorites. Many examples bear the Northwood trademark, but an equal number are unsigned.

Collar-based 8" – 9" bowls may be found either with a plain background or stippled, ruffled or with a pie crust edge. Three different exteriors were used: Basketweave, plain or ribbed. The ruffled bowls with a plain background are still widely available in marigold, amethyst, and green. Most of the other colors will be difficult to find, but clambroth, lavender, horehound, and honey amber examples surface from time to time. Smoke, cobalt blue, white, lime green, aqua opalescent, and pearlized custard are all rare colors. The pie crust edge examples are known in a somewhat more limited range of colors. Like their ruffled counterparts, they are still fairly abundant in marigold, amethyst or green. Lime green, cobalt blue, and smoke are the rarities here. Most examples of the non-stippled bowls will be found with the Basketweave exterior, but a fair number with plain exteriors may also be found. Most of the more unusual colors, like honey amber, lavender, and smoke, will have plain exteriors.

Aside from the stippling itself, the collar-based ruffled and pie crust edge bowls differ in that they have a band of three fine, raised ribs encircling the pattern. Most examples are found with the ribbed exterior. They are harder to find than the non-stippled version, in any color, but the ruffled ones do turn up most often in marigold, amethyst, cobalt blue, and, surprisingly, white. The green, lavender, pearlized custard, and aqua opalescent are all very scarce. Ice blue, teal, and sapphire blue are all very rare, as are a couple of reported horehound examples. Pie crust edge stippled bowls are harder to find in any color, even marigold. Amethyst, cobalt blue, horehound, and green are tougher still, and the ice blue and russet (olive) bowls are rare.

The second known bowl shape rests on a raised, dome foot. Measuring 8" – 9" in diameter, these bowls are often found with an unusual superimposed, double exterior pattern. At first glance they appear to merely have the Basketweave exterior, but look close-ly. You will find faint portions of the Vintage Grape pattern, one of the moulds Northwood purchased from Jefferson in 1908, showing through the Basketweave design. These bowls are still fairly plentiful in marigold, amethyst, green, and even white. Scarcer examples include horehound and honey amber. Ice green is the least often seen, but even they are not considered particularly rare.

The third known bowl shape is often referred to as Three Fruits Medallion. The center spray of cherries is replaced by a sprig of three leaves on this version, which rests on three, spade-like spatula feet. The exterior pattern is Meander which Northwood purchased from Jefferson in 1908. Here again, both plain and stippled examples exist. The plain version is still easily available in marigold, amethyst, and green.

Shapes & Colors Known

Bowl, 8" – 9", collar base, ruffled: marigold, amethyst, green, cobalt blue, white, clambroth, lavender, horehound, smoke, honey amber, lime green, pearlized custard, aqua opalescent

Bowl, 8" – 9", collar base, pie crust: marigold, amethyst, green, cobalt blue, lime green, smoke

Bowl, 8" – 9", collar base, ruffled, stippled: marigold, amethyst, green, cobalt blue, white, ice blue, teal, lavender, sapphire blue, lavender, horehound, pearlized custard, aqua opalescent

Bowl, 8" – 9", collar base, pie crust, stippled: marigold, amethyst, green, cobalt blue, ice blue, horehound, russet

Bowl, 8" – 9", dome-footed: marigold, amethyst, green, white, ice green, horehound, honey amber

Bowl, 8" – 9", spatula-footed: marigold, amethyst, green, cobalt blue, white, ice blue, ice green, aqua opalescent, lavender, pearlized custard, ice blue opalescent, ice green opalescent

Bowl, 8" – 9", spatula-footed, stippled: marigold, amethyst, cobalt blue, white, ice blue, ice green, aqua opalescent

Plate, 9" – 9½": marigold, amethyst, green, cobalt blue, lavender, horehound, aqua opalescent

Plate, 9" – 9½", stippled: marigold, amethyst, green, cobalt blue, ice blue, ice green, lavender, horehound, honey amber, clambroth, aqua, teal, violet, sapphire blue, aqua opalescent, ice blue opalescent, ice green opalescent

Lavender, cobalt blue, and white are scarce. While seen far less often than the aforementioned colors, aqua opalescent examples turn up in fair quantities — everyone seems to want one. The rarest colors include pearlized custard, ice blue, ice green, ice blue opalescent, and ice green opalescent, the latter two topping the rarity list. The stippled version turns up most often in marigold, amethyst, and occasionally, cobalt blue and white. Ice green and aqua opalescent are very scarce, but ice blue is the least often seen here.

Collar-based 9" – 9½" plates are also found in both plain or stippled versions. Most of the plain ones will have the Basketweave exterior, but a fair number with plain exteriors turn up as well. Again, marigold, amethyst, and green are by far the most available colors. Cobalt blue, lavender, and horehound are quite scarce, but aqua opalescent examples win the top honors here, with just a few examples known. Like their bowl-shaped counterparts, the stippled plates have the band of three raised ribs encircling the pattern. These nearly always have the ribbed exterior and are actually found in a far greater variety of colors

than the non-stippled version. Marigold and amethyst are the most available, but even they are much harder to find than non-stippled examples. A fair number of cobalt blue examples turn up, but virtually all the other known colors range from very scarce to extremely rare. Lavender, clambroth, and horehound would all fit the very scarce category. I would personally consider the aqua opalescent and honey amber plates as rarely found but not really in the extreme category. Most of the others fit well into the extremely rare category, and these include aqua, teal, violet, green, and sapphire blue. Topping the list are the ice blue and ice green plates. I personally have heard of only two in ice blue and one in ice green.

As you can see, there is certainly a lot to hunt for, and entire collections have been built around this pattern. No wonder it is a favorite with today's collectors. The variety of colors combined with shape and design variations provides for a nearly limitless array of items to find. As an interesting sideline to your carnival Three Fruits pieces, be on the lookout for some lovely non-iridized pieces as well. Collar-based bowls are also known in non-iridized crystal, blue opalescent,

Two versions of the Three Fruits plate: the amethyst one, on the left, is one of the more easily found colors. The stippled cobalt blue example on the right is harder to find, but a fair number do turn up.

and custard glass. The dome-footed bowls are known in blue opalescent glass. The spatula-footed bowls can be found in clear to white opalescent, blue opalescent, and custard glass.

Fenton also produced a carnival version of Three Fruits in both bowl and plates. They have a plain exterior and a distinctly 12-sided effect to the edge shape. They are known in marigold, amethyst, green, and cobalt blue.

Even Northwood's beautiful aqua opalescent can vary a great deal in color tone, iridescence, and opalescence. The rare aqua opalescent Three Fruits bowl above has a rich butterscotch overlay to the iridescence, and the opalescence is confined to the tips. The bowl on the right is one of the very few examples known in smoke, always a rare color for Northwood.

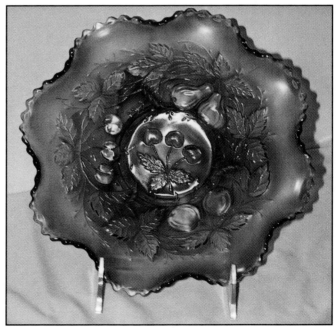

Reminiscent of a stylization found on some of the more expensive art glass vases of the period, Northwood's Tornado vase dates from the 1911 – 1912 period. It has never been particularly plentiful in any color, and the variety of known colors is also very limited. Still, the existence of a couple of examples in stretch iridescent colors tells us that some limited production of the design occurred as late as 1916. Add to that the number of variations in size, shape, and style that are known, and the production circumstances become most intriguing. Height may vary from 6" to 6½". Some examples are found with a distinct collar base (marie), while others do not have one, but rest upon the base of the body of the piece and appear to have a ground base. An even rarer variation with a ribbed background is known. Rarer still is a version that rests on a distinct pedestal foot. Most are shaped with a triangular crimp to the top edge, but the two

known examples with the stretch effect to the iridescence are cone shaped. It seems like an awful lot of variation for an item that was apparently not produced in anywhere near the numbers of most Northwood carnival items. Perhaps there were moulding problems with it, and they kept experimenting with variations on size, shape, and style in an attempt to rectify the situation. If so, Harry Northwood certainly took his time in doing so, as this highly limited production spanned at least four to five years! The mysterious circumstances surrounding the production of this vase will likely remain unsolved, but that somehow only adds to its appeal. Most examples will bear the Northwood trademark.

The standard Tornado vase, with a plain background and triangular crimped top, is most often found in green. Amethyst is harder to find and marigold even more so. White examples are extremely

Shapes & Colors Known

Vase, 6" – 6½", plain background: marigold, amethyst, green, white
Vase, 6" – 6½", ribbed background: marigold, amethyst, cobalt blue, white, ice blue
Vase, whimsey, cone-shaped, flared top: marigold, lavender, celeste blue
Vase, pedestal footed: marigold

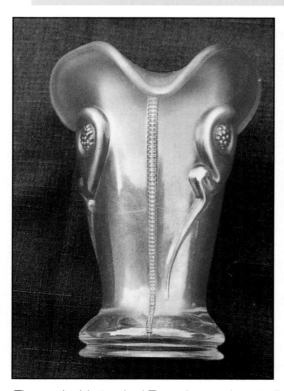

The marigold standard Tornado vase is actually found far less often than its amethyst or green counterparts. The white tornado vase shown here is extremely rare and one of only a few known examples in this color.

rare. Examples with the ribbed background and triangular crimped top are rare in any color, but amethyst seems to turn up the most. Blue and marigold are very rare and white extremely so, but ice blue tops the list here, with only two or three examples known.

An extremely rare version is that of a cone shape, with a flared out top. Some collectors have dubbed these as whimsies, and they certainly qualify as such. These have a plain background, and only three examples are currently known to exist: one each in marigold, lavender, and celeste blue. The lavender and celeste blue examples have a pronounced stretch effect to the iridescence, indicating that the shaping was done after the iridescent spray was applied.

The fourth variation rests on a distinct pedestal foot, with the body of the vase tapering downward towards the base. Only three examples are confirmed, and all are in marigold.

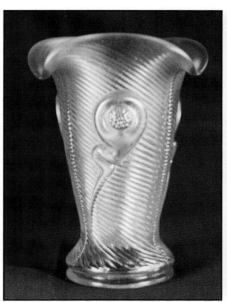

The ribbed variant of the Tornado vase is rarely found in any color, but the ice blue one shown here is extremely rare, one of only two or three reported. The cone-shaped, flared Tornado whimsey in lavender is the only one known in this color. Note the distinct stretch effect to the iridescence, a result of being shaped after the piece was sprayed with the iridizing solution.

This is the extremely rare Tornado Variant vase in marigold. Note that it rests on a distinct pedestal foot. This is one of only three known examples with a triangular pinched top. One example is also known with a four-ruffled pinched top.

PATTERN: TOWN PUMP

The overall concept of this unique vase enjoyed a long history in the hands of Harry Northwood. The idea of such a spouted, handled vase first became a reality at Northwood's Ellwood City, Pennsylvania factory in 1894. It was a delicate, hand-blown piece that was marketed with an even more delicate bail-handled glass bucket to hang from the spout. Few, if any of these at all, have survived the years. In 1899, Northwood produced a second version of the Town Pump. This one was pressed, patterned in a tree bark design, rested on four twig-like feet, and came with a matching, footed trough. They were made in non-iridized opalescent colors. In recent years this version was reproduced by L.G. Wright.

The carnival glass version that Harry made at Wheeling early in 1912 differs considerably from the earlier Town Pumps. It is pressed, rests on a distinct marie (collar base), and is patterned with ivy leaves. The Northwood trademark is always present, and the pumps stand approximately 6" tall. Examples in perfect condition are very hard to find, as the spout and handle are highly prone to damage. Amethyst is the most available, but even these are tough to find. Marigold Town Pumps are rare and always in demand, but the green examples are the hardest of all to find. For some reason the green ones seem to be even more prone to damage than the amethyst or marigold pumps. I have seen far more damaged green ones over the years, especially with the spout missing, than in either of the other two colors.

Don't expect too many bargains on these. The amethyst examples are rapidly closing in on four-figure price tags, and the marigold and green pumps are already well into that range. Demand for perfect examples is very high as these unique vases rapidly vanish from the market. I have yet to find any ads for these vases in any of the known wholesale catalogs of the period. It is also unusual that this vase has not surfaced in any of the pastel colors, as it was in production at the height of their popularity. I suspect that the carnival version of the Town Pump was likely a one shot deal, made for a specific customer and not marketed for the general trade.

Shapes & Colors Known

Vase, 6": marigold, amethyst, green

Always a favorite with collectors, Northwood's Town Pump in amethyst.

Tree Trunk vases must have been very popular sellers for Harry Northwood. They first appeared in 1908 and remained in the Northwood line throughout the entire span of the firm's iridescent production. They were also produced in non-iridescent opalescent colors and custard glass. They are also very popular items with collectors today. Most examples are signed.

They are actually six different size and shape variations of Tree Trunk vases, made from three different size base moulds. Size classification is actually determined by the base diameter rather than height. They are as follows: The standard size base was used for three variations. These items have a base diameter of from 3⅜" to 3¾". The first variation is that of the vases in the 8" – 12" height range. These are the most often found size and are available in a wide range of colors, some easily found and some very rare. Examples in marigold, amethyst, and green are the most common, but a fair number of cobalt blue and white examples surface as well. Ice blue and ice green vases are rarely found, and sapphire blue, teal and aqua opalescent examples are rarer still. The same mould was also used to fashion the squat vases, which are only from 5" to 7" in height. Here again, marigold, amethyst, and green are the most available. Cobalt blue is scarce and ice blue very rare in this size. The third variation made from this mould is that of a Jack in the Pulpit or jester cap shape. These examples have the back edge pulled up and the front edge turned down. These are extremely rare and reported in only two colors to date. I know of one in marigold and two in amethyst.

The midsize vases have a base diameter of 4¾" and are generally found in the 11" to 14" height range. These are much harder to find than the standard size vases. Even the most available colors, marigold, amethyst, and green, are becoming scarce now. Cobalt blue examples are very scarce, and vases in

horehound and lime green are rare. Ice blue and ice green are very rare, as are the sapphire blue vases, but aqua opalescent and marigold on custard come very close to taking the top honors here with only a few examples known. Close, but no cigar! The top spot goes to a single known example in iridized blue slag.

The true funeral vases have a base diameter of 5¼", and these are the rarest of all the Tree Trunk sizes. These massive items are very rare and desirable in any color. All will sell in the multi-thousand dollar range! Heights are generally in the 16" to 21" size range. Amethyst is the most often seen, oddly followed by cobalt blue. Marigold examples are actually

Shapes & Colors Known

Standard base
Vase, 8" – 12": marigold, amethyst, green, cobalt blue, white, ice blue, ice green, sapphire blue, aqua opalescent, teal
Vase, squat, 5" – 7": marigold, amethyst, green, cobalt blue, ice blue
Vase, Jack in the Pulpit, 6" – 7": marigold, amethyst

Midsize base
Vase, 11" – 14": marigold, amethyst, green, cobalt blue, ice blue, ice green, aqua opalescent, lime green, horehound, sapphire blue, marigold on custard, iridized blue slag

Funeral size base
Vase, 16" – 21": marigold, amethyst, green, cobalt blue, white, ice blue, ice green, marigold on custard
Vase, elephant's foot, 7½" – 10": marigold, amethyst, green, cobalt blue?

An interesting assortment of Tree Trunk vases. The five standard vases are in amethyst, sapphire blue, cobalt blue, marigold, and ice blue. The squat vase is also in cobalt blue. The vase in the center is the rare elephant's foot vase, with a 5¼" base size, in amethyst.

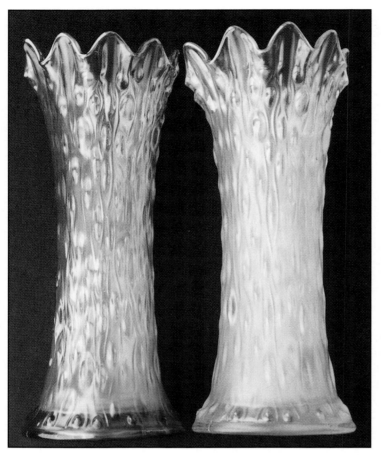

harder to find. White and ice green are very rare, and only a few green examples are known. The top spot unquestionably goes to the two known examples in ice blue. Mention should also be made of two known examples in marigold on custard. Though both stand less than 16" in height, they were made from the 5¼" base size, so they technically qualify as funeral vases.

The sixth size was also made from the 5¼" base size. These unusual vases have been dubbed as elephant's foot vases. They generally measure only 7¼" to 10" in height, with the top sometimes flared out to a diameter equal to or even surpassing the height. These are extremely rare in any color, but amethyst is the most often encountered. A couple of green examples are also known as is at least one confirmed in marigold. Cobalt blue has been reported, but not confirmed as of this writing.

Two midsize Tree Trunk vases (at left) in lime green (extremely rare) and white (rare). These stand roughly 13" tall. By comparison, the squat Tree Trunk vase (below right) in green is just 5½" tall.

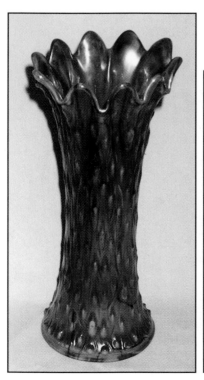

Two views of the only known midsize Tree Trunk vase in iridized blue slag.

One of the few iridized designs of its type to emerge from the Northwood factory, Valentine combines stylized and geometric motifs into a single pattern and dates early in the carnival era, circa 1908 – 1909. It was previously made in non-iridized crystal in 1906 and was one of the patterns rushed into iridescent production in order to gain an early share of the new market. Its production run in iridized form was very short.

The design is found only on the exterior surface of large and small berry bowls, both ruffled and non-ruffled. The interior is plain, and the Northwood trademark is usually present. Marigold is the only reported color, to date. Other iridized shape variations are certainly possible, as evidenced by the non-iridized crystal assortment included here from the 1906 Northwood factory catalog. Any of these shapes might well surface in iridized form.

This page from the 1906 Northwood catalog illustrates an assortment of pre-carnival, non-iridized Valentine shapes. To date, the only iridized shapes known closely match the top two. I have included this to illustrate the possibilities. As these were all standard production shapes, an iridized example of any of these could well exist.

No. 14 Superb Crystal Berry Assortment

BIG VALUE TEN CENTERS

BEAUTIFUL high class design and finish, and we do not hesitate to say that for quality of the glass and the velvety fire polish of its surface it surpasses any such assortment you have ever had.   It consists of :—

⅜— 9½ inch	Shallow Dish	
⅜— 8½ "	Flared Berry	
⅜— 7½ "	Regular Shaped Berry	
⅜— 9½ "	Square Berry	
⅜— 7½ "	Cupped Berry	
⅜—10 "	Cake Plate	
Total 5 dozen at 80c		$4 00
	Bbl	35
Weight 100 lbs.		— $4.35

Shapes & Colors Known

Bowl, 9" – 11": marigold
Bowl, 5" – 8": marigold

Northwood's #14 pattern, called Valentine by carnival glass collectors.

139

PATTERN: VINTAGE GRAPE

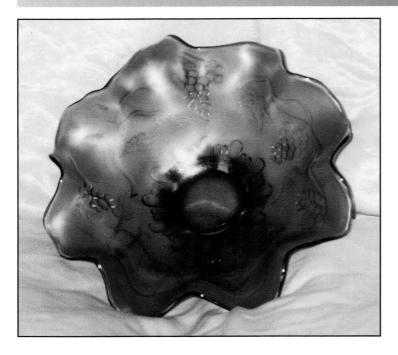

Vintage Grape, one of the moulds Northwood purchased from Jefferson in 1908, is usually found as an exterior pattern on dome-footed bowls with different interior designs. This beautiful example, in green with the Alaskan iridescent treatment, is to date the only reported example with a plain interior.

This one of several pattern moulds that Harry Northwood purchased from the Jefferson Glass Co., early in 1908. It is normally found only as a secondary or exterior pattern in combination with a different primary or interior design. As such, it is found most often on the exterior surface of dome-footed bowls with patterns like Star of David on the interior surface. However, it is also found as the primary pattern on the very rare bowl shown here. This piece has a plain, unpatterned interior, so the exterior Vintage Grape design becomes the primary pattern. This bowl is in green with the Alaskan iridescent treatment, and I might add is one of the finest, most beautiful examples of that iridescent treatment that I have ever seen on a piece of Northwood carnival! Unlike many examples of the Alaskan iridescent treatment that tend to have a rather lifeless, dull, bronze-like tone to them, this piece seems to jump right out at you. The effect of the marigold over green color blend is positively beautiful! This is the only example of a Vintage Grape bowl without a primary interior design that I have ever had reported to me. Others, possibly in marigold or amethyst, may well exist, but they remain unconfirmed as of this writing.

A special note of thanks goes to Gary Parsons for reporting and sharing this unusual find.

Shapes & Colors Known

Bowl, 8½", dome-footed: green

This design holds the distinction of being the very first full line pattern to undergo iridescent production, in 1908. However, that honor does not belong to Harry Northwood. Fenton was the first to market this design in iridized form, in water sets, berry sets, table sets, and a wide variety of bowls and novelty shapes. Northwood was quick to capitalize on its success however, and by 1909 his own version of the design was in iridized production, albeit a very short one.

Northwood's version of Waterlily & Cattails is known only in a water set. The pitcher is distinctly different from Fenton's version. It is taller and cone-shaped. Fenton's version of the tumbler has a distinct basketweave effect around the base of the pattern area, and the Northwood tumbler lacks this. The Northwood trademark is present on both the pitcher and matching tumblers. Marigold is the usual color, and the water pitchers are very scarce, but the tumblers turn up in fair numbers. Only one confirmed example of the pitcher in cobalt blue is known and only about seven or eight cobalt blue tumblers. The cobalt blue tumblers are often found with a name and date etched around the top band, usually 1909, which is very early for Northwood cobalt blue carnival production.

The Northwood water set can also be found in non-iridized blue opalescent glass. All other Waterlily & Cattail shapes were made by Fenton.

Shapes & Colors Known

Water pitcher: marigold, cobalt blue
Tumbler: marigold, cobalt blue

Northwood's version of Waterlily & Cattails. The cobalt blue tumbler is one of only about six known in that color and has a name and the date 1909 etched on it.

Northwood's version of Waterlily & Cattails pitcher.

To say that the production of this ultra-rare Northwood carnival design is shrouded in mystery would be a considerable understatement! Only four examples of the pattern, in three shapes, are known to exist, in any form, iridized or not! Why would Harry Northwood go to the expense of having at least three moulds made for this design and then produce so little of it? It remains one of the great unsolved mysteries of carnival glass. From the shapes and colors that are known, we can be pretty safe in saying we know the approximate date of production, and that's about it. The pattern likely dates from about 1910 – 1911, the same time frame for Northwood's Grape & Cable. Two of the three known shapes are identical in size and configuration to known Grape & Cable items.

Two examples of a covered sweetmeat, one in amethyst and one in green and identical in shape to the Grape & Cable sweetmeat, are known to exist at present. An unusual covered serving bowl in amethyst is also known. The third item only recently surfaced, an amethyst pedestal-footed sherbet, identical in size and configuration to the Grape & Cable sherbet. As I understand it, this piece turned up for sale at one of the carnival glass conventions. That's it! No other pieces of this pattern in any type of glass are known to exist. There must surely be other pieces, so keep your eyes peeled. You might just come up with a real sleeper!

Shapes & Colors Known

Covered sweetmeat: amethyst, green
Covered serving bowl: amethyst
Sherbet, pedestal-footed: amethyst

Both of these pieces are one-of-a-kind in their respective colors. The Wheat sweetmeat in green is identical in configuration to the Grape Cable sweetmeat, and the covered serving bowl is in amethyst. The production of this ultra-rare Northwood carnival pattern remains shrouded in mystery.

PATTERN: WIDE PANEL

The most well-known and eagerly sought item here is the positively magnificent four-lily epergne. These stately items stand roughly 14" – 15" tall and are comprised of five separate pieces: an 11" – 12" diameter base, with four fitting holes; and a tall center lily and three matching, angled side lilies. They are of course, due to the number of pieces, highly prone to damage, so complete, perfect examples are almost non-existent. They usually must be found and assembled piece by piece, which can be quite a challenge indeed. The Northwood trademark is often present on the underside of the base but may be very difficult to detect. It is found deep in the center of the recessed base. The epergne in iridescent form made its debut in 1909 and continued in the Northwood line through 1914.

Green is by far the most frequently found color, and for good reason. It had the longest production run of any of the known colors, appearing in the wholesale catalog for three years running. Marigold and amethyst are the next most available, in that order. White and cobalt blue examples are very rare, but ice blue and ice green are extremely so. The

Shapes & Colors Known

Epergne, four-lily: marigold, amethyst, green, cobalt blue, white, ice blue, ice green, aqua opalescent
Vase, standard: marigold, amethyst, green, white, ice blue
Vase, midsize: marigold, amethyst, green, cobalt blue, white, ice blue, ice green, teal, aqua opalescent
Vase, funeral: marigold, amethyst, green, white, celeste blue, vaseline

crowning glory here is the single known complete example in aqua opalescent.

The Wide Panel epergne may also be found in non-iridized blue, green, and white opalescent colors.

The pattern is also found on vases in three sizes: standard, midsize, and funeral. The standard vases have a base diameter of roughly 3½" and will usually be found in heights varying from 7" to 11". I have seen them in marigold, amethyst, green, white, and ice blue. The midsize vases have a 4½" base diameter and generally range in height from 10" to 14". Colors known include marigold, amethyst, green, cobalt blue, white, ice blue, ice green, teal, and a couple of extremely rare aqua opalescent examples. The funeral vase has a 5" base diameter and ranges in height from 16" to about 20". They are known in marigold, amethyst, green, white, celeste blue, and vaseline, the latter two colors often found with stretch effect to the iridescence. The midsize vases are the most often seen, and most of the green ones will have the Alaskan iridescent treatment.

Wide Panel epergnes in green, the most available color; marigold, which is harder to find; and white, a very rare color.

PEARL IRIDESCENT EPERGNE OR TABLE CENTERPIECE.

Has the exclusive art principles of the expensive imported ware.

C2139—11 in. fluted bowl, 4 lily design, removable holders, crystal, blue and green glass, pearl iridescent finish, 3 in bbl., asstd., — lbs. Each, **$1.25**

Ads for the Wide Panel epergne, in green only, appeared in Butler Brothers catalogs from 1909 through 1912. Nearly four straight years of production in that color certainly explains why the green examples are the most often found today. In the spring of 1912, this ad appeared noting that it was now available in crystal, blue, and green, all with a pearl iridescent finish. This combination of these three colors and the term pearl iridescent is a direct reference to three colors that had been introduced by Northwood in 1912: white, ice blue, and ice green.

PATTERN: WILD ROSE

This is another of Northwood's early iridescent efforts, first appearing in the wholesale catalogs during the 1908 – 1909 period. It was one of the patterns carried over from opalescent production circa 1905 – 1906. However, the existence of cobalt blue and ice blue examples tells us that some iridescent production of the design occurred at least through 1912. The pattern is very similar in concept to Northwood's Blossom & Palm and is found only on the exterior surface of three-footed bowls of varying shape with a reticulated or open edge. Three different interiors are known. It may be plain, carry a variation of Stippled Rays, or have a design comprised of alternating stippled and non-stippled rays. The Northwood trademark is usually present, but not always.

The most often encountered shape has the reticulated edge flared outward in varying degrees. On some, this edge is near flat while others may be shaped to a 45-degree angle or more. Green seems to be the most often found color, followed by marigold and amethyst. Cobalt blue examples are very scarce and ice blue very rare.

The nutbowl shape has the reticulated edge pointing straight up. Here again, green is the most common color followed by marigold and amethyst. Cobalt blue is rarely seen, and ice blue is very rare. An example in horehound has also been confirmed.

The rosebowl shape has the reticulated edge cupped inward and is found far less often than the previously mentioned shapes. Green is the most available and amethyst tougher to find. Marigold examples are surprisingly scarce, and ice blue very rare. Topping the list here is a single known example in sapphire blue.

The rarest shape of all here is that of the footed plate, completely flattened out. Green is the only reported color, and only a couple of these are known.

Wild Rose can also be found in non-iridized blue, green, white, and vaseline opalescent. They make for a colorful go-along to the carnival examples.

Shapes & Colors Known

Footed bowl: marigold, amethyst, green, cobalt blue, ice blue
Nutbowl: marigold, amethyst, green, cobalt blue, ice blue, horehound
Rosebowl: marigold, amethyst, green, ice blue, sapphire blue
Plate: green

 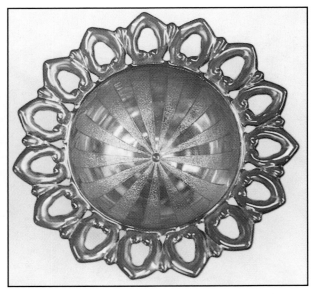

The cobalt blue Wild Rose piece on the left is the nutbowl shape and has the Stippled Rays interior pattern. The cobalt blue example on the right is the bowl shape with the reticulated edge more widely flared outward. It also has a previously unreported interior pattern of alternating stippled and smooth panels.

This is the only known Wild Rose rosebowl in sapphire blue. Note how the reticulated edge is turned inward to form the rosebowl shape.

PATTERN: WILD STRAWBERRY

Because it is found in the pastel colors, we know that this close cousin to Northwood's Strawberry must have been in production during the 1912 – 1913 time frame. The design has a slightly more whirling effect to it and also contains more foliage and small blossoms which are absent on Northwood's Strawberry. Although a few examples are known with a plain exterior, most will have the Basketweave back, and the Northwood trademark is usually present.

The design is most often found on large, 9" – 10" ruffled bowls and a small, 5" – 6" counterpart. They make a most attractive ruffled berry set. Although the amethyst examples usually sell for higher prices than their marigold counterparts, they are actually more easily found. Green is found far less often, and white examples are very scarce. Ice blue and ice green ones are rarely seen.

A handgrip plate with one edge turned up is the only other reported shape. Amethyst is the most often found, with green and marigold, in that order, somewhat harder to find. No pastels have yet been reported in this shape.

Shapes & Colors Known

Bowl, ruffled, 9" – 10": marigold, amethyst, green, white, ice blue, ice green
Bowl, ruffled, 5" – 6": marigold, amethyst, green, white, ice blue, ice green
Handgrip plate: marigold, amethyst, green

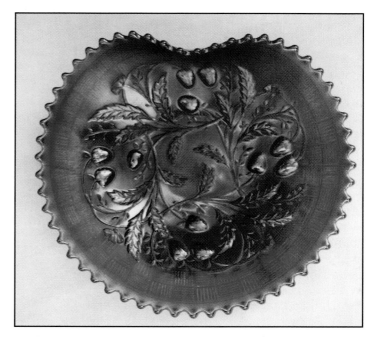

Great iridescence really shows off the pattern detail on this amethyst Wild Strawberry handgrip plate.

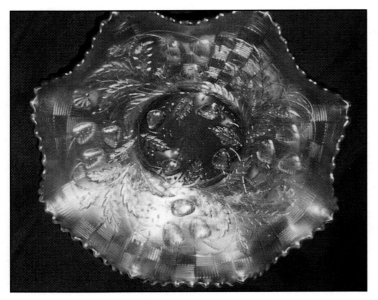

The large 9½" bowl in ice green is rarely found.

PATTERN: WISHBONE

This very popular Northwood creation first appeared during the 1911 – 1912 pattern boom years, and at least some production of it occurred as late as 1914 – 1915. It was made in a reasonably wide variety of shapes including a water set, footed bowls and plates, collar-based bowls and plates, a handsome single-lily epergne, and even a triangular-footed whimsey plate. The Northwood trademark is found on most examples, but some are unsigned.

Three-footed ruffled 8" – 9" bowls apparently enjoyed the most prolific production of the known shapes in this design. They are known in the widest variety of colors and are the most often found of the known shapes. The exterior carries the Ruffles & Rings pattern, one of the moulds Northwood purchased from Jefferson in 1908. Marigold, amethyst, and green are the most available colors. Virtually all the others will present a challenge, but there are quite a few of them. Cobalt blue is very scarce as are lavender and white examples. Horehound is scarcer still while ice blue and ice green bowls are rarely encountered. A few very rare lime green examples are also known, but top rarity honors go to the aqua opalescent bowls. Only two or three examples have been reported.

Shapes & Colors Known

Bowl, 8" – 9", footed: marigold, amethyst, green, cobalt blue, white, ice blue, ice green, aqua opalescent, lavender, horehound, lime green, smoke

Plate, 9", footed: marigold, amethyst, green

Plate, 8" – 9", triangular: marigold, amethyst

Bowl, 9" – 10", collar base, ruffled: marigold, amethyst, green, sapphire blue

Bowl, 9" – 10", collar base, pie crust: marigold, amethyst, green, cobalt blue, clambroth, white, smoke

Chop plate, 10" – 10½": marigold, amethyst, green

Epergne: marigold, amethyst, green, white, ice blue, ice green

Water pitcher: marigold, amethyst, green

Tumbler: marigold, amethyst, green, pearlized custard

The same mould was used to fashion a three-footed 9" plate. These are very scarce and reported in only three colors to date. Amethyst examples actually do turn up in reasonable numbers, but green and marigold are really quite rare. Triangular-shaped whimsey plates have also been documented in amethyst and marigold.

Collar-based 9" – 10" bowls with a Basketweave exterior and ruffled or pie crust edges are not as often found as the footed bowls. The ruffled ones are most often found in amethyst or green. Marigold examples are a little tougher. A single known sapphire blue example also exists. The pie crust edge examples are known in a slightly wider variety of colors. Marigold and green seem to be the most available, more so than amethyst. White and clam-broth are next in line, but quite scarce, and cobalt blue examples are rarely found. I know of at least one example in smoke, always a rare color for Northwood.

The collar-based plates usually measure 10" – 10½" in diameter, qualifying them as true chop plates. They are very rare in any color and to date have been reported only in marigold, amethyst, and green, with the green ones particularly rare.

The handsome, two-piece, single-lily epergne is a highly treasured item with collectors. The exterior has the Basketweave pattern, while the Wishbone design is found both on the interior of the base and on the lily. Like all epergnes, perfect examples are very hard to find in any color, but amethyst and marigold seem to be the most available, with green close behind. White is rare, but ice blue and ice green are extremely so. Take your pick for the top honors.

Water sets are the only other known shapes in this design. While the tumblers can be found without too much difficulty, there seems to be a shortage of pitchers, bulbous in shape and mould-blown with a separately applied handle. Marigold, amethyst, and green are the only colors reported for the pitcher, but a single known example of the tumbler exists in pearlized custard. This not only leads to speculation that a matching pitcher may be out there, but also confirms some production of this pattern during 1914 – 1915 when Northwood custard glass production was revived.

The Northwood Wishbone 9" footed plate in marigold is surprisingly rare. I doubt there are more than 15 to 20 of these known.

The Northwood Wishbone water pitcher and tumbler in green.

147

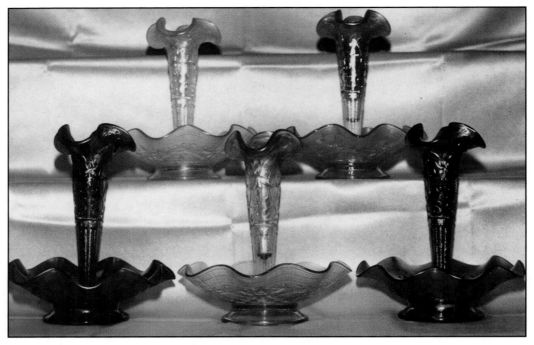

A beautiful array of Wishbone epergnes in green, marigold, amethyst, ice blue, and white. None of them is very plentiful, but the ice blue is particularly rare.

PATTERN: WISTERIA

If you have ever wondered what might be considered the rarest of all Northwood carnival water sets, look no further. Here it is! It is very similar in design concept to Northwood's Grape Arbor with wisteria flowers replacing the grapes. The pattern definitely dates from the 1912 – 1914 era, but production of it was extremely limited. Examples of the tankard water pitcher, which is mould-blown with a separately applied handle, are almost non-existent. Only a handful is known and only in ice blue and white. Most of the known examples also have damage. A perfect one would be a fantastic find!

The tumblers are also extremely rare. Ice blue examples seem to outnumber the white, ice green, and a few reported lime green tumblers. To date, no ice green water pitcher has surfaced. It would be one of the all-time great finds.

Only two other pieces of this pattern are known to exist and both are whimsies. A single known vase fashioned from the tankard pitcher mould sans handle surfaced in 1991 at a local antique auction in Ohio, not far from Wheeling, West Virginia. It is in dark green, the only item in this pattern known in a non-pastel color. The only other item known is a most unusual whimsey bank in white, fashioned from the tumbler mould. The top is tightly pinched in and slotted to accommodate coins. Both of these items would certainly be in contention for the honors of rarest Northwood carnival items known!

Shapes & Colors Known

Tankard pitcher: white, ice blue
Tumbler: white, ice blue, ice green, lime green
Whimsey vase: green
Whimsey bank: white

Rare Wisteria tumblers in ice blue and white.

The Northwood Wisteria tumbler and water pitcher in ice blue, one of the rarest of all Northwood carnival pitchers. Very few perfect examples are known.

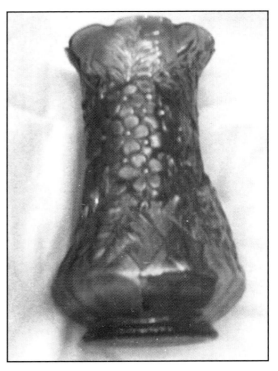

Without question one of the rarest treasures in all of Northwood carnival is the one-of-a-kind Wisteria vase, fashioned from the pitcher mould, in green. It's a double rarity in that it is also the only known piece in this pattern in a color other than a pastel.

ADVERTISING PIECES

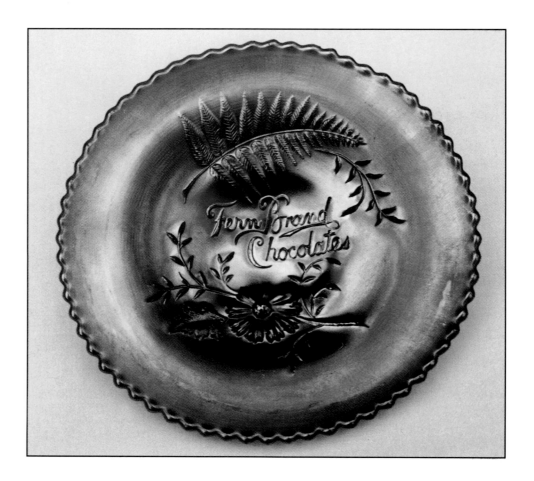

Carnival glass advertising pieces, or lettered pieces as they are sometimes called, are actually a testament to just how popular this innovative form of glass was during the 1908 – 1910 period, when it was still relatively new to the market. Many companies were eager to have their products promoted on this new art form, and Harry Northwood was more than willing to accommodate them. During the 1909 – 1910 period, Northwood was comissioned to produce several such items, for at least 10 different firms. The various firms involved used these pieces as promotional or give-away items.

Eight of the 10 firms involved chose to have items made that promoted their product or company name on the interior surface of the piece. These items are known in small 5" – 6" bowls, small 6" – 7" plates, or small 6" – 7" handgrip plates. All carry Northwood's famous Basketweave exterior, and all are known only in amethyst. All of them are very difficult to find today, some much more so than others, and all are highly treasured when found.

Listed here, in alphabetical order, are the known Northwood interior lettered advertising pieces. The bold names are exactly as they appear on the piece.

BALLARD-MERCED, CAL: These pieces were made for the Merced, California office of the Simeon M. Ballard Insurance and Real Estate Company. It is known on ruffled bowls and flat plates. The interior is plain, save for the lettering "Ballard-Merced, Cal."

WE USE BROEKER'S FLOUR: John Resnik, in his pioneer book titled *The Encyclopedia Of Carnival Glass Lettered Pieces,* made a valiant effort to establish exactly where the Broeker Flour Company was, but apparently these efforts met with limited success. His research did narrow the field to four possible locations for this company: Minnesota, Nebraska, Iowa or Kansas. The firm obviously no longer exists and may have been absorbed by one of the larger food corporations. Also, many Midwestern firms that produced agricultural products, such as flour, went belly-up during the dustbowl years of the 1930s. Only plates, with a plain interior save for the lettering, are known and only about a dozen of them.

DAVIDSON'S SOCIETY CHOCOLATES: Here again we do not know the location of this company, but it was likely somewhere in the Midwest. This is found only on a handgrip plate and seems to be one of the more frequently found Northwood advertising pieces.

DREIBUS PARFAIT SWEETS: Parfait Sweets was a line of candy made by the Dreibus Candy Company of Omaha, Nebraska. The company was founded in 1884 by Anton C. Dreibus, a German immigrant. Records and mention of the firm come to an abrupt halt around 1930 – 1931, so the company was likely a casualty of the Great Depression. This is found on ruffled bowls, flat plates, and handgrip plates. Another of the more available Northwood advertising pieces.

EAGLE FURNITURE COMPANY 282-284 SOUTH MAIN ST.: The Eagle Furniture Company still exists today, though it is now known as J. J. Haverty Co. It was established in Memphis, Tennessee, in 1900 by James J. Haverty. By the 1930s, it had grown to a chain of 22 stores in 18 Southern cities. These pieces are known in bowls, plates, and handgrip plates. The ruffled bowl seems to be the rarest of them.

FERN BRAND CHOCOLATES: This producer of fine confections was established in June 1900 in Burlington, Iowa. They remained in business until 1955. The spray of ferns above the lettered logo is unique to this particular item. No other Northwood advertising piece has it. Plates are the only reported shapes here, and they do turn up from time to time.

E. A. HUDSON FURNITURE CO. 711 TRAVIS ST.: Clarence D. Hudson established this firm in 1897, in Houston, Texas. His son Eugene took it over in 1903 and thus it became E.A Hudson. It operated as a furniture company until World War II when it became a moving and storage company. It ceased operation entirely in 1953. These very scarce pieces are known in bowls, plates, and handgrip plates.

These are the only two unpatterned Northwood advertising pieces: Ballard Merced, Calif. and "We use Broeker's Flour."

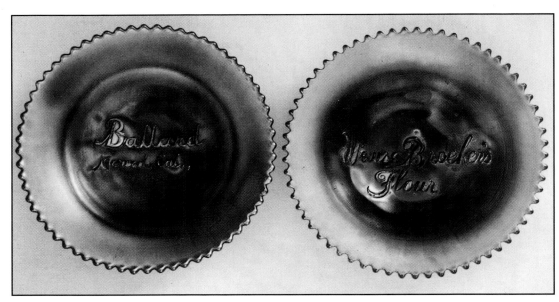

JOCKEY CLUB: All current evidence points to Jockey Club as a brand of perfume marketed by a California firm in the early 1900s. Current evidence also indicates that the famous Northwood Good Luck pieces may have come about as a re-tooled, more highly evolved version of this unique mould. (See the text on Good Luck for more information.) Found on bowls, plates, and handgrip plates, these interior lettered pieces are some of the scarcest Northwood advertising items.

Four advertising plates: E.A. Hudson Furniture, Dreibus Parfait Sweets, Fern Brand Chocolates, and Eagle Furniture Co.

Davidson's Society Chocolates handgrip plate and the Jockey Club plate.

A closer view of the Davidson's Society Chocolates handgrip plate in amethyst.

EXTERIOR LETTERED ADVERTISING PIECES

There are also two Northwood advertising items on which the lettering appears on the exterior surfaces. These also differ from the others in that they were not made from specialty moulds, but they are found on the exterior surface of two patterns that were both moulds from Northwood's standard production lines.

HOWARDS FURNITURE COMPANY: This lettering is found on the underside of the base on some Four Pillars 9" – 12" vases. Green is the only reported color, and these are probably the most easily found of all Northwood advertising items.

OLD ROSE DISTILLERY: This lettering is found on the center portion of the underside of the marie (collar base) of some Northwood Stippled Grape & Cable flat plates. Here again, green is the only reported color. These are scarce, but not classified as rare. They do turn up from time to time.

NORTHWOOD DECORATED CARNIVAL GLASS

Garden Swirl tankard water pitcher, the most elaborately painted of any of Northwood's decorated patterns. The pitcher itself is actually Northwood's Swirl Rib Variant #2. This is the only example known at present.

Like most of his major competitors, Northwood produced a variety of hand-painted, enamel decorated carnival glass pieces, starting around 1909. All but two of these designs are confined exclusively to mould-blown water sets. At present, there are at least 42 different decorated patterns known, but sorting out just exactly who made what can be a real challenge and, in some cases, next to impossible. Both Fenton and Dugan also made a number of these designs, often in virtually identical shapes and with nearly identical decorations. Compounding the problem is the fact that many of the decorators who painted these designs are known to have moved from factory to factory as the availability of work dictated. So, virtually identical decorations can appear on products from more than one firm.

Among the most valuable tools in researching and identifying glass patterns and their makers are the wholesale catalogs from the carnival glass production era, such as Butler Brothers and Charles Broadway Rouss. These catalogs offer assortments of glass, all of which were packed at the factory of origin. Thus, the process of crediting a pattern to a specific manufacturer becomes relatively simple, in most cases. If you find a previously unidentified shape or pattern grouped within an assortment of other known Northwood designs, then you know for certain that the pattern in question must have also been a Northwood product. Sadly, this process does not work when it comes to the enamel decorated items. Most of these items appear in the catalogs individually, or worse still, often in groupings with other enamel decorated pieces that are also of uncertain origin. Back to square one! Perhaps one day a Northwood factory catalog from the carnival production era will surface, and we will finally be able to conclusively sort this all out.

Included in this section are only the eight enamel decorated patterns for which we currently have some conclusive evidence pointing to a Northwood origin. There are likely others from the Northwood factory, but without something definite to indicate that, I have not included them here.

APPLE BLOSSOM: This pattern holds several distinctions. First, it is one of only two Northwood enamel decorated designs that are pressed and not mould-blown. Second, it is the only one made in a full line, rather than just water sets. It holds a more impressive distinction in that virtually all pieces are very rare, far more so than any other Northwood enamel decorated creation. The glass itself has smooth, raised panels on the interior and a plain exterior, which nicely accommodates the painted decoration. The mould is actually a revival of a 1904 – 1906 Northwood pre-iridescent line that the late William Heacock named Barbella. It is found on berry sets, table sets, and water sets, and the only reported color is cobalt blue. All are rarely found. In fact, the first examples of the table set pieces only surfaced in 1995. All of the Apple Blossom pieces are virtually identical in configuration to Northwood's Grape & Gothic Arches, and one can't help but wonder if that pattern actually came about as a result of a re-tooling of the Barbella moulds.

Apple Blossom water pitcher, tumbler, master berry bowl, and small berry bowls.

CHERRIES & LITTLE FLOWERS:
A mould-blown, bulbous or cannonball-shaped pitcher, this one causes some confusion as Fenton is known to have produced a nearly identical set. The tumblers have a factory ground base and are occasionally found with the Northwood trademark. Cobalt blue is by far the most available color, but scarce marigold and rare amethyst examples are also known.

COSMOS: This is a mould-blown cylindrical pitcher with a sharply defined shoulder where the body of the pitcher joins the neck, identical in shape to that of the Northwood Swirl Variant #5. The tumblers have a factory ground base, and marigold is the only reported color on this scarce set.

DAISY & LITTLE FLOWERS: Another cannonball-shaped, bulbous pitcher, identical in shape to the Cherries & Little Flowers. The pressed tumblers are of a unique tapered shape, resting on a flared base. Known only in cobalt blue, and the tumblers are particularly tough to find.

GARDEN SWIRL: This extremely rare tankard pitcher has, to the best of my knowledge, never been named, so I'm taking the liberty of assigning it the name Garden Swirl. (We have to call it something!) It seems appropriate as the mould for this pitcher is that of the Northwood Swirl Variant #2, and the decoration is composed of a number of different flowers. It has the raised swirls on the inside and is by far the most elaborately painted of any of the Northwood decorated pitchers. Only one example of this pitcher has been confirmed, and I'm pleased to show it on page 154. Marigold is the only reported color and to date, no matching tumblers have surfaced.

GROUND CHERRIES: This is the second of Northwood's decorated water sets that is pressed and not mould-blown. Both pitcher and tumbler share the same basic tapered, rounded shape. The tumbler mould is the same as that used for the Daisy & Little Flowers. This rare set is known only in cobalt blue.

Cherries & Little Flowers water pitcher and tumbler in cobalt blue. Fenton made a virtually identical set.

PERIWINKLE: This painted design is known on three differently shaped pitchers. The first one is a tall, cylindrical tankard that is virtually identical in shape to Dugan's Lattice & Daisy Tankard, so I'm convinced that this version is of Dugan origin. The second is that of the bulbous or cannonball shape. That shape was made by both Northwood and Fenton, so the jury is still out on this version. The third shape is definitely a Northwood product. It is a mould-blown, cylindrical shape with the defined shoulder where the body joins the neck, identical in shape to Northwood's Swirl Rib Variant #5 and the Cosmos pitcher. The tumblers have a factory ground base, and marigold is the only reported color.

PRETTY PANELS: This pattern is actually so named because of the tumbler. It has smooth, raised panels on the inside, is pressed rather than mould-blown, and is actually the same Barbella mould used for the Apple Blossom water set. The pitcher is a bulbous, mould-blown shape. Marigold is the only reported color.

NORTHWOOD CARNIVAL LIGHT SHADES

While H. Northwood & Co. produced a wide variety of lighting accessories, the firm's production of iridescent light shades was surprisingly limited. To date, only three different electric light shades in iridescent form can be conclusively attributed to Northwood. All three can be dated to a 1912 production time frame. Two of these are primarily found in a line that Northwood called Luna. Introduced early in 1912, this Luna line is a satiny translucent off-white color, quite dense in texture, yet not quite fully opaque. It produced an even lighting effect, very similar to today's soft-white light bulbs. The patterns are called Pillar & Drape and Flared Panel. They are found with two different iridescent treatments, a soft, delicate pastel iridescence, very similar to that found on pearlized custard, or a rich marigold iridescent overlay. Both may often be found with the name Northwood molded in block letters around the fitting collar as shown in the illustration here.

The third light shade, not shown, is identical in shape, but absolutely plain, with no pattern whatsoever. It, too, often has the Northwood block letter signature around the fitting collar, but has not been reported in the Luna color. Marigold is the only reported color.

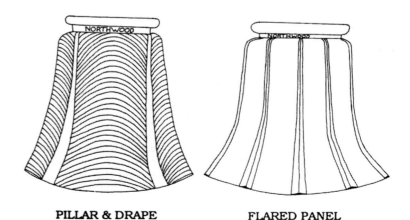

PILLAR & DRAPE   FLARED PANEL

Northwood's Luna carnival light shades.

Burns Auction Service. Auction catalogs 1984 – 2000.

Burns, Carl O. *Collector's Guide to Northwood's Carnival Glass.* LW Books, Gas City, IN. 1994.

———. *Imperial Carnival Glass — Identification & Values.* Collector Books, Paducah, KY. 1996.

———. *Dugan/Diamond Carnival Glass 1909 – 1931 — Identification & Values.* Collector Books, Paducah, KY. 1998.

Butler Brothers wholesale catalogs. "Our Drummer," various issues, 1900 – 1925.

Charles Broadway Rouss. Wholesale catalogs, various issues 1905 – 1919.

Doty, David. *A Field Guide to Carnival Glass.* The Glass Press Inc., Marietta, OH. 1998.

Edwards, Bill & Mike Carwile. *Standard Encyclopedia of Carnival Glass, 6th Edition.* Collector Books, Paducah, KY. 1998.

Freeman, Larry. *Iridescent Glass.* Century House, Watkins Glen, NY. 1956.

Hartung, Marion. *Carnival Glass Pattern Series Vols. 1 – 10.* Currently published by Heart of America Carnival Glass Association.

Heacock, WIlliam. *Collecting Glass.* Vols. 1-3, Antique Publications, Marietta OH, 1984 – 1986.

———. *The Glass Collector.* Vols. 1-6, Antique Publications, Marietta, OH, 1982 – 1983.

———. *Pattern Glass Preview.* Vols. 1-6, Antique Publications, Marietta, OH, 1980 – 1981.

Heacock, William; James Measell; Berry Wiggins. *Harry Northwood – The Early Years 1881 – 1900.* Antique Publications, Marietta, OH. 1990.

———. *Harry Northwood — The Wheeling Years 1901 – 1925.* Antique Publications, Marietta, OH. 1991.

Heart of America Carnival Glass Association. Carnival Glass Pattern Notebook.

———. Carnival Glass Newsletters, various issues, 1973 – 2000.

International Carnival Glass Association. Newsletters, various issues, 1973 – 1998.

Jennings, Steve. *Catalog Reprint of the Dugan Glass Co. (1907) and H. Northwood & Co. (1906).* 1988.

Madeley, John; Dave Shetlar. *American Iridescent Stretch Glass — Identification & Value Guide.* Collector Books, Paducah, KY. 1998.

Measell, James; W.C. Roetteis. *The L. G. Wright Glass Company.* The Glass Press Inc., Marietta, OH. 1997.

Moore, Donald E. *Carnival Glass — A Collection of Writings.* Heart of America Carnival Glass Association.

Lincoln-Land Carnival Glass Association. Newsletters, various issues, 1988 – 2000.

Mordini, Tom & Sharon. *Carnival Glass Auction Price Reports.* 1988 – 2001.

Olsen, O. Joe. *Carnival Glass News & Views.* Various issues, 1973 – 1981.

Owens, Richard. *Carnival Glass Tumblers.* Richard Owens, 1973.

Pottery, Glass & Brass Salesman (trade journal), various issues 1905 – 1925.

Resnick, John. *Encyclopedia of Carnival Glass Lettered Pieces.* 1989.

San Diego Carnival Glass Association. Newsletters, various issues, 1990 – 1998.

Thistlewood, Glen & Stephen. *Carnival Glass: The Magic and the Mystery.* Schiffer Publishing Ltd., Atglen, PA. 1998.

VALUE GUIDE

This guide is just that: a guide. It is not intended to establish values and is included here solely for the purpose of giving the reader a sense of perspective with regards to the scarcity, desirability, and average prices paid for the items listed. The prices quoted represent an average value based on actual prices paid at carnival glass auctions, shops, shows, and internet auctions and through private sales. However, none of these are written in stone. Prices can vary widely by region, and some items are more available in some areas than in others.

The premium prices often realized at carnival glass specialty auctions tend to represent the top of the food chain, so to speak. When you have 200 – 300 serious carnival glass buyers gathered in one place with the sole intent of concentrating on the most desirable items offered, bidding competition becomes fierce, and prices can often be driven to unrealistic levels. All it takes is two people, both of whom have made up their minds that they simply have to own a piece, and the result is a very high price. Carnival glass auction prices have played a key role in compiling this guide but are tempered with a grain of salt. Only in the case of extreme rarities can equally high prices be realized on the open market.

Some shapes and colors listed in the main text of this book are not represented in this guide. In some instances, no examples of items in certain colors have sold publicly for many years and are therefore not included in the guide. To do so would be nothing more than pure speculation and that does not belong in an accurate pricing guide.

Prices quoted here are for glass in ABSOLUTELY PERFECT condition with TOP QUALITY IRIDESCENCE. Pieces with average or below average iridescent quality will not bring anywhere near these prices. To quote the motto of the San Diego Carnival Glass Club, "Iridescence is the Essence."

Every effort has been made to ensure an accurate price representation in this guide, but neither the author nor the publisher assumes any responsibility for any transactions conducted as a result of using the values quoted in this guide.

ABBREVIATIONS USED IN THE OTHERS COLOR COLUMN

AM – Amber	PO – Peach Opalescent
AQ – Aqua	PE – Persian Blue
IBO – Ice Blue Opalescent	PB – Powder Blue
IGO – Ice Green Opalescent	VB – Venetian Blue
L – Lavender	R – Russet
S – Smoke	BA – Black Amethyst
M/C – Marigold on Custard	TL – Teal
LG – Lime Green	C – Coke Bottle Green
SB – Sapphire Blue	VI – Violet
CB – Celeste Blue	CL – Clambroth
VA – Vaseline	SO – Sapphire Opalescent
H – Horehound	BS – Iridized Blue Slag
RB – Renninger Blue	HA – Honey Amber
J – Jade	TO – Topaz
PRL – Pearl	CIT – Citrine

Pattern & Shape	marigold	amethyst	green	cobalt	white	ice blue	ice green	aqua opal.	others
ACORN BURRS									
Master Berry Bowl	130	190	250						
Small Berry Bowl	30	45	50						
Butter Dish	275	325	375						
Covered Sugar	135	185	200						
Creamer	100	140	165						
Spooner	100	140	165						
Punch Bowl & Base	700	1,000	2,650		4,000	5,000	7,000	50,000	10,000 LG
Punch Cup	40	45	75	150	100	150	160	2,250	200 LG
Water Pitcher	450	600	750						
Tumbler	55	65	75						
Whimsey Vase		2,000							
BASKET OF ROSES									
Bonbon	425	475							
Bonbon, Stippled	500	525		575					
BASKETWEAVE (PLAIN INT. RAINBOW)									
Bowl, 8" – 9"	45	50	60						
Compote	45	50	60						
Plate, 9"	75	95	100						
BEADED CABLE									
Candy Dish, Ruffled	35	50	55	85	100	125	165	275	
Rosebowl	100	110	135	160	350	475	1,200	425	10,000 PO
									8,000 M/C
									150 L, 500 TL
									1,500 IBO
									1,750 IGO
									600 AQ
									2,000 PE
BEADS									
Bowl, 8 – 9"	35	55	30						
BLACKBERRY									
Compote	90	125	160	300					
BLACKBERRY & RAYS									
Compote	400	450	550						
BLOSSOMS & PALMS									
Bowl, 8" – 9"	35	55	45						
BLOSSOMTIME									
Compote	265	325	475						
BULLSEYE & LEAVES									
Bowl, 7½" – 9"	30		40						
BUSHEL BASKET									
Round	125	150	450	135	75	600	250	300	2,650 VA
									2,000 SB
									700 S

Pattern & Shape	marigold	amethyst	green	cobalt	white	ice blue	ice green	aqua opal.	others
									400 H
									1,500 CB
									400 LG
									2,500 IGO
									500 TL
									400 AQ
									300 L
									2,200 IBO
Eight-Sided	125	150	475	225	135	425	450		1,800 AQ
									375 H
									600 RB
Round, Plain Handle		400	650						
Eight-Sided, Plain Handle		400							
BUTTERFLY									
Bonbon, Plain Ext.	65	100	125						475 S
Bonbon, Threaded Ext.	600	265	1,050	600		3,750			
CHERRY & CABLE									
Berry Bowl, Lg	125								
Berry Bowl, Sm.	40								
Butter Dish	300								
Covered Sugar	175								
Creamer	175								
Spooner	175								
Water Pitcher	1,200								
Tumbler	155								
CONCAVE DIAMONDS									
Tankard Pitcher, Covered									300 VB
									600 TO
Tumbler									40 VB
									170 TO
									75 R
Guest Set, 2 Piece									525 VB
									600 TO
									400 R
									700 J
Pickle Castor w/Frame	775								
Vase									100 VB
									275 TO
									300 J
CORN VASE									
Vase, 6½", Plain Base	900	650	950		350		450		1,300 AQ
									1,000 C
									600 LG
Vase, 6½", Husk Base	1,500.	900	1,000		300	1,800	375	5,000	2,500 TL
									1,250 AQ
									425 LG
									1,500 BA
CORN HUSK VASE									
Vase, 7½"		18,000.	20,000						
Vase, 7½", Open Husks		25,000							

Pattern & Shape	marigold	amethyst	green	cobalt	white	ice blue	ice green	aqua opal.	others
DAISY & DRAPE									
Vase, Footed	475	1,000	7,000	725	225	2,500	3,500	700	500 AQ
DAISY & PLUME									
Candy Dish, Footed	50	140	80		350	700	950		800 LG
Compote, Plain Int.	40	55	50						
Rosebowl, Footed	100	125	100	400	700	1,200	1,100	18,000	1,000 AM
Rosebowl, Stemmed	45	85	100	350					225 AM
DANDELION MUG									
Mug, Plain Base	275	250	475	450				500	400 H
									900 IBO
Mug, Knights Templar	325					550	850		
DANDELION WATER SET									
Tankard Pitcher	500	700	1,250	2,000	5,000	7,000	10,000		900 H
Tumbler, Plain Int.	45	55	80	250	150	250	425		175 H
DIAMOND POINT BASKET									
Footed Basket	2,000	3,500		2,400					
DIAMOND POINT VASE									
Vase, 8" – 12" Standard	50	65	75	145	195	350	275	1,650	800 SB
									225 AQ
									500 TL
									700 RB
									475 S
									275 H
Vase, 6" – 7½", Squat	135	100	100	450	375	500	425		225 AQ
DOUBLE LOOP									
Creamer	225	275	300	550				675	
Open Sugar	100	125	150	135				200	
DRAPERY									
Berry Bowl, Small					200				
Candy Dish, Tri-shaped	175	200	375	425	125	150	200		
Rosebowl	275	225	700	225	350	650	2.000	250	3,500 RB
									500 L
Vase, 7" – 9"	135	250	400	325	175	450	225	600	1,500 SB
									500 AQ
									650 TL
									400 LG
Tumbler					2,800				
DRAPERY VARIANT									
Vase, 8" – 10"	125	165		275					
ELEGANCE									
Bowl, 8" – 9", Ruffled						2.500			
Bowl, 8" – 9", Ice cream shape	2,500								
Plate, 8" – 9"						3,500			

161

Pattern & Shape	marigold	amethyst	green	cobalt	white	ice blue	ice green	aqua opal.	others
EMBROIDERED MUMS									
Bonbon					1,000				
Bowl, 8" – 9"	375	425		500	2,000	850	1.050	3,200	3,400 IGO
									2,800 SB
									3,400 IBO
Plate, 9"				9,000	1,500	2,200	2,000		
FEATHERS									
Vase, 6" – 12"	40	150	45		725	500			
FERN									
Compote	100	125	150						
FINECUT & ROSES									
Candy Dish, Plain Int.	40	55	65	250	100				175 PRL
Candy Dish, Fancy Int.	75	90	350	375	100	225	300	450	
Rosebowl, Plain Int.	125	100	135	600	200				150 PRL
Rosebowl, Fancy Int.	145	175			375	275	2,000	2,500	600 H
									900 PRL
									325 VI
									250 L
FINE RIB									
Vase, 6" – 18"	35	50	55	150	100		200		350 SB
FLUTE									
Berry Bowl, Lg.	65	100							
Berry Bowl, Sm.	20	35							
Butter Dish	250								
Covered Sugar	100		125						
Creamer	65		75						
Spooner	50								
Breakfast Creamer		75							
Breakfast Sugar, Open		75							
Celery Vase	70								
Nut Cup	65	85							90 VA
Salt, Master	95	135							175 SB
									150 VA
Salt, Small	25	40							50 SB
									35 VA
Sherbet	5	30	45	75	55				70 VA
Vase, 8" –14"	50	300	75	375	200			1,000	450 SB
Water Pitcher	175	325							
Tumbler	40	75	75						
FOUR PILLARS									
Vase, 9" – 12"	40	95	60	175	225	300	350	150	50 R
									2,500 M/C
									900 IGO
									500 VA
									550 SB
									225 TL
									45 CIT
VASE, 5" – 7", Squat		375	450						

Pattern & Shape	marigold	amethyst	green	cobalt	white	ice blue	ice green	aqua opal.	others
FOUR PILLARS (cont.)									
Vase, 9" – 12", Howard's Furniture Adv.			225						
FRUITS & FLOWERS									
Bonbon, Stemmed	95	110	125	135	275	475	700	725	275 R
									1,200 SB
									500 AQ
									1,100 IBO
									325 CL
									575 S
									475 L
Bonbon, Stippled	135		475	400					700 RB
Bowl, 9" – 10"	65	135	155		575		1,750		400 VI
Bowl, 7"	45	65	100	175			475		500 SB
Bowl, 7", Stippled	75		175						
Handgrip Plate or Card Tray	200	145	250						
Plate, 8" – 9"	175	265							
Plate, 7" – 7½"	100	175	275	450		3,500			500 M/C?
GOOD LUCK									
Bowl, 8" – 9", Ruffled	200	300	350	400	6,000	2,800	5,000	4,500	2,000 SB
									550 H
									800 L
									1,850 TL
									1,500 AQ
									1,250 LG
Bowl, 8" – 9", Pie Crust Edge	225	350	375	425		4,200		8,500	1,750 RB
									800 H
Bowl, 8" – 9", Stippled	300			575					1,650 RB
Bowl, 8" – 9" Variant	3,000								
Plate, 9" – 9½"	500	600	775	1,750		12,000	20,000		900 H
Plate, 9" – 9½", Stippled	900	1,200		2,000					
GRACEFUL									
Vase, Pedestal-ftd.	40	60	45						
GRAPE & CABLE									
Banana Bowl	135	200	300	425	365	500	600		325 PRL
Banana Bowl, Stippled	175		500	265					600 AQ
									650 RB
Berry Bowl, Lg.	100	150	185	450			1,200		400 PRL
Berry Bowl, Sm.	20	25	40	125			250		75 PRL
Berry Bowl, Lg., Ruffled	125	175	225	300	400	550	625		
Berry Bowl, Sm., Ruffled	25	30	45	100	200	300	325		
Bonbon	75	100	120	175	275			3,000	9,500 PO
									600 PRL
Bonbon, Stippled	100	120	175	175	425				3,500 M/C
									500 VI
									500 AQ
Bowl, 10" – 12", Salad	250	275	300						
Bowl, 7" – 7½" Ruffled	40	65	75			650		5,000	
Bowl, 8" – 9", Ruffled	55	75	85	650	900	700	600	3,000	400 R
									375 L

Pattern & Shape	marigold	amethyst	green	cobalt	white	ice blue	ice green	aqua opal.	others
GRAPE & CABLE (cont.)									
Bowl, 8" – 9", Pie Crust Edge	75	100	90	800	1,000	1,200	1,500	3,500	
Bowl, 8" – 9", Ruffled, Stip.	165	225	700	1,500	1,200	1,100	2,500	2,100	
Bowl, 8" – 9", Pie Crust, Stip.	200	250	850	1,700	1,200	1,200	3,000	3,400	2,600 SB
									1,250 AQ
Bowl, 8" – 9", Tendril Var	85	135	175	425		1,250		2,500	175 L
									1,000 TL
Bowl, 8" – 9", Leaf Center	75	125	145	450					225 L
Bowl, 8" – 9", Spatula-ftd.	55	85	100	250			1,000		
Breakfast Creamer	50	65	75						
Breakfast Sugar, Open	50	65	75						
Candlestick, 6" 1	00	145	125						
Candle Lamp, Complete	850	1,000	700						
Card Tray, 6" – 8"	100	135	150						150 L
Centerpiece Bowl, Lg., Ftd.	275	350	550	450	650	1,250	700		
Chop Plate, Footed					6,000				
Cologne Bottle	150	235	275			950			
Compote, Lg. Covered	1,500	400							
Compote, Lg. Open	475	325	850						
Compote, Whimsey from									
Sweetmeat Base	200	135							
Cracker Jar	300	350		750	1,100		2,500	20,000	700 S
Cracker Jar, Stippled	400								
Cup & Saucer	250	325	425		500	575	525		
Dresser Tray	200	250	475		1,800	1,200			
Fernery, Lg. Footed	750	825			1,000	1,800	20,000		800 PRL
Fruit Bowl, Ftd. Shallow	150	180	250	350	475	1,450	625		450 R
Fruit Bowl, Ftd. Deep	265	350	575	625	800		1,000		
Fruit Bowl, Ftd. Banded	300			500					
Hatpin Holder	275	250	325	1,100	2,500	2,250	1,950	15,000	850 L
									2,250 LG
									400 BA
Hatpin Holder, Banded	300	375		1,200					
Hat Shape, Ruffled	50	75	65						
Humidor	375	475		750				15,000	
Humidor, Stippled	525			650					
Ice Cream Bowl, Lg. 10" – 11"	250	325	450	1,500	225	2,500	2,250		
Ice Cream Bowl, Sm. 5" – 6"	100	125	200	175	150	350	325		
Nappy, Handled	45	50	75			900			
Pin Tray	200	265	375		1,200	8.00			400 PRL
Pin Tray, Banded	300	325							300 PRL
Plate, 6" – 6½"	135	175	200						
Plate 7" – 7½"	1,000	145	200						2,500 M/C
									225 H
Plate, Handgrip 7" – 8"	100	140	175						
Plate, 8" – 9"	145	200	275			3,000			225 CL
									750 L
Plate, 8" – 9" Stippled	575	650	800	1,000					4,000 SB
									2,500 S
Plate, 8" – 9" Spatula-ftd.	125	165	185	500			625		
Powder Jar, Covered	135	165	250	750		1,500	1,000	3,000	
Punch Bowl & Base, Sm.	375	450	1,000		5,000	14,000	15,000	100,000	
Punch Bowl & Base, Sm.,									
Stippled	600			2,700					

Pattern & Shape	marigold	amethyst	green	cobalt	white	ice blue	ice green	aqua opal.	others
GRAPE & CABLE (cont.)									
Punch Bowl & Base, Mid.	575	850	1,450	1,750	4,750	10,000	12,000		2,000 TL
Punch Bowl & Base, Mid.,									
Stippled	700	1,000		1,350					
Punch Bowl & Base, Banquet	1,500	2,000	4,500	8.000	10,000	25,000	18,000		
Punch Cup	30	35	45	55	75	125	100	2,000	
Sherbet, Pedestal-ftd.	35	40	50						
Shot Glass	135	185							
Spittoon Whimsey	3,250	3,750	4,500						
Sweetmeat, Covered	1,500	275							
Table Set									
Butter Dish	125	165	250			1,500			
Covered Sugar	80	120	135			500			
Creamer	100	80	100			500			
Spooner	80	80	100			500			
Triangular Whimsey, Ftd.		2,500							
Vase, Ftd. Whimsey		5,000	6,500						
Water Pitcher, Standard	200	275	325				15,000		1,000 S
Water Pitcher, Tankard	550	700					5.000		
Tumbler, Standard	35	40	55				350		175 H
Tumbler, Tankard	60	65	125				500		
Tumbler, Stippled	75	100							
Whiskey Decanter, Hndl.	400	675							
GRAPE & GOTHIC ARCHES									
Berry Bowl, Lg.	60	125	175	150					175 PRL
Berry Bowl, Sm.	15	35	50	40					45 PRL
Butter Dish	110	200	375	180					250 PRL
Covered Sugar	60	100	175	90					100 PRL
Creamer	45	90	125	75					75 PRL
Spooner	40	90	125	75					75 PRL
Water Pitcher	175	300	600	250					400 PRL
Tumbler	35	75	125	45					85 PRL
GRAPE ARBOR									
Tankard Pitcher	375	600		9,000	875	1,100			
Tumbler	35	50		350	90	165	275		150 AQ
									100 L
									250 PRL
Hat Shape	75			175	135		300		
GRAPE FRIEZE									
Bowl, 10" – 11", Ftd.									500 PRL
GRAPE LEAVES									
Bowl, 8" – 9", Ruffled	45	65	100	500		2,000			300 L
									175 AM
									100 CL
Bowl, 8" – 9", Three In One									
Edge Crimp	80	135	200	650					
GREEK KEY									
Bowl, 7" – 9", Dome-ftd.	45	75	50						
Bowl, 8" – 9", Collar Base	135	175	225	375			750		

Pattern & Shape	marigold	amethyst	green	cobalt	white	ice blue	ice green	aqua opal.	others
GREEK KEY (cont.)									
Plate, 9", Collar Base	600	550	525	1,200					
Water Pitcher	1,200	950	1,000						
Tumbler	110	145	150						
HEARTS & FLOWERS									
Bowl, 8" – 9" Ruffled	400	450	2,000	750	285	375	900	13,000	1,500 AQ
									1,000 LG
									3,000 RB
Bowl, 8" – 9", Pie Crust Edge	600	775	1,400	3,400	475	425	1,750		2,750 LG
Compote	250	550	1,500	450	165	875	1,000	575	3,500 LG
									3,750 PB
									2,400 RB
									5,000 M/C
									7,000 SO
									4,500 SB
									1,500 IBO
									1,150 L
Plate, 9"	1,750	2,200	2,500	7,500	3,000	2,000	3,000		4,000 LG
									10,000 SB
									25,000 VA
Whimsey Plate, Stemmed					2,000				
HOLIDAY									
Tray, Large Round	75								
INTAGLIO LINE, Strawberry									
Cherry, Peach & Pear									
Bowl, Lg. 10"	90								
Bowl, Sm. 4" – 5"	45								
JESTER CAP									
Vase, JIP Shape	95	165	275	300					
Vase, Cone Shape	60								
Vase, 4 Ruffles	65	100		200					
Vase, 6 Ruffles	75	100	145	200					
LEAF & BEADS									
Bowl, 7" – 8" Dome-ftd.	45	75	50						
Bowl, Ftd., Ruffled	45	75	50	300	400				
Nutbowl, Ftd.	120	150	200	475	450			2,250	
Plate, 9" Dome-ftd.			150						
Rosebowl, Plain or Rayed	100	150	125	200	600	1,250	1,200	400	1,000 SB
									500 TL
									850 RB
									475 L
									2,000 IBO
									2,300 IGO
									700 S
Rosebowl, Sunflower Int.	125	165	200						1,500 SB
									350 R
									1,200 TL
Rosebowl, Beaded Edge	250			500					
Rosebowl, Smooth Edge	250	285							375 PRL

Pattern & Shape	marigold	amethyst	green	cobalt	white	ice blue	ice green	aqua opal.	others
LEAF COLUMNS									
Vase, 6" – 7", Squat	275	325	400		450	1,400	950		1,750 SB
									750 L
Vase, 8" – 12"	90	125	175	1,000	250	575	500		800 SB
									500 TL
LINN'S MUMS									
Bowl, 8" – 9" Footed		2,000							
LOTUS LAND									
Bonbon, 2-Hndl.	1,850	1,400							
LOVELY									
Bowl, Ftd., Round	950	750	1,000						
Bowl, Tri-shape		1,250							
LUSTRE FLUTE									
Bowl, 5"	15	30	20						
Bonbon	30	55	35						
Creamer or Sugar	20	45	25						
Custard Cup	20	40	15						
Hat Shape	20	45	25						
MEMPHIS									
Berry Bowl, Lg.	100	300						6,000	
Berry Bowl, Sm.	25	50							
Compote, Lg.		3,000							
Covered Sugar		350							
Fruit Bowl & Base	375	400	750		2,500	4,500	10,000		
Punch Bowl & Base	450	600	2,000		2,500	9,000	16,000		12,000 LG
Punch Cup	30	35	45	100	75	125	175		100 LG
NORTHWOOD NEARCUT									
Compote	135	200	275						
Goblet	200	225							
Water Pitcher	2,000								
Tumbler	250	300							
NIPPON									
Bowl, 8" – 9" Ruffled	175	225	350	1,200	325	350	600		
Bowl, 8" – 9" Pie Crust Edge	275	475	550		225	475	650	5,000	2,500 TL
									950 LG
Plate, 9"	850	950	1,100		1,850	10,000		15,000	
OCTET									
Bowl, 7" – 9"	160	200	260		475		625		
ORIENTAL POPPY									
Tankard Pitcher	400	750	1,000	1,450	1,100	2,000	5,000		8,000 LG
Tumbler	45	60	75	225	90	200	250		900 LG
PANELED HOLLY									
Bonbon, 2-Hndl.	55	100	40						
Covered Sugar		400							

Pattern & Shape	marigold	amethyst	green	cobalt	white	ice blue	ice green	aqua opal.	others
PANELED HOLLY (cont.)									
Creamer		400							
Spooner	300	300							
Water Pitcher		10,000							
PEACH									
Berry Bowl, Lg.				250	165				600SB
Berry Bowl, Sm.				50	35				275 SB
Butter Dish					275				
Covered Sugar					175				
Creamer				250	175				
Spooner	250			250	125				
Water Pitcher				950	750				
Tumbler	350			165	135				
PEACOCK & URN									
Bowl, 8" – 10" Ruffled	400	650	950						
Chop Plate, 10½" – 12"	1,500	1,000	3,000	5,000					
Ice Cream, Lg., 10" – 11"	500	575	4,000	900	475	1,000	1,350	30,000	
Ice Cream, Lg., Stippled	600			1350		1,250			3,000 S
									2,800 RB
									9,000 SB
									1,500 H
									1,700 HA
Ice Cream, Sm., 5" – 6"	75	100	650	90	135	250	300	4,000	
Ice Cream, Sm., Stippled	200			150					1,600 RB
Plate, 6" – 7"	600	900		1,150					
Plate, 6" – 7" Stippled				1,250					
PEACOCK AT THE FOUNTAIN									
Berry Bowl, Lg.	150	200	350	300	325	475	600		
Berry Bowl, Sm.	30	40	80	45	50	120	150		
Butter Dish	150	265	550	425	450	1,250			
Covered Sugar	100	200	325	250	300	500			
Creamer	100	200	300	225	300	350			
Spooner	80	145	300	200	300	250			
Compote	475	850	2,000	750	500	1,500	1,650	3,800	
Fruit Bowl, Lg., Ftd.	450	675	3,500	750	1,750		3,000	12,000	
Fruit Bowl, Points Straight	800	1,450							
Fruit Bowl, Points Turned In		5,500							
Punch Bowl & Base	500	725	5,000	1,250	3,500	5,000	6,500	60,000	
Punch Bowl & Base, Points Up	1,000	1,750			4,000				
Punch Cup	35	45	300	70	100	125	300	2,000	
Spittoon Whimsey		16,500	18,000						
Water Pitcher	375	450	4,000	500	900	2,500	5,000		
Tumbler	45	65	300	75	135	250	500		
PEACOCKS									
Bowl, 8" – 9" Ruffled	250	425	850	625	700	1,100	1,500	1,300	1,600 S
									3,800 IGO
									3,000 IBO
									1,250 AQ
									1,750 RB

Pattern & Shape	marigold	amethyst	green	cobalt	white	ice blue	ice green	aqua opal.	others
PEACOCKS (cont.)									
Bowl, 8" – 9" Pie Crust Edge	300	475	1,500	800	950	1,250	1,600	2,750	9,000 PB 15,000 BS 1,250 H 1,100 S 1,250 RB 1,300 L 1,600 LG
Bowl, 8" – 9", Ruffled, Stippled	350	750		650				5,000	1,100 RB
Bowl, 8" – 9", Pie Crust Edge, Stippled	400	1,250		800					1,200 RB
Plate, 9"	575	700	1,750	900	500	2,000	475		1,000 L 850 H 10,000 SB 2,000 S
Plate, 9" Stippled	700			1,400					2,200 RB
PETALS									
Compote	50	70	125	550		2,500			
PLUMS & CHERRIES									
Covered Sugar		1,250							
Spooner				1,250					
Tumbler				1,000					
POINSETTIA LATTICE									
Bowl, 8" – 9" Footed	600	475	10,000	625	10,000	3,000		9,000	1,500 H
POPPY									
Oval Pickle Dish	135	350	375	225	250	625		3,250	3,100 M/C 750 AQ 375 L 450 AM 550 TL
POPPY SHOW									
Bowl, 8" – 9" Ruffled	675	1,150	2,000	1,350	375	1,200	1,700	10,000	500 CL 1,000 LG
Plate, 9" – 9½"	1,500	1,250	3,300	1,600	475	1,350	2,400	15,000	
POPPY VARIANT									
Bowl, 6" – 7"	25	45	40						
RASPBERRY									
Milk Pitcher	135	200	265		1,400	3,500	4,000		
Occasional Piece, Ftd.	150	200	250						
Water Pitcher	175	275	300	4,000	1,400	1,650	5,000		
Tumbler	40	55	75	1,000	800	275	500		100 H 150 L
ROSE SHOW									
Bowl, 8" – 9" Ruffled	475	700	1,750	1,000	375	1,800	1,650	1,200	4,000 IGO 3,000 H 2,500 SB

Pattern & Shape	marigold	amethyst	green	cobalt	white	ice blue	ice green	aqua opal.	others
ROSE SHOW (cont.)									
Plate, 9" – 9½"	1,250	1,000	3,250	1,300	550	3,000	3,100		2,200 IBO 14,000 M/C 1,000 AQ 2,800 LG 20,000 VA 12,000 IGO
ROSE SHOW VARIANT									
Bowl, 8" – 9"	900	850							1,200 RB
Plate, 8" – 9"	1,550	3,000							2,500 RB
ROSETTE									
Bowl, 7" – 8½" Ftd.	100	70	150						
RUFFLES & RINGS									
Bowl, 8" – 9", Ftd.									1,000 PO
SINGING BIRDS									
Berry Bowl, Lg.	150	275	200						
Berry Bowl, Sm.	30	45	35	200					
Bowl, Ice Cream, Lg.	650								
Butter Dish	200	325	425						
Covered Sugar	150	200	225						
Creamer	100	140	125						
Spooner	100	140	125						
Mug	75	85	135	125	700	425		1,400	150 L 450 H 750 S
Mug, Stippled	150	325	450	225					1,500 RB
Sherbet, Pedestal-ftd.	300								
SMOOTH RAYS									
Bowl, 9" – 10", Ruffled	30	80	40						
Bowl, 5" – 6" Ruffled	10	30	15						
Bonbon, 2-Hndl.	30	50	35						
Compote	25	50	30	75					50 LG
Hat Shape	20	35	25						
Plate, 6"	50	80	75						
SPRINGTIME									
Berry Bowl, Lg.	150	200	250						
Berry Bowl, Sm.	35	45	50						
Butter Dish	300	350	425						
Covered Sugar	165	225	265						
Creamer	125	175	225						
Spooner	125	175	225						
Water Pitcher	650	950	1,200						
Tumbler	130	150	160						
STAR OF DAVID									
Bowl, 7" – 8½", Dome-ftd.	200	100	140						

Pattern & Shape	marigold	amethyst	green	cobalt	white	ice blue	ice green	aqua opal.	others
STIPPLED RAYS									
Bowl, 8" – 9", Collar Base	30	50	65	135	225	375	600		
Bowl, Dome-ftd.	40	55	45						
Bonbon, 2-Hndl.	30	45	40	75					
Compote	30	50	40	85					
Plate, 6½"	300	350							
STRAWBERRY									
Bowl, 8" – 9", Ruffled	85	110	140		3,000		1,400		950LG 800 H 700 L, 650 S
Bowl, 8" – 9", Ruffled, Stippled	150	400		750			1,900	10,000	750 H 1,300 LG 1,600 RB
Bowl, 8" – 9" Pie Crust Edge	110	150	175						350 VI 1,000 S
Bowl, 8" – 9", Pie Crust Edge, Stippled	375	450	850	575					750 H
Plate, 9"	175	220	250						800 PO 400 L
Plate, 9", Stippled	2,100	1,100	1,500	5,000		25,000			
Handgrip Plate, 6" – 7"	175	250	300						
SUNFLOWER									
Bowl, Spatula-ftd.	75	135	175	650		2,500			1,700 RB 425 CL 900 TL
Plate, 9" Spatula-ftd.	3,000								
SWIRL RIB & INTERIOR SWIRL & PANEL									
Water Pitcher Var. #1	150	650	375						
Water Pitcher Var. #2	135								
Water Pitcher Var. #3	175								
Water Pitcher Var. #4	175								
Water Pitcher Var. #5	175								
Water Pitcher Var. #6	200								
Water Pitcher Var. #7	150								
Water Pitcher Var. #8	150		225						
Tumbler	30	100	75						
THIN RIB									
Vase, 3" – 3½" b, 5" – 7" h	40	75	60	90	150	350	475		550 LG
Vase, 3" – 3½" b, 8" – 12" h	30	60	50	125	150	200	265		50 R 400 SB 400 VA, 300 TL 175 AQ
Vase, 3" – 3½" b, JIP shape	325	250	450	650					500 TL
Vase, 4¼"– 4½" b, 6½" h		800							
Vase, 4¼"– 4½" b, 11" – 15" h	200	225	250	325	550	850	1,200	2,000	2,400 SB 825 VA 1,650 LG
Vase, 4¾ –5" b, 16" – 21" h	750	1,250	2,000	3,000	3,500			5,000	3,600 SB 2,500 VA

Pattern & Shape	marigold	amethyst	green	cobalt	white	ice blue	ice green	aqua opal.	others
THREE FRUITS									
Bowl, 8" – 9" Ruffled	75	100	120	575	1,000			900	475 L 375 H 350 HA 600 PRL 800 LG 175 CL 750 S
Bowl, 8" – 9" Pie Crust Edge	85	125	150	700					900 S 800 LG
Bowl, 8" – 9", Ruffled, Stippled	200	250	775	500	625	2,600		1,400	600 LG 2,000 SB 950 PRL 650 L 575 H 1,500 TL
Bowl, 8" – 9" Pie Crust, Stippled	400	600	1,000	700		8,000			650 H 750 R
Bowl, 8" – 9" Dome-ftd.	100	135	145		250		375	700	175 H 225 HA
Bowl, 8" – 9" Spatula-ftd.	90	140	165	425	375	900	500	600	1,100 IGO 1,000 IBO 300 L
Bowl, 8" – 9" Spatula-ftd., Stippled	135	165		500	600	1,000	800	600	650 SB 375 PRL
Plate, 9"	155	185	225	1,200				3,000	300 L 550 H
Plate, 9" Stippled	350	550	700	950		7,000	10,000	4,500	2,000 SB 800 L 1,850 AQ 1,300 VI 300 CL 4,000 TL 2,500 HA 1,200 H
TORNADO									
Vase, Plain Background	550	550	450		8,000				
Vase, Ribbed Background	2,250	1,500		3,500	10,000	6,500			
Vase, Whimsey Cone Shape, Flared Top	3,000								3,500 L 3,500 CB
Vase, Variant, Pedestal-ftd.	2,500								
TOWN PUMP									
Vase, 6" Pump Shape	2,250	950	4,000						
TREE TRUNK									
Vase, 3¼" b, 5" – 7" h	65	100	125	800	275	750	1,300		
Vase, 3¼" b, 8" – 12" h	50	60	100	600	165	550	500	1,300	600 SB 750 TL
Vase, 3¼" b, JIP shape	3,000	4,000							
Vase, 4¾" b, 11" – 14" h	350	325	375	725	1,200	1,600	2,000	4,000	600 H

Pattern & Shape	marigold	amethyst	green	cobalt	white	ice blue	ice green	aqua opal.	others
TREE TRUNK (cont.)									
									1,250 SB
									1,250 LG
									20,000 BS
Vase, 5¼" b, 16" – 21" h	4,500	2,200	5,000	3,000	4,500	25,000	10,000		
Vase, Elephant's Foot	5,000	2,600	4,500						
VALENTINE									
Bowl, 9" – 11"	200								
Bowl, 5" – 6"	150								
VINTAGE GRAPE									
Bowl, 8" – 9" Dome-ftd.			200						
WATERLILY & CATTAILS									
Water Pitcher	700	6,500							
Tumbler	50	475							
WHEAT									
Covered Serving Bowl		10,000							
Covered Sweetmeat Compote		10,000	12,000						
Sherbet, Pedestal-ftd.		2,000							
WIDE PANEL									
Epergne, 4-Lily	1,000	1,200	800	2,500	2,750	15,000	15,000	35,000	
Vase, 3½" b, 7" – 11" h	35	100	50		200	350			
Vase, 4½" b, 12" – 16" h	150	225	175	450	375	425	450	2,000	575 TL
Vase, 5" b, 16" – 20" h	550	775	500		1,000				900 VA
									700 CB
WILD ROSE									
Bowl, Footed	45	120	45	250		1,200			
Nutbowl, Footed	135	100	65	325		1,500			225 H
Rosebowl, Footed	250	375	145			2,500			6,000 SB
Plate, Footed			1,000						
WILD STRAWBERRY									
Bowl, 9" – 10"	85	145	235		400	1,200	1,600		
Bowl, 5" – 6"	35	75	100		125	200	325		
Handgrip Plate	185	250	225						
WISHBONE									
Bowl, 8" – 9" Footed	135	175	185	1,000	625	1,400	1,250	5,000	750 S
									550 H
									350 L
Bowl, 9" – 10" Collar Base, Ruffled	145	225	300						4,000 SB
Bowl, 9" – 10" Collar Base, Pie Crust Edge	200	300	250	1,400	475				750 S
									450 CL
Chop Plate, 10" – 11"	1,800	2,500	4,000						
Epergne, Single Lily	425	650	750		1,800	4,500	6,500		
Plate, 9" Footed	1,000	350	750						
Plate, 8" – 9", Triangular	600	550							
Water Pitcher	700	1,800	1,400						

Pattern & Shape	marigold	amethyst	green	cobalt	white	ice blue	ice green	aqua opal.	others
WISHBONE (cont.)									
Tumbler	75	95	150						2,200 PRL
WISTERIA									
Tankard Pitcher					5,000	7,000			
Tumbler					575	650	700		
Whimsey Bank					5,000				
Whimsey Vase			15,000						
ADVERTISING PIECES									
BALLARD – MERCED, CAL.									
Bowl		950							
Plate		2,200							
BROEKER'S FLOUR									
Plate		2,200							
DAVIDSON'S SOCIETY CHOCOLATES									
Handgrip Plate		1,300							
DREIBUS PARFAIT SWEETS									
Bowl		500							
Plate		550							
Handgrip Plate		600							
E. A. HUDSON FURNITURE									
Bowl		1,300							
Plate		2,000							
Handgrip Plate		1,500							
EAGLE FURNITURE CO.									
Bowl		750							
Plate		1,250							
Handgrip Plate		2,000							
FERN BRAND CHOCOLATES									
Plate	1,200								
JOCKEY CLUB									
Bowl		1,700							
Plate		2,000							
Handgrip Plate		1,800							
HOWARD FURNITURE CO.									
See Four Pillars Vase									
OLD ROSE DISTILLING									
Plate, Grape & Cable Int.			700						

Pattern & Shape	marigold	amethyst	green	cobalt	white	ice blue	ice green	aqua opal.	others
ENAMEL DECORATED PATTERNS									
APPLE BLOSSOM									
Berry Bowl, Lg.				300					
Berry Bowl, Sm.				50					
Butter Dish				450					
Covered Sugar				200					
Creamer				175					
Spooner				150					
Water Pitcher				750					
Tumbler				125					
CHERRIES & LITTLE FLOWERS									
Water Pitcher	275	400		165					
Tumbler	50	75		30					
COSMOS									
Water Pitcher	275								
Tumbler	40								
DAISY & LITTLE FLOWERS									
Water Pitcher			280						
Tumbler			50						
GARDEN SWIRL									
Tankard Pitcher	325								
GROUND CHERRIES									
Water Pitcher			450						
Tumbler			60						
PERIWINKLE									
Water Pitcher	265								
Tumbler	35								
PRETTY PANELS									
Water Pitcher	200								
Tumbler	30								

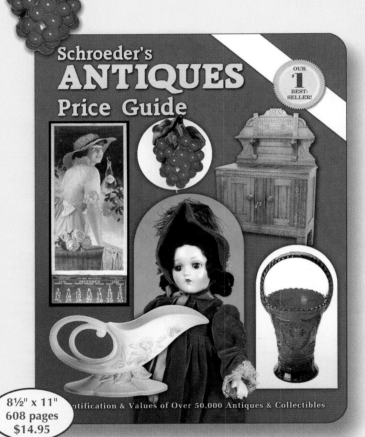